THEOLOGY AFTER COLONIZATION

Notre Dame Studies in African Theology

*Series co-editors: Rev. Paulinus Ikechukwu Odozor, C.S.Sp.,
and David A. Clairmont*

DE NICOLA CENTER
for ETHICS AND CULTURE

Under the sponsorship of the de Nicola Center for Ethics and Culture,
and in cooperation with the Notre Dame Department of Theology, this
series seeks to publish new scholarship engaging the history, the contemporary situation, and the future of African theology and the African
church. The goal is to initiate a global and interdisciplinary conversation
about African theology and its current trajectories, with special attention
to its interreligious and multicultural context on the African continent
and in the African diaspora. The series will publish works in the history
of the African church and in African perspectives on biblical studies,
liturgy, religious art and music, ethics, and Christian doctrine.

THEOLOGY AFTER COLONIZATION

Kwame Bediako, Karl Barth,
and the Future of Theological Reflection

TIM HARTMAN

University of Notre Dame Press

Notre Dame, Indiana

University of Notre Dame Press
Notre Dame, Indiana 46556
undpress.nd.edu

Published in the United States of America

Library of Congress Control Number:2019948650

ISBN: 978-0-268-10653-9 (hardback)
ISBN: 978-0-268-10656-0 (WebPDF)
ISBN: 978-0-268-10655-3 (Epub)

For Saranell
Simeon, Elliana, and Jeremiah

CONTENTS

ACKNOWLEDGMENTS

"If you want to run fast, go alone. If you want to run far, go together." As I consider this African proverb and remember how far I and this project have come, many faces come to mind of those who have run with me, without whom this book would not be in your hands. This book's story begins on February 21, 2012, when as a graduate student at the University of Virginia, I was sitting in Alderman Library with an inkling of how I might contribute to contemporary theological reflection. A series of questions ran through my mind: What if I could combine my upbringing in the Presbyterian Church in the United States of America with my experiences with African Christianities? Could I put two theologians in dialogue, one from Africa and one from North America or Europe? Maybe Karl Barth, and who else? I had been reading Kwame Bediako's writings but knew that if this was a viable direction I would need to visit the Akrofi-Christaller Institute (ACI) in Ghana. I hastily composed an email to the person I knew with the most connections to the Christian church worldwide, Tim Dearborn. I asked him if he had ever heard of Kwame Bediako or knew anyone I could talk with about Bediako. That very afternoon, I was copied on an email from Tim to Gillian Mary Bediako, Kwame's widow, that began, "Dear Gillian, Meet my friend Tim. . . ." The journey that started that day has been supported by many people and institutions. I am deeply grateful to everyone who has helped this book come to be.

First, the hospitality, grace, and generosity shown to me by Dr. Gillian Mary Bediako has made this book possible. Both during my research trips to ACI and during my ensuing visits, I received encouragement for my work, helpful interpretation of Kwame's thought, and access to countless unpublished documents. Thank you, Mary.

I thank Tim Dearborn for his initial email of introduction and Tim and Kerry Dearborn for first teaching me about the unlimited and unconditional grace of God through Karl Barth's doctrine of election.

I am deeply indebted to the Ghanaians who taught me and encouraged me as I learned about Kwame Bediako: Maurice Apprey, Kwabena Asamoah-Gyadu, John Azumah, Rudolf Kuuku Gaisie, Griselda Lartey, Mercy Amba Oduyoye, Kofi Asare Opoku, and Benhardt Y. Quarshie.

This project began as a dissertation, and I wish to thank my adviser, Paul Dafydd Jones, for his unflagging enthusiasm for this project from the beginning and his attentive reading and incisive comments, as well as my committee, Maurice Apprey, Cindy Hoehler-Fatton, Charles Marsh, and Chuck Mathewes. The labor of dismantling the dissertation and writing the book was greatly aided by the insights of Randi Rashkover and Ted Smith. The style of the final manuscript benefited from the work of my research assistants, AJ Shortley and Hannah Trawick, and the editorial skills of Ulrike Guthrie. I am grateful to Stephen Little and the team at the University of Notre Dame Press for believing in this project and shepherding it through the production process. I am deeply honored to have this book selected to inaugurate the Notre Dame Studies in African Theology series.

Institutional support has been essential in the completion of this project. I am grateful for three awards from the Graduate School of Arts and Sciences at the University of Virginia that funded research visits to Ghana and supplied encouragement and financial support at important stages of the project. I gratefully acknowledge the support of a Dissertation Fellowship from the Louisville Institute that enabled me to complete my dissertation in a timely manner. My three academic deans at Columbia Seminary, Deb Mullen, Christine Roy Yoder, and Love Sechrest, have been faithful champions of my scholarship in words, time, and grants. Many thanks to the library staff at the University of Virginia, the Akrofi-Christaller Institute, and Columbia Theological Seminary who obtained numerous documents for me over the years from libraries around the world. This research would literally not have been possible without their efforts.

On a personal level, I am grateful to my parents, Dave and Kitty Hartman, for their support throughout this work, with special gratitude to my mother for transcribing three of Bediako's lectures from audio files. My wife's parents, Doug and Alleene Kracht, also enabled me to run the long road of research and writing through their encouragement and help with my family, especially during my research trips to Ghana. Finally, and most important, I am grateful to my children, who welcomed me home at the end of each day of work with a hug, a smile, a ball, or a toy—and know how to keep me humble and on my toes. I dedicate this work to them and to Saranell, my wife and partner in life's journey. I could not have conducted this research or written it up without her unconditional love, her daily support, her constant encouragement and belief in me, and her loving and generous spirit. My hope is that this book may contribute to theologies that encourage human flourishing for our children and the world they will inhabit through the good news of Jesus Christ.

ABBREVIATIONS

All biblical quotations are from the New Revised Standard Version.

Works by Kwame Bediako

CiA   *Christianity in Africa: The Renewal of a Non-Western Religion* (Edinburgh: Edinburgh University Press, 1995)

JAC   "Jesus in African Culture: A Ghanaian Perspective," in *Jesus and the Gospel in Africa* (Oxford: Regnum, 2000)

TI   *Theology and Identity: The Impact of Culture on Christian Thought in the Second Century and Modern Africa* (Oxford: Regnum, 1992)

Works by Karl Barth

I/1   *Church Dogmatics*, vol. I, part 1, 2nd ed. (Edinburgh: T&T Clark, 1975)

I/2   *Church Dogmatics*, vol. I, part 2 (Edinburgh: T&T Clark, 1956)

II/1   *Church Dogmatics*, vol. II, part 1 (Edinburgh: T&T Clark, 1957)

II/2   *Church Dogmatics*, vol. II, part 2 (Edinburgh: T&T Clark, 1957)

III/1   *Church Dogmatics*, vol. III, part 1 (Edinburgh: T&T Clark, 1958)

III/2   *Church Dogmatics*, vol. III, part 2 (Edinburgh: T&T Clark, 1960)

III/3   *Church Dogmatics*, vol. III, part 3 (Edinburgh: T&T Clark, 1960)

III/4   *Church Dogmatics*, vol. III, part 4 (Edinburgh: T&T Clark, 1961)

IV/1   *Church Dogmatics*, vol. IV, part 1 (Edinburgh: T&T Clark, 1956)

IV/2   *Church Dogmatics*, vol. IV, part 2 (Edinburgh: T&T Clark, 1958)

IV/3   *Church Dogmatics*, vol. IV, part 3 (Edinburgh: T&T Clark, 1961)

IV/4   *Church Dogmatics*, vol. IV, part 4 (Edinburgh: T&T Clark, 1969)

TCL   *The Christian Life: Church Dogmatics IV.4, Lecture Fragments*, ed. Hans-Anton Drewes and Eberhard Jüngel, trans. Geoffrey Bromiley (London: T&T Clark, 2004)

INTRODUCTION

Colonization and Christendom are interrelated phenomena that have shaped the history of Christianity over the past seventeen hundred years. The impulses to expand and to rule have reinforced each other through a hegemonic cultural consensus that has defined the boundaries and content of Christian theological reflection. A key feature of this complex has been the confusion of Christianity with North Atlantic white culture. Particularly during the past five hundred years, this consensus has been disintegrating when confronted with the impact of secularization and globalization.

Christendom and colonization are not merely parallel processes. Though distinct, they are interrelated, interdependent, and mutually reinforcing. As the Christian faith became yoked to imperial political power, there was a push to expand and dominate. On the night before the decisive battle of the Milvian Bridge that allowed Emperor Constantine I to consolidate his power, he saw a vision of the cross of Jesus Christ with the words, "In this sign, [you shall] conquer."[1] At the moment that Constantine ordered crosses placed on the shields of his army, the Christian faith became tethered to military conquest. A year later, in 313, Constantine issued the Edict of Milan, declaring Christianity an officially tolerated religion within the Roman Empire. By 380, Christianity became the sole authorized religion of the Roman Empire. The once-persecuted community on-the-way—as the Acts of the Apostles described the early church—was co-opted to support power and privilege. Since this institutionalization of the Christian church, including formalized doctrines and structures of authority, Christianity has been inseparable from the quest to expand and conquer.

The first part of this book demonstrates how the loss of cultural hegemony through rising pluralism and secularization has undermined the interconnection of the Christian faith and political power and how globalization has undermined the expansive (and expanding) mind-set of colonization. The second part then engages two twentieth-century theologians who opposed this complex from within their own social locations—sometimes in strikingly similar ways (though the similarities themselves are not the subject of this book). The Swiss-German theologian Karl Barth (1886–1968) responded to the challenges of Christendom and the increasing secularization of Europe by articulating an early post-Christendom theology that based his dogmatic reflections on God's self-revelation in Jesus Christ, not on official institutional structures (including the church) or societal consensus. Instead, he used Christian theology to counter claims made by the Nazi-sympathizing state church. In a similar way, the Ghanaian theologian Kwame Bediako (1945–2008) offered a post-colonial theology. He wrote from the Global South as the Christian faith grew exponentially after the departure of Western missionaries from Africa. For Bediako, the infinite translatability of the gospel of Jesus Christ led to the renewal of Christianity as a *non-Western* religion, not as a product of colonization.

Bediako and Barth each responded to the coupling of Christian faith and political power, which was manifested in externally focused imperial colonization and internally focused cultural hegemony. While for many in the West this conflation of gospel and culture was, and has been, so pervasive as to be imperceptible, theologians in the Global South have identified Western Christianity as deeply syncretistic, with capitalism and cultural domination defining how the gospel of Jesus Christ has been understood. The Christian faith has been all too willing to aid the ever-expanding growth of capitalism in its attempts to serve its own aims. As one example, the nineteenth-century British missionary David Livingstone proudly proclaimed that he was bringing the three C's to southern Africa: Christianity, civilization, and commerce.[2]

Christian theologies that are wedded (or indebted) to this colonial-Christendom complex—often without knowing it—currently find themselves struggling. Assumptions embedded in these theological systems are based on power, privilege, and societal consensus. They are not accustomed to being challenged or having to explain themselves. Often, theological knowledge has been based on centralized or top-down structures. These theologies (and I would include most Western theologies here) find themselves unable to respond to increasing secularization and intensifying globalization because they are based on the very assumptions of uniformity and parochialism (sometimes called orthodoxy) that are being challenged.

This book turns to Kwame Bediako and Karl Barth as prophets of alternative ways of theological reflection. Though the church historian Andrew Walls wrote, "Kwame Bediako was the outstanding African theologian of his generation,"[3] Bediako's insights and theological acumen nonetheless remain at the margins of contemporary theological reflection in the West. Barth is widely considered the most significant Protestant theologian of the twentieth century. Both men developed Christian theologies that were not dependent on the colonial-Christendom complex, even before it collapsed socially and materially. Accordingly, they can serve as helpful guides for contemporary theological reflection in this time when the consensus surrounding this complex is disintegrating further. Collectively, their work points the way toward contemporary theological reflection that is Christological, contextual, cultural, constructive, and collaborative.

PART I

Western Christian Theology Today

ONE

A Crisis of (Shifting) Authority

*The Decline of Christendom and the Rise of
Secularization and Globalization*

One month after his twenty-fifth birthday, a young man from West Africa found himself in Bordeaux, France, crying in the shower. He was struggling to write his master's thesis on Francophone literature. Raised just outside the capital city in the Gold Coast (present-day Ghana), young Bediako excelled in school and was admitted to Mfantsipim, the top high school in the country, where Kofi Annan (later, secretary-general of the United Nations) was a few years ahead of him.[1] Graduating at the top of his class, Bediako matriculated at the University of Ghana, where he studied French language and literature. Deeply influenced by French existentialism, he became an avowed atheist. His intellectual heroes were Jean-Paul Sartre, Simone de Beauvoir, Albert Camus, and André Malraux. He received a grant for postgraduate study at the University of Bordeaux with the stipulation that he would return to Ghana to teach French. He studied the work of the Congolese poet Tchicaya U'Tamsi, who was in exile in Paris, and became immersed in the authors of *négritude*: Aimé Césaire, Léopold Senghor, Léon-Gontran Damas, and, with particular fondness,

Frantz Fanon.[2] In his master's thesis, he sought to gain a greater under-standing of négritude and its application to African personal identity in light of the cultural and religious challenges of the twentieth century.

Consumed by writer's block that August day during his summer break, Bediako decided to take a shower to clear his mind. Before he could turn on the faucet, his feet were wet with his tears. Instead of gaining the in-sight he had expected, he "experienced a rather sudden and surprising conversion to Christ,"[3] wherein he learned that "Christ is the Truth, the integrating principle of life as well as the key to true intellectual coher-ence, for himself, and for the whole world."[4] Within two months of his conversion, his thesis was completed and work on his doctorate had begun. However, the course of his life had changed.

Later in his life, Kwame Bediako reflected, "When Jesus Christ be-came real to me nearly thirty-five years ago, I discovered that I was re-covering my African identity and spirituality."[5] In his last public ad-dress, he referred to his own "personal Damascus road [experience] . . . where in becoming Christian, I was becoming African again."[6] In hind-sight, Bediako understood that the lasting impact of colonization on him was atheism, not Christianization. Contrary to colonial missionary hopes, Bediako's journey had taught him that one could be "Western" without God or religion. Yet he believed that to be African was to be incurably religious.[7] By renouncing atheism and becoming a Christian, Bediako understood himself to be recovering his African identity and the African spiritual view of life. His future theological vocation can be understood as an extended exercise in seeking to "understand what had happened to [him]"[8]—and to many other Africans. By becoming Christian, he be-came more African—and less Western.[9]

On a similar August day, fifty-six years earlier, in 1914, a twenty-eight-year-old pastor in the working-class town of Safenwil, Switzerland, experi-enced an awakening of his own that radically changed the course of his life. As Kaiser Wilhelm II made machinations of war, ninety-three German intellectuals publicly declared their support for his military policy. On that list young Karl discovered almost all his theological teachers. He reflected on the significance of this discovery some forty years later: "In despair over what this indicated about the signs of the time I suddenly realized that I could not any longer follow either their ethics and dogmatics or their understanding of the Bible and of history. For me at least, nineteenth-century theology no longer held any future."[10] For Karl Barth, Christian theology should have been able to resist warmongering, not support it. For him, this moment revealed a fatal flaw in the theology that he had been taught. There was a gap between belief and action, an inability for one's convictions to give one the confidence to stand against the temporal ruler. The church needed to confront the state, not support it.

Primarily, Barth's theological work sought to counter what he took to be the misleading impact of "cultural Protestantism" (*Kulturprotestantismus*) on the task of theology.[11] This reorientation of Barth's thought began through his study of the Bible, particularly the Epistle to the Romans; he then demonstrated his opposition to cultural Protestantism in particular moments of protest, first against the theologians endorsing the Kaiser's war effort and later against the German Christians' cooperation with Adolf Hitler and the Nazi Party. In essence, Barth was protesting their claims that asserted human reasoning over against God's self-revelation. These movements in Germany shared with colonial officials in Africa an overconfidence in the human interpretation and application of revelation over against, or in addition to, God's self-revelation in Jesus Christ.

Western Protestant theological reflection—of which Barth is a product and a representative example—has typically been an insular affair. There is a canon consisting of the Patristics; Nicaea, Chalcedon, and other ecumenical councils; and Augustine, Luther, Calvin, and Schleiermacher, which is then interpreted and debated. Barth is often read as someone who is an heir to that legacy and as someone who is either more or less faithful to the tradition. Barth's deep immersion in and engagement with the tradition led Pope Pius XII to call him the greatest theologian since St. Thomas Aquinas.[12]

The tumultuous events of the twentieth century (two world wars, the Holocaust, nuclear warfare, apartheid, colonial independence movements, etc.) suggested that many of the plausibility structures of Western Christianity had collapsed. In this context, both Karl Barth and Kwame Bediako sought to articulate anew the gospel of Jesus Christ amid societies in which one's religious beliefs are determined in some sense over against others, not received by fate. In the twenty-first century, holding multiple beliefs or professing no belief at all is a real possibility. From across the colonial divide, both Bediako and Barth responded to the failings they saw and experienced in nineteenth- and twentieth-century European theology. In Germany and Switzerland, Barth criticized the lack of self-critical reflection in theological discourse regarding "religion" expressed through cultural Protestantism. In Ghana, Bediako criticized an intensification of a different kind—one that sought to "civilize" Africans through colonialism, as conveyed by European missionaries. Both authors appealed to an understanding of God's revelation. Both believed that their adversaries had confused revelation and culture in the name of religion by using religious arguments to privilege cultural assumptions over a genuine wrestling with divine communication. And their shared hope was that through a fresh approach to revelation, Christian theology could once again be rooted in the story of Jesus Christ, over against the religion of nineteenth-century European Protestants.[13]

For both Bediako and Barth, the critique of European Protestantism was as much about identity as religion. As the historian John Largas Modern has noted, "Any viable description of the nineteenth century must account for how one's identity becomes bound up with one's relationship with the religious."[14] Bediako's and Barth's responses to nineteenth-century European Protestantism are intriguingly similar: both sought to uncouple the connection between the gospel of Jesus Christ and culture that had been forged in the name of colonization in Africa and religion in Europe. Both theologians sought to answer quite similar questions about revelation, religion, and culture despite very different cultural backgrounds. Barth sought to articulate a new theology at the end of the era of modern Christendom; Bediako sought to articulate theology in the aftermath of the colonial period. The similarities of their responses are not coincidental; European Christendom and colonization were not parallel processes but an interconnected whole.

The Colonial-Christendom Complex

Christendom and colonization were both fueled by the use of authority in explicit ways (e.g., conquest) and implicit ways (e.g., defining what children were taught about the world). To buttress the colonial-Christendom complex, narratives arose to legitimate its authority. These narratives took various forms, including but not limited to cognitive superiority, racial superiority, and cultural superiority, all of which privileged Eurocentric ways of knowing and living.

Over the past five hundred years, the Western cultural and religious consensus around Christianity has been crumbling and has nearly collapsed entirely. In Europe, the Christian church has dramatically lost power and influence. Even though the United States remains a deeply religious society, church attendance and membership are declining, as well as trust in the church as an institution.[15] Sociologists have posited that previously accepted plausibility structures have been rejected or abandoned and belief in God has become one option among many.[16] In such a cultural environment, theological systems whose emphases were birthed in the context of medieval Europe require updating and reorientation if they are to address contemporary contexts and cultural concerns.

While this process of secularization has meant the recession of Christianity in Europe and North America, there has been unprecedented, exponential growth of Christianity in the Global South over the past fifty years, particularly in sub-Saharan Africa. In a development that few saw coming, the end of colonization and the withdrawal of many missionaries led to a dramatic *increase* in the numbers of adherents to Christianity throughout the formerly colonized world. Colonization essentially intended to extend the reach of Christendom outside of Europe. The process of globalization—which began with the early "explorers" over five hundred years ago—has intensified during the past fifty years as developments in the technologies of transportation and communication have brought into even greater proximity peoples who live far apart and have enabled regular, rapid exchanges with others near and far. The process of colonization is as significant an aspect of globalization as the spread of European languages, systems of thought, and governmental structures. Then, in the mid-twentieth century, formerly colonized peoples emigrated to the former colonial powers in a process that the Jamaican poet Louise Bennett described in her 1966 poem, "Colonization in Reverse." These new citizens brought their customs, worldview, and religious traditions with them as they "settle in de mother lan." And, as Bennett saw, they posed a question to the old colonial powers: "What a devilment a Englan! / Dem face war an brave de worse; / But ah wonderin how dem gwine stan/Colonizin in reverse."[17]

A Failed Narrative

The indicators of the end of a Christendom-era consensus based in a white, Western European Christianity are all around us.[18] The loss of cultural hegemony, the rise of religious pluralism, increased levels of immigration, and appeals to experience and culture as sources of theological reflection are all evidence of a shift in the West away from the Christian church as the political, social, and intellectual center of society. In the United States, the religious landscape has dramatically changed over the past half century. The percentage of Americans who claim that they are Christians continues to decline. Most of the growth in North American Christianity has come from immigration and the births of babies of color.[19] Meanwhile, in Africa and other areas of the Global South, Christianity is growing exponentially. Rather than bemoan the end of Christendom or seek to reinstate it (either in the Global North or the Global South), I argue that the collapse of Christendom is not a threat but an opportunity for Christian theology to let go of the Western cultural shackles and embrace a plurality of perspectives and theologies from around the world.

My approach contrasts sharply with the long-standing narrative of European-led progress to which Christianity yoked itself in the nineteenth century. Three twentieth-century events demonstrated the delegitimization of this narrative: World War II, the Holocaust, and movements for colonial independence. All three "simultaneously delegitimized the West as axiomatic center of reference and affirmed the rights of non-European peoples straining against the yoke of colonialism and neocolonialism."[20] Nazism and the Holocaust revealed the "internal sickness" of Europe as a site of racist totalitarianism, while the movements for colonial liberation, especially in Africa and Asia, revealed the "external" revolt against Western domination, "provoking a crisis in the taken-for-granted narrative of European-led progress."[21] Many—predominantly white—Christians have allowed this narrative of European-led "progress" to replace the narrative of the gospel of Jesus Christ. This false narrative has many guises, including American exceptionalism, manifest destiny, and various forms of well-meaning ecclesial mission programs. The collapse of this taken-for-granted narrative has left many Christians (again, predominantly white) asking questions about how the church and Christian theology can survive.

A Crisis of Authority

Indeed, the roots of what will later be called secularization can be found at the very origins of the Christian faith. As Marcel Gauchet expressed it, "Christianity proves to have been *a religion for departing from religion.*"[22] There is something inherent to the Christian faith that seeks to undermine religion itself. The sociologist Peter Berger locates the origins of secularization even earlier: "The roots of secularization are to be found in the earliest available sources for the religion of ancient Israel. In other words, we would maintain that the 'disenchantment of the world' begins in the Old Testament."[23] In the early centuries of the Christian church apologetic writings offered a rational defense of the Christian faith aimed primarily at those who practiced Greco-Roman religions.

After the biblical authors, the most significant apologists in the early church were Justin Martyr (ca. 100–165) and Origen of Alexandria (ca. 185–254). Once the Christian faith was legalized and declared the official religion of the Roman Empire in the early fourth century, the need to persuade people of the truth of the Christian faith disappeared. Adherence to Christianity was assumed and the authority of the church (backed by the ruling authorities) unquestioned. Though certainly not without significant historical moments of dissension, this trust in the church and this willingness to allow the church to interpret the revelation of God continued until the sixteenth century. The Protestant Reformers' challenge to the authority of the Roman Catholic Church, among other factors, led to a growing uncertainty about the centrality of the Christian faith to individuals and society as a whole. In fact, the Reformation was a significant moment in the secularization of Western society,[24] for the subsequent splintering of the Western church affirmed the choice of correct doctrine over accepted church tradition. Even so, until the seventeenth century most Europeans assumed that the Christian faith and most religious arguments were largely intra-Christian questions.

Beginning with writers such as Blaise Pascal (1623–62), it was then that the genre of apologetics was revived from dormancy. Pascal and other apologists were responding to a need that they perceived. They were responding to people (in Pascal's case, two of his friends) who questioned the Christian faith or did not believe in God in Jesus Christ.

The sociologist James Davison Hunter identified a connection between such apologetics and those who questioned authority in general. He wrote, "A rise in apologetic activity can be understood as a tacit recognition of a growing implausibility of religious authority."[25] The late twentieth century has seen an explosion of apologetic materials, often aimed at preserving a theological or political status quo.[26]

A combination of factors has caused the dramatic shifts within the religious culture of North America today: the rise in secularization and the collapse of plausibility structures for religion, Christianity's loss of cultural hegemony and the advent of pluralism, a shifting of individual authority from external to internal, and the relativization of morality. None of this would surprise Berger, who understood that when "religion can no longer be imposed [it] must be marketed. . . . [T]he religious institutions become marketing agencies and the religious traditions become consumer commodities."[27] Through the process of secularization, religious institutions have lost their monopoly on claims to truth and worldview and have been forced to compete with each other by pitching their ideas to individual consumers of faith-based goods and services.

With their "products" no longer taken for granted, a new word has entered the religious lexicon: *relevance*. Following the rise of secularization, apologists need to be concerned not only with the content of their message (and its conformity to scripture and tradition) but also with what is heard by their intended audience. If an audience does not understand or rejects the plausibility of an apologetic, then the message is deemed irrelevant. Apologists have to consider adapting their message and its form, since, as Berger writes, it pays "to sell out on certain features of the tradition."[28]

Within these intra-Christian debates, we see a microcosm of the larger conflict in American culture: a conflict "over the range and limits of acceptable pluralism; over where and how and on what terms the boundaries of acceptable diversity would be drawn," according to Hunter.[29] Instead of varieties of cultural or political diversity, for apologists, this cultural conflict has been waged over theological and ecclesiological issues. In the same way that "the culture war can be read as a negotiation over what will come next," so too this (apologetic) culture war is contending over what will come next for Christianity.[30]

The Collapse of Plausibility Structures

If broad swaths of entire societies have determined that religious claims are no longer plausible, then we must fundamentally rethink how to understand and interpret divine revelation. If the Christian message is no longer passively received by the masses through osmosis, then we must interrogate the process by which people hear the revelation of God in Jesus Christ. This shift away from passive (and partial) assent to cultural Christianity to a more deliberate and vigorous engagement with the revelation of God in Jesus Christ can spur positive and fruitful contemporary theological reflection.

The shift that secularization theorists identified is that whereas for thousands of years religion "played a strategic part in the human enterprise of world-building,"[31] in the second half of the twentieth century organized, institutional religion rapidly receded and secularization increased (again, most notably in Europe). The way in which individuals were socialized in Europe and North America no longer assumed Christianity as self-evident truth. Not since the early fourth century had Christianity's truth claims been fundamentally questioned. By the late twentieth century many people deemed implausible the worldview and the claims of Christianity.

The shift was significant and dramatic, but it is not entirely unwelcome. Though Christian institutions are losing their authority and influence and secularization is leading to the privatization of religion, we have an opportunity to rethink entrenched, calcified approaches to theological reflection. Charles Taylor described what he meant by contemporary society's secular age when articulating the goal of his book: "The change I want to define and trace is one which takes us from a society in which it was virtually impossible not to believe in God, to one in which faith, even for the staunchest believer, is one human possibility among others."[32] Taylor noted that the impact of secularization was that "belief in God is no longer axiomatic. There are alternatives."[33] These alternatives were not merely theoretically present, but were equally present in shaping "new conditions of belief [,] . . . a new context in which all search and questioning about the moral and the spiritual must proceed."[34] Faith, or belief, is now (in a secular age) characterized as a quest, full of searching and questioning, not simply a matter of socialization or consent, as in the Constantinian era.

Commonly held beliefs as well as the context in which those beliefs are held, which had been taken for granted, have been drastically and dramatically altered. Instead of "Christian" being used as an adjective to describe nations, rulers, and ways of life, its meaning is no longer assumed and in fact is challenged on every front. More generally, religion as a social phenomenon currently lacks the authority to shape a common world for all society. Increasing numbers of people in the West are pushing aside the overarching narrative of religion, and of Christianity in particular.

Claims that Christianity had made for centuries, particularly about salvation and the divinity of Christ, Western culture now deems exclusivist and out of order in the public realm. The basis of the claims (the scriptures) has not changed, but their reception in society has changed from implicit acceptance to hostile resistance. The collapse of these plausibility structures affects not only the faith claims themselves but also the worldview and societal assumptions based on them. Thus there is now an absence of assumptions shared by all (or even a majority) within Western societies, and that collapse is causing fragmentation and disorientation throughout society—but also innovation and a shift from external to internal authority. The decline of Christendom coincides with a rise in secularization and increasing globalization. In order to understand the contemporary context, secularization and globalization must be considered together, not as isolated phenomena as is often the case. In the rest of the book I employ the *theological* responses of Bediako and Barth to globalization and secularization to cast a vision for contemporary theological reflection; the decline of colonial Christendom presents numerous opportunities for contemporary theological reflection.

Secularization

Understanding the complexity (and ongoing debates) of both secularization and globalization is essential for theological thinking today. If Christendom can be described as the process of Christianity ruling (parts of) the world (both formally and informally) from one center, then this chapter tells the story of Christianity losing its cultural hegemony in Europe and North America while simultaneously expanding its global reach. In the West, Christianity went from being *the* faith to one faith among many others. The transition from singularity to plurality over the past four centuries led to a crisis of authority for the church and Christian theology. The first half of this chapter examines this transition; the second half examines the exporting of the Christian faith from Europe to the Global South, noting ways that the exponential growth of Christianity in Africa, Asia, and Latin America has led to a "shift in the center of gravity" of the Christian faith to multiple centers in that region. This chapter argues that the conditions of possibility for contemporary theological reflection have irrevocably changed. That changed context calls for a revised theological method and emphases.

Over the past five hundred years the context of belief and the content of those beliefs have changed dramatically in light of increasing secularization and intensifying globalization. The task of Christian theology has changed as well. No longer is the task of Christian theology to articulate the mysteries of God for those who already believe amid a culture of fellow believers. In this sense, theology has been faith-seeking-understanding. Rather, the task of contemporary theological reflection is to articulate human understandings of divine revelation in particular contexts.

In *A Secular Age*, Taylor describes the collapse of the implicit and often unacknowledged structures within Western societies that encouraged belief in the Christian faith. As Taylor writes:

Belief in God isn't quite the same thing in 1500 and 2000. I am not referring to the fact that even orthodox Christianity has undergone important changes (e.g., the "decline of Hell," new understandings of the atonement). Even in regard to identical creedal propositions, there is an important difference. This emerges as soon as we take account of the fact that all beliefs are held within a context or framework of the *taken-for-granted*, which usually remains tacit, and may even be as yet unacknowledged by the agent, because never formulated.[35]

Theology after Colonization is about the nature and possibility of belief in differing cultural contexts. Specifically, I explore the collection of beliefs known as the Christian faith and how—in the face of increasing secularization and globalization—belief in the God of Jesus Christ can be plausibly held and articulated. As such, this book begins by offering a theological reading of the history of what is often called Christendom.

I am using the term "Christendom" to designate the yoking of the Christian faith to political power and cultural hegemony that began in the fourth century with Constantine I.

In the 1930s, Karl Barth wrote that the "*Christian*-bourgeois or *bourgeois*-Christian age has come to an end[;] . . . that is, Christendom no longer exists in the form we have known. . . . The world is reclaiming . . . its freedom (from the church). . . . But with that, the gospel's freedom over against the world has been restored to it."[36] Barth sensed that in Germany, at least, the relationship between the church and the world had changed radically.[37] There was increased separation between world and church beginning with the departure of the church from public spheres. This departure, removal, or abandonment of the church from public spaces is one aspect of secularization, the aspect that Taylor calls the "subtraction theory" of secularization. This understanding of secularization relates to Barth's experience of his theological teachers who Barth felt did not have the fortitude to confront the Kaiser. However, as the sociologist José Casanova suggests, there are two other aspects of secularization as well.[38] The second is the decline of religious belief and practice and captures Bediako's main critique of Western Christianity,[39] and the third is the privatization of religion. Taylor has built on these aspects of secularization to describe the changed cultural context resulting from the first two aspects as "*secularity 3*," where belief is "one [option] among many."[40] Not only has the content of belief been changed, but the possibility of belief or nonbelief has been introduced. Taylor describes this as "a titanic change" in Western civilization, for Christianity is no longer assumed but is understood as simply one of the options. This recalibrating of religious and cultural authority away from the Christian church helpfully describes the dramatically changed context for contemporary theological reflection in Europe and North America.

My interest, however, is different from Taylor's. Taylor examines what it *feels like* to live in a secular age. I ask about the *content* of theological belief in a secular (and globalized) age. If what it means to *believe* has changed, what impact does that development have on what is believed? As the theological questions have changed, so too have the answers that theology provides. Just as there is now the unprecedented option to choose belief or nonbelief, what one believes does not come prepackaged but is à la carte, a matter of choice.[41] Indeed, belief itself has become more fragile since 1500; now many share "the undermining sense that others think differently" than them.[42] Taylor has insightfully expressed both the changes in the conditions of the possibility of belief (i.e., to believe does not mean the same thing in the sixteenth century that it does in the twenty-first) and the unprecedented option to choose belief or nonbelief.

The Shift from External to Internal Authority

With the society-shaping power of religion undermined in the late modern world, a dramatic shift from the communal to the individual occurred. No longer was meaning legitimated by society (external to the individual), but now individuals legitimate meaning for themselves. The locus of authority had been internalized. Thus individual, personal concerns became elevated above communal concerns.

The "new center" of human understanding and being is the "self," not the "spirit or soul."[43] This move—and the many others like it—is neither innocuous nor semantic but instead has wide-ranging implications for the understanding of human society and for faith and religion in particular. For example, "to be entertained . . . bec[a]me the highest good and boredom the most common evil."[44] "Love yourself" replaced the command to "Love thy neighbor." The standard becomes, "Not the good life but better living."[45] Epitomizing these changes was Sheila Larson's description of her faith as "Sheilaism. Just my own little voice," reported in *Habits of the Heart*.[46]

The contrast between the two approaches that Philip Rieff outlined is stark: "Religious man was born to be saved; psychological man is born to be pleased."[47] The cry of the ascetic, "I believe," was replaced by "I feel," the caveat of the therapeutic.[48] The goal of living became to gain clarity about oneself, not to devote oneself "to an ideal as the model of right conduct."[49] Self-knowledge and personal authenticity (living out of one's center as a self) became valued over conformity to societal or religious norms and ideals. There is no external moral code, only be true to yourself. It is not so much that morality is relativized as that it is has become personalized and in being personalized has, essentially, evaporated.

Rieff identifies a connection between the evaporation of morality and the minimizing of guilt. Without an overarching moral demand system, there is no longer a theological category of sin for the therapeutic individual. Rieff writes, "Sin is all but incomprehensible to [the individual] inasmuch as the moral demand system no longer generates powerful inclinations toward obedience or faith, nor feelings of guilt when those inclinations are over-ridden by others for which sin is the ancient name."[50] An act that a religious person might once have called "sin" would for the therapeutic be an "unhealthy choice." All morality—whether ascetic or hedonistic—loses its impact.[51] Gluttony, whether of food or consumer goods, becomes not a sin against God that requires forgiveness (and penance for some) but instead an unhealthy lifestyle choice. In the case of both the religious and the therapeutic, the individual should consume less but each for a different referent. For the sin of pride, a religious person acknowledges the sin of putting oneself on a pedestal as an idol instead of God, whereas an overinflated self-image leads to an inauthentic self-understanding and perhaps difficult social relations for a therapeutic individual.

Rieff's insights have three implications for a contemporary understanding of authority and revelation:

(1) The legitimating authority moves from the communal to the individual.
(2) The subjective trumps the objective. Personal feelings and emotions supersede truth claims and even at times historical facts, as personal memories reshape history.
(3) Sin is no longer part of the therapeutic individual's vocabulary.

In short, (2) while modern humans may be intellectually advanced, they have significant skepticism regarding matters of faith and belief. For them, the purpose of religion is no longer to pursue ultimate truth (which may or may not exist) or to be saved from one's sin (since it is impossible for a "self" to sin) or to gain admittance to an afterlife (which is too far into the future) but to help one feel better about daily life in the here and now. Though constantly aware of one's impending death, the therapeutic wants his or her anxiety to be soothed, comforted, and entertained, not to seek a long-term solution to a metaphysical, cosmic problem.

Concomitantly, (3) as authority moves from the communal to the individual, sin is replaced by neurosis.[52] Indeed, "all destinies . . . become intensely personal and not at all communal."[53] There is a connection between one's external symptoms and the inner conditions responsible for that symptom. While a soul or a spirit was in relationship with the divine and a religious community and could, through unrighteous action, separate itself from them, a self is only responsible to itself. What this means is that "the religiously inclined therapists are themselves engaged in the absurd task of trying to teach contented people how discontented they really are."[54] For if people do not think in terms of sin or guilt, apologists must first convince people of the problem before offering a salvific solution. The therapeutic individual cannot hear the Christian gospel as "good news," until first she is convinced of the "bad news" that must precede it. So for many modern-day evangelists and apologists, the cultivation of anxiety takes the place of sin.

Rieff identifies how the cultivation of anxiety has been a key element in evangelistic strategies. "Throughout the history of Christian evangelism," he writes, "anxiety has been exploited for apologetic purposes."[55] In today's context, anxiety about cultural change provides fertile soil for modern-day apologists. Regardless of how someone defines the "problem" (the particular thing he is anxious about: relationships, injustice, wealth, comfort, health, etc.) in the world or in his own life, there is a religious solution crafted to be the answer to the problem.

This shift from sin to anxiety is huge. An understanding of sin has been the bedrock of most Christian dogmatics, particularly since the sixteenth century. To have sin removed from the therapeutic individual's vocabulary and consciousness has tremendous theological implications. For without sin, there is nothing from which to be saved, and we must rethink the entire understanding of salvation. Western Christian missionaries to indigenous cultures without understandings of guilt or sin have in the past introduced the notion of guilt in order to then offer the "Christian" solution to alleviate the guilt.[56]

Offering that solution in the past has come through preaching. But Rieff concludes that late-modern culture "renders preaching superfluous"[57] and by extension all Christian apologetics as well. James Davison Hunter has paraphrased Rieff to say that "all moral and religious convictions lose their force when subject to the therapeutic."[58] If the Christian faith is reduced to such cultural consensus, expecting divine revelation to come to peoples through Western culture, and in this case therapeutic culture, then the Christian faith will evaporate from history as secularization continues—at least in the West.

Berger saw only two options for religious communities amid this rise of secularization: either they can accommodate by modifying their "products" in accordance with human demands or they can refuse to accommodate and "continue to profess the old objectivities as much as possible as if nothing had happened."[59] On the surface, neither option looks promising. It appears that either Christianity will have to abandon the message and claims of the past two thousand years and find new ones (which sounds like a sort of religious reinvention) or Christianity will have to stick its head in the sand and pretend that nothing is happening in the wider culture. Can contemporary theological reflection offer a third option (neither accommodation nor the status quo) through an understanding of divine revelation that is relevant to varying cultural contexts *and* faithful to the gospel? Before responding to this question, we must explore further the impact of globalization on contemporary contexts.

Intensifying Globalization

Rapid changes in technology and travel have "shrunk" the world and brought diverse peoples, their ideas and cultures, into closer proximity to one another. These changes, coupled with the exponential growth of the Christian faith in the Global South, complicate further the task of contemporary theological reflection. Not only is there a crisis of authority within Western theological understandings (thanks to secularization), but there are also increased pressures from the rest of the world (thanks to globalization) to articulate broad and varied theological understandings.

"Globalization" is the name given to the complex social, economic, cultural, and political factors that are combining to shape today's world. Definitions of globalization, its causes, history, and meaning, are all intensely debated—yet what is clear to all is that the world has changed dramatically during the past half century, perhaps more rapidly than at any other time in human history. The implications of these cultural changes for the understanding of divine revelation and the contemporary task of Christian theological reflection are significant and yet rarely considered.[60] Globalization is a fact of our times. Whether one is wholeheartedly embracing the flattening of the world like the *New York Times* columnist Thomas Friedman, who celebrates the rapid exchange of ideas, finances, and peoples,[61] or rejecting it like the anthropologist James Ferguson, who understands globalization as a powerful arm of neoliberal capitalism that is making the rich richer and the poor poorer, there is no denying that technological changes have made it possible for information and people to interact across wider spaces in less time than ever before. Globalization has economic consequences (offshore production, call centers in India, and the global economic crisis, as three examples), political consequences (starting with European exploration and colonization and current post-colonial movements), military consequences (the 9/11 attacks and the wars in Iraq and Afghanistan), environmental consequences (from the impact of deforestation in Brazil to the effect of global warming at Mount Kilimanjaro, the Arctic, the Antarctic, and elsewhere). Social scientists and others have amply documented many of these consequences. Historians, sociologists, and theologians in the developing world have demonstrated and documented the rapid growth of Christianity in the Global South.

Friedman's historical schema begins in 1492 with Christopher Columbus and his enthusiasm focused primarily on the present. Alternatively, the sociologist Roland Robertson offered a long history of globalization in five phases. For Robertson, the "overall processes of globalization . . . are at least as old as the rise of the so-called world religions two thousand and more years ago."[62] Robertson's historical narrative allowed the literary critic Paul Jay to claim the banality of globalization. Jay wrote, "Cultures have always traveled and changed. . . . [T]he effects of globalization, as dramatic as they are, only represent in an accelerated form something that has always taken place: the inexorable change that occurs through intercultural contact, as uneven as the forms it takes may be."[63] For Jay, globalization has been around for over six hundred years and has occurred across cultures. The present significance is the "accelerating convergences"[64] of these globalizing forces and their multinational and multicultural origins.[65]

Jay identified the myopic error of many interpreters who equate globalization with Western neoliberal capitalism. "To see globalization as a recent eruption," Jay wrote, "is to mistake not only the date but the nature of its emergence, for it leads us to miss the extent to which earlier world systems outside the West produced forms of knowledge and technology integral to the later phases of globalization."[66] Many of the advances in science and technology that are often attributed to the West are based on insights and innovations from China, India, and Arabic peoples. The economist Amartya Sen agreed: "Is globalization really a new Western curse? It is, in fact, neither new nor necessarily Western; and it is not a curse. . . . [A]n immaculate Western conception is an imaginative fantasy."[67] The false theorization of globalization as a Western creation is instructive for a consideration of Christian theology today. Neither globalization nor Christian theology is a Western invention.

Nearly all of the earliest Christian thinkers would be referred to today as "people of color." Jesus of Nazareth was of Semitic descent and likely had olive-colored skin. Athanasius of Alexandria and Augustine of Hippo were both from North Africa—likely with olive or black skin. The work of Christian theology is based on the contributions of many and diverse persons in the early centuries and today. However, much like in discussions about globalization, the peoples of Africa are rarely mentioned as significant contributors to our Christian theology, though Christianity is waxing there even as it wanes in the Global North.[68]

While Christianity is receding in the West (in terms of both influence and numbers of adherents), it is growing exponentially in the Global South. Some empirical data are telling. In 1910, 66 percent of Christians worldwide lived in Europe and North America. In 2010, 61 percent of Christians lived in the Global South (63 percent of Africans are Christians).[69] While the number of Christians worldwide has quadrupled over the past century to 2.2 billion, the proportion of the world population that is Christian has remained constant at about one-third. Yet, in a dramatic change few saw coming, there are now nearly twice as many Christians in the Global South as in the Global North.

The rapid growth of Christianity in Africa began to receive scholarly attention in the 1970s. David Barrett first identified the shift in "centre of gravity" in 1970. "By AD 2000," he wrote, "the centre of gravity of the Christian world will have shifted markedly southwards, from Europe and North America to the developing continents of Africa and South America."[70] Shortly thereafter, the British church historian Andrew Walls expanded and interpreted Barrett's observation.[71] Walls wrote, "Within the last century there has been a massive southward shift of the center of gravity of the Christian world."[72] The implications of this shift were clear to Walls: the peoples of Latin America, sub-Saharan Africa, and Asia were going to show the future of Christian theology. While the theology of European Christians may remain important to them, it will only serve as a historical footnote to the theologies written in the developing world.[73]

Bediako was grateful for this shift from the North to the South, as he saw it preserving the Christian faith that had come under threat in Europe. Bediako often deployed the language popularized by Walls. Bediako wrote, "The present shift in the centre of gravity may have secured for Christianity a future that would otherwise be precarious in the secularized cultural environment of the modern West."[74] As the trajectory of nineteenth-century European Protestantism reached its nadir in the crises of the twentieth century, increasing secularization and decreasing participation in Christian churches, Bediako saw new possibilities for Christianity arising from Africa.

By 2002, Philip Jenkins, in his widely read *The Next Christendom: The Rise of Global Christianity*, applied the phrase to the whole of Christianity in the Global South as he anticipated a shift in ecclesial power from Europe and North America to Africa, Asia, and South America.[75] Jenkins described the new "southern" Christianity as "exotic, intriguing, exciting, but a little frightening."[76] While Jenkins hints that these changes will have a significant impact on future theological discussions (and though his follow-up book softened many of his earlier claims),[77] he offers little on the content of this impact. Barrett also noted the racial-ethnic impact of these demographic changes: "Christianity, long a religion of predominantly the white races, will have started to become a religion of predominantly the non-white races."[78] My interest, then, lies in the implications of these sociological changes for contemporary theological method and reflection.

Bediako and other African theologians, while thankful that many Westerners were finally noticing the rapid growth of Christianity in the Global South through Jenkins's books, strongly disputed Jenkins's predictions of a "next Christendom." They claimed that his conclusions resulted from his lack of experience of religious pluralism. Jenkins, from the United States (a Roman Catholic turned Episcopalian), lives in a society that is predominantly Christian, has historical roots in Christianity, and is experiencing increased religious pluralism that some find threatening. However, Bediako, as is typical for sub-Saharan Africans, grew up amid religious pluralism. Traditional African religions and Islam, in addition to Christianity and African Independent Churches (AICs), are found throughout Ghana. Thus, for Bediako and other theologians in the Global South, Christianity can—and often already does—coexist with other religious traditions, and does so without seeking political domination. Indeed, since the experience of African Christianity has always included religious pluralism, in the form of both primal religions and Islam, Bediako suggests that Africa can help the West in the remaking of its theology. In such a process of remaking, the complex character of Christianity is laid bare for fresh exploration and appraisal.

For Bediako, the core failure of Jenkins's work was how it "polarizes . . . [the] conservative, and probably innocent South, and the more sophisticated, liberal North. . . . [This] persistent 'us and them' frame of reference . . . obscures the polycentric character of Christian presence in the world."[79] Bediako repeatedly referred to Christendom as a "disaster"[80]—Barth also offered stinging criticism of the "deep shadow" of Christendom (IV/3, 19–20)—and was certain that "Africa has not produced and is not likely to produce, a new Christendom" (*CiA*, 249).[81] On Bediako's reckoning, then, the growth of the Christian church in the Global South is *not* a "new Christendom"; rather, it is an authentic, indigenous expression of the Christian faith—*outside* of Europe and North America and *within* a religiously pluralistic environment—that creates *multiple* centers (or *no* geographic center!) of Christianity.

Through an emphasis on the role of the primal imagination and African mother tongues, Bediako pushed for the remaking of Christian theology.[82] Most fundamentally, Bediako insisted that Christianity is indigenous to Africa, not imported from Europe, and that expressions of Christianity in Africa—in both practices and beliefs—had significant contributions to make to the worldwide understanding of the Christian faith. The growth of Christianity in Africa, for Bediako, then, was about faithfulness to the gospel, not about power, contrary to Jenkins's assertions in *The Next Christendom*. Bediako challenged Jenkins's understanding of the nature of the Christian faith when he wrote, "Christianity can be seen as having no one permanent centre. Every centre is a potential periphery and every periphery a potential centre."[83] Appealing to the growing presence of Christians in all parts of the world, Bediako used the familiar trope of center and periphery from postcolonial theory to demonstrate that Jenkins's understanding of Christianity was still bound by colonial categories. In response to the crumbling, former center of Christianity in Europe, Jenkins sought a new center in the Global South. Bediako resisted the guiding assumption of Jenkins's argument. Simply put, he insisted that Christianity did not require a single center in the Global North *or* the Global South. Everywhere Christianity is found is both a center of theological reflection and a peripheral recipient of the ongoing theological reflection in every other center.

While the Christendom-colonial complex has been unraveling, two other interrelated trends have been growing: increasing Western secularization and intensifying globalization. In isolation, secularization has been undermining Christendom while pluralism brought by globalization has upended colonialization. In tandem, the contemporary context for Christian theological reflection has been radically altered—particularly in the West. Authority has shifted from external institutions to within individuals and local faith communities. Authority has increasingly shifted from the Global North to the rapidly growing bodies of Christians in the Global South. Authority has shifted from European dogmatics to grassroots theologies in a more conversational tone. The story of these shifts in authority, how they have delegitimated the narratives supporting the Christendom-colonial complex, points toward the future of theological reflection. Bediako's experience of feeling more African (and less Western) by embracing the Christian faith and Barth's realization that "nineteenth-century theology no longer held any future" are instructive.[84]

Both theologians were convinced that all theology is contextual, that is, that the social location of a theologian and that of her audience deeply shape the questions that she asks of God, humanity, and the world, as well as the answers that are offered. The same is true of North America today in the early twenty-first century. Given this premise, below I describe the conditions of Christian theological reflection in the twenty-first century in the United States, conditions in which secularization and globalization feature strongly. There is much for us to learn from Barth's and Bediako's insights.

The Interconnectedness of Secularization and Globalization

Already, these brief encounters with Barth and Bediako have demonstrated that theories of secularization and globalization are not neatly separated. Though Barth's theological project was motivated by secularization and addressed to secularizing Europe, at the end of his life he pointed to the need for contributions from outside Europe, specifically from the developing world. Bediako, a product of globalization, was both deeply influenced by and then deeply critical of European secularization. Both theologians demonstrate the need to think about secularization and globalization together, a point that has been missed by many social scientists.

To appropriately engage secularization, scholars from the non-Western world are needed. José Casanova has noted, "Understandably, most discussions of the secular and secularism are internal Western Christian secular debates about patterns of Christian Western secularization."[85] He also acknowledged the "Western-centrism" of his work on secularization.[86] In addition, Casanova acknowledged the impact of colonization on processes of secularization that are missed by Taylor.[87] The sociologist Sara Mahmood captures the interrelated nature of these phenomena when she writes, "Missionary work in regions colonized by European powers was not simply an extension of a stable Christian essence into foreign traditions and cultures but transformative of Western Christianity itself."[88] The global changed the local. The lived experience of sending Europeans to far-off lands and receiving their reports of what was encountered in these lands changed Europeans' self-understanding, their view of God, and their view of themselves. By leaving out any account of colonialism in both its political and religious forms, Taylor ignored a shaping factor in the process of European secularization. His focus on Latin Christendom neglected the recipients of the colonial project. Secularization did not occur in a vacuum but in regular contact with the wider world. Secularization and globalization need to be considered together in our contemporary context.

Similarly, globalization theorists have a history of neglecting its connections with secularization and with religion more broadly.[89] Peter Beyer and Lori Beaman noted that "during the roughly two decades that globalization has risen to its currently iconic status, religion as irrelevant or as outsider to whatever globalization might mean has been the prevailing orientation."[90] One of the reasons for this broad neglect of religion (to say nothing yet of secularization) is an overreliance on an understanding of globalization as solely the expansion of Western capitalism or Western cultural imperialism. Revised understandings of globalization based on "world consciousness"[91] or on having "very distinctive religious overtones"[92] have opened new lines of inquiry. These newer approaches demonstrate that the trends and phenomena called globalization did not simply affect religion: instead religion, including secularization, has affected globalization as well. These effects are often manifested in local instances of negotiation between cultures and religious traditions.[93] The concept of reverse mission—where missionaries from formerly colonized countries, such as South Korea or Nigeria, are sent to Europe or North America for evangelizing, missionary activities—is one example of how globalization in travel and access allowed a response to secularization. Indeed, as Casanova noted, "Under conditions of globalization, world religions do not only draw upon their own traditions but also increasingly upon one another."[94] Further, Casanova identified the opportunities and threats that globalization presents, "insofar as globalization entails the de-territorialization of all cultural systems and threatens to dissolve the essential bonds between histories, peoples, and territories that have defined all civilizations and world religions."[95]

The combination of the internal crumbling of cultural consensus around Christianity and social norms attributed to the Christian faith (secularization) and the external pressures brought by exposure to other cultures and religious beliefs (globalization) has led to a crisis of authority within the church and for the task of Christian theology. Truth is no longer solely mediated by ecclesial authorities. Such changes necessitate a rethinking of theological method and a rearticulation of the doctrine of revelation, one that is not simply self-referential, but listens to outside voices with attention and respect. By "outside voices," I am referring not to familiar and ancient controversies over heresies in the early church: Marcionites, Arians, Nestorians, Donatists, and the like. Over forty years ago, the Kenyan John Mbiti noted, "We [Africans] feel deeply affronted and wonder whether it is more meaningful theologically to have academic fellowship with heretics long dead than with the living brethren of the Church today in the so-called Third World."[96] Instead, I juxtapose the Ghanaian theologian Kwame Bediako's insights about the remaking of Christian theology and his analysis of the causes of the recession of the church in Europe to those of the Swiss theologian Karl Barth in order to provide Western readers with more tools to respond to the globalization and secularization of their world.

Pluralism in Western Society

The context of pluralism is unprecedented in the history of the Christian church. Never before have Christians not known the dominant societal narrative. In the first centuries, the apologists spoke in the context of the

Roman Empire. Then, following Constantine, Christendom ruled—in various forms—until crumbling under the pressures of late modernity. Even during the expansion of the Christian church in Communist China, there was a dominant culture. In late modern North America, there is no consensus on the presenting issues, no dominant culture. Instead, a type of thin pluralism exerts a weak hegemony wherein everyone feels outside of a perceived dominant culture. Hunter describes this situation: "Religious and philosophical pluralism—at least in late modern America—exists without a dominant culture, at least not one of overwhelming credibility or one that is beyond challenge."[97] Institutional pressures will cause institutions to try to preserve the problem to which they are the solution, making the matter more intractable.[98] Part of the energy behind the polemics is a propping up of the opposition in order to give one's position greater plausibility (conservatives need liberals and vice versa). The apologists write to each other because in pluralism they are lacking an obvious interlocutor. There is no dominant culture asking Christianity for a defense. In fact, for "the foreseeable future, the likelihood that any one culture could become dominant in the ways that Protestantism and Christianity did in the past is not great."[99] If it is unlikely that there will soon be another dominant culture, then the Christian church must find a new way of relating to the world or else the apologists will continue to be talking to themselves—with no one else listening, making the claims of Christianity even less engaging.

The onset of pluralism marks the beginning of a new religious culture that (following Rieff) calls for a new apologetic.[100] In a pluralistic society, religious belief is possible, but it must be different.[101] Christian churches and their apologists cannot assume that the claims of Christianity, or the forms in which those claims are made, can be taken for granted. The cultural context of late modern North America requires a new self-understanding for the church, its mission and its message. Using history as a guide, in order to remain viable the church must preserve its core teachings while introducing and embracing innovations. Further, these innovations are most successful when they "build on the unique history and traditions of the religious organization and cite core teachings as the source of inspiration."[102] There are significant resources within the scriptures, theologies, and traditions of all the churches. As social and historical contexts change, so must contemporary theological emphases. Christendom-era answers ought not to be offered in response to post-Christendom (or postmodern) questions. The blank stares and quizzical looks on the faces of the inquisitive betray their deep theological disconnection from the church. The doctrines of Christian theology must be reassessed for their relevance and relative significance today.

Throughout history, the Christian faith has adapted from one context to another through processes of translation. In contrast to the Islamic faith that spreads by assimilation—new converts must learn Arabic in order to read the Koran, adhere to specific traditions regarding clothing and community life, and pray five times a day facing Mecca—the Christian faith translates the Bible into vernacular languages, reappropriates indigenous customs, and often claims that God has been at work for generations in the "host culture."[103] In order to perform the challenging theological work of translating the message of the Christian faith for the twenty-first century, Western theology must be examined for the cultural and Christendom-based assumptions guiding its self-understanding. Only when old practices and biases are laid aside can new approaches to contemporary questions and problems be considered. Only in this way can an understanding of the Christian faith that is generative and seeks human flourishing and the common good be articulated.

World Christianity(-ies)

There are (and should be) multiple centers of Christianity in the world, not just one and certainly not just one in the West.[104] Instead, as Bediako recognized, "the emergence of a 'world Christianity' [is] the result of diverse indigenous responses to the Christian faith in various regions of the world."[105] Each indigenous culture offers a distinct response to its own faithful contextualization of the gospel of Jesus Christ.

The emergence of a "world Christianity" suggested to Bediako an opportunity for the developing world to *help* the West.[106] In fact, Bediako stated his conviction even more strongly. As a graduate student, he wrote, "It may well require a more active partnership with Third World churches to effect the rescue of Western churches from their captivity to culture."[107] This quotation foregrounded Bediako's central claim about Western Christianity: its captivity to culture. For him, the West had traded the good news of the gospel for a poor substitute. Instead of the Western church placing its foundation on the unchanging gospel of Jesus Christ, it had placed its confidence in the shifting sands of culture. For Bediako, the gospel of Jesus Christ does not change, but its cultural form *must* change as the gospel is translated from one host culture to the next. Consequently, "all Christian theology is a synthesis, an 'adaptation' of the inherited Christian tradition in the service of new formulations. . . . [N]o Christian theology in any age is ever simply a repetition of the inherited Christian tradition" (*TI*, 434). As a synthesis, the timeworn category of syncretism is revealed as hollow. While Bediako does not give up on the term—he still seeks "relevance without syncretism"—he primarily articulates an understanding of Christianity that is "a synthesis" (*TI*, 434).

For Bediako, the considerable intellectual shift toward adjustment of a non-Western Christianity and the process of reverse globalization encourage and demand a *universalizing in reverse*. Since, for him, the gospel is universal and applies everywhere, it can be translated from Greek and Hebrew and understood in Africa as God speaks in every tongue. Then, once understood in Africa, the implications for the meaning of Christianity worldwide can be universalized as a non-Western religion. Bediako's articulation of this claim relies on Revelation 7:9: "After this I looked, and there was a great multitude that no one could count, from every nation, from all tribes and peoples and languages, standing before the throne and before the Lamb, robed in white, with palm branches in their hands." He interprets this verse in light of the growth of world Christianity to mean that "though Christianity has always been universal in principle it can be seen to have become universal in practice only in recent history."[108]

We cannot overestimate the impact of this transition. Bediako considers the universalizing of the Christian faith in practice "a fact that is not only unique among the world's religions, it is a new feature for the Christian faith itself. One must therefore also not underestimate what the outworking of a global, Christian identity might involve."[109] The shaping of a new identity requires significant work, and the growth can be awkward at times. As Christianity moved from being theoretically applicable worldwide to manifesting diverse forms throughout the world, Bediako went beyond trying to establish and articulate an *African* Christian identity to establishing "a global, Christian identity." Yet even a broader Christian identity is not abstract, somehow apart from its host culture(s). Instead, as always, this universalizing from the bottom up, or at least from Africa to the world, *must* be particular.

And indeed African Christianity has something particular, and unique, to offer to the conversation about universality. Bediako writes, "In order to understand Christianity as a religious faith, one needs to understand African Christianity. . . . African indigenous knowledge systems may have something to contribute here in their holistic, integrating and reconciling nature, and their profound tolerance of diversity. African indigenous knowledge systems could become a positive resource in a new polarized world."[110] In this "new era in Christian history," Africa can help Christianity connect with the primal substructure of the Christian faith and positively engage the religiously pluralistic contexts of the twenty-first century world.

With that, we turn to Karl Barth, who though he rarely mentioned the non-Western world in his *Church Dogmatics*, yet has something important to contribute to this conversation, which might have even surprised him.

Barth: The Future of Theology Lies outside the West

Barth mentioned Africa just twenty times in his *Church Dogmatics*, and in most of these cases he referred either to missionaries or to Africa as an object of missionary outreach. Having died before Bediako published any work, Barth could not engage him, but neither did he address any other twentieth-century African theologians. Barth did not seem to consider the possibility that modern African theology could be a rich source for theological reflection. Africa was a destination for missionaries, and a difficult one at that. At the turn of the twentieth century, anthropologists were just returning to Europe from other parts of the world with accounts of the religious practices and beliefs they encountered.[111] At this time, Africa and Asia were seen mostly as destinations for missionaries and sources of raw data for Western theories of religion. The peoples of these lands were not seen as partners in theological discussions; they were to be *consumers* of theology, not *producers* in the fields of Christian thought.

Yet toward the end of his life, Barth offered two glimpses of a contrary, developing view—that non-Westerners, and particularly non-Europeans, may have significant contributions to offer to Christian theological reflection. In his 1963 address to foreign students in Basel, most of whom were from Africa, Asia, and Latin America, Barth concluded by saying, "The day may come when [Christianity] will be better understood and better lived in Asia and Africa than in our old Europe. Meanwhile try to learn, not from us, but with us, that the horizon and hope of us all also includes this: that God is for us and with us."[112] Further, just three weeks before his death in 1968, Barth wrote a letter to "Southeast Asian Christians" in which he encouraged them to do theology for themselves. He wrote:

> In my long life I have spoken many words. But now they are spoken. Now it is your turn. Now it is your task to be Christian theologians in your new, different and special situation with heart and head, with mouth and hands. . . . You truly do not need to become 'European,' 'Western' men, not to mention 'Barthians,' in order to be good Christians and theologians. You may feel free to be South East Asian Christians. Be it![113]

Even though Barth did not offer sustained attention to the theological developments taking place in Africa or Asia, his earlier suspicions—or at the least omissions—lessened as he acknowledged that the future of Christian theology may lie in these lands. Bediako represents an expression of that future.

Responding Theologically to Globalization and Secularization

While the voice of Barth may be quite familiar, many readers are not as familiar with or appreciative of his account in the last completed part-volume of his *Church Dogmatics* (IV/3) of the necessity and possibility of culture in God's self-revelation, an account evident in his all-pervasive understanding of Christ as Prophet. As for Bediako, the overriding theme, in his (even less familiar) corpus, is the interrelationship between revelation, religion, and culture. In short, both theologians were asking three questions: (1) How does God speak?, (2) What is God saying?, and (3) How do we know it? Central to addressing these questions is the issue of the role that human cultures and cultural media play in divine communication. Barth and Bediako engaged these similar themes but from very different contexts. Whereas Bediako wrote from Africa with the Christian faith growing rapidly and sending her peoples all around the world, Barth wrote from Europe as the Christian faith was receding numerically and losing credibility. Both offered strong responses welcoming the end of Christendom and presenting new possibilities for Christian theological reflection. Bediako wrote as a result of and in response to globalization, while Barth wrote as a result of and in response to secularization.

Bediako and Barth both exemplify how changes in their context necessitated changes in the content of their beliefs. Over the past five hundred or more years, there has been a shift in authority within Western culture from power and influence emanating from the Christian church (Christendom) to a cultural norm where not only is Christianity not assumed, but instead belief itself is just one option among many (post-Christendom). This shift in authority in the West (primarily in Europe and also in North America) has taken place in a variety of ways:

1. The state governments are now assuming functions in society that had been performed by ecclesial institutions.
2. There is a decline of religious belief and practices in Europe and segments of North American Protestantism.
3. Religious belief and practice have become more personal and private.
4. The conditions of possibility of religious belief have changed.
5. There is an increase in religious pluralism that sometimes corresponds to increasing ethnic diversity.
6. Single centers of religious authority (Rome, Canterbury, etc.) have been replaced by multiple concentrations of influence disrupting tidy distinctions between the center and the periphery.

The first four shifts get lumped together under the label of secularization, while the final two shifts are (generally speaking) results of globalization. Getting a sense of what these two concepts signify can provide a fuller description of the contemporary context for theological reflection.

Barth is known for his strong assertion of God's otherness and for the role of his doctrine of revelation in his theology. Reading only his early work (typically his *Epistle to the Romans* and *Church Dogmatics* I) misses his understanding of religion and culture presented in his discussion of Jesus Christ and the Light of Life in *Church Dogmatics* IV/3. For Barth, the light of Christ shines on truth and enkindles knowledge of God in true words and parables of the kingdom. In his last decade of life, Barth wrote of the value of voices from outside of Europe and North America to shape future theological understandings.

Indeed, the works of Bediako and Barth, each in their own ways, anticipated the postcolonial critique of universalizing standards and mores in Christian theological reflection and the Christian life, yet offered a surprising alternative: namely, Jesus Christ as the only universal. I treat Bediako and Barth as theological peers who generate significant theological engagement that transcends cultural and geographic boundaries; I imagine an intra-Protestant conversation that has broad implications. In my attention to three themes—revelation, religion, and culture—this book exemplifies a practice of theological reflection for the twenty-first century that is not hegemonic and that advocates instead for representatives of multiple perspectives and contexts in the task of constructive theological inquiry.

Individually and together, Bediako and Barth suggest new alternatives and provide resources to contemporary theological conversations. That forms the main body of the book. Following the detailed analysis of Bediako's and Barth's insights for understanding revelation and culture, amid secularization and globalization, I conclude by appealing to imagination to offer an updated understanding of revelation and a theological understanding of culture for the twenty-first century.

For Bediako, African Christianity offered hope and guidance to those stuck in a Christendom mind-set that assumed that a single "center of gravity" must exist and was based on a society focused on a single faith tradition. His work was a concerted attempt to understand the universal revelation of Jesus Christ in the translatability of the gospel into all cultures, the continuity of Christianity with traditional African religions, and the indigenous primal imagination as the substructure of African Christianity (as collectively expressed in his ancestor Christology), with implications for engaging religious pluralism, understanding Christianity as a non-Western religion, and the emergence of a world Christianity. Bediako understood Western Christianity to have been fatally wounded by the elimination of religious difference. He wrote, "When the context of religious pluralism is succeeded by . . . a Christendom from which all possible alternatives are presumed eliminated, not only from the context, but from theological existence too, [then] the theological enterprise ceases to need to make Christian decisions. Because no other kinds of decisions are conceivable, the character of theology itself becomes changed" (*CiA*, 257).

The total conquest and Christianizing of Europe eviscerated Europeans' primal religious pasts: groups like the Celts in present-day Ireland become the exception that proves the rule. A significant result of this character of Christendom theology can be an inability of Christian theologians to speak intelligibly with people outside the Christian faith. Likewise, a non-Christian will not be able to "encounter Christ except on the terms of a Christian theology whose categories have been established with little reference to the faiths of others" (*CiA*, 257). The implication of Bediako's claim, then, is that Western Christianity cannot continue to operate, ecclesiologically or theologically, on a Christendom-era model.

Bediako's theology is pertinent for contemporary theological reflection in Africa and in the United States. The influence of Christians of non-European descent on the practices of American Christianity has been increasingly documented.[114] As immigrants have migrated to the United States, they have brought their religious traditions and beliefs with them. No longer can the trajectory of Christianity in America be understood as a linear development of European denominations and faith traditions.

This changed cultural context calls for new theological reflection. Blindly continuing onward with centuries-old questions and answers treats Christianity as a static religion, not a living faith. Bediako and Barth offer new possibilities, new ways forward. Bediako describes the dynamic encounter between gospel and culture as the "infinite translatability of the gospel of Jesus Christ." Barth describes the ongoing prophetic activity of Jesus Christ as God's enkindling presence that shines light throughout the world.

Engaging Bediako and Barth together, I argue that Bediako's postcolonial theology and Barth's postmodern theology[115]—with *post-* in both cases used primarily in a historical rather than theoretical sense— together offer helpful resources for engaging twenty-first century questions centered on three themes: revelation, religion, and culture. Bediako's corpus is an example of writing from the margins of the empire back to the center of theological power and production in the West.[116] Although

Barth found himself geographically and culturally near the center, his theological work placed him outside the center, criticizing the liberal Protestant consensus. Both theologians used their understandings of God's revelation to confront accepted and prevailing norms in religion and culture. Their economic, social, political, and cultural contexts shaped their identities and interests; they wrote specifically for those settings.

TWO

Transcultural Theology through Juxtaposition

The shards of a broken cultural order, in isolation and in new juxtapositions, illuminate reality by an oddly refracted light.
— Larry Bouchard, *Tragic Method, Tragic Theology*

In September 1827, at the age of twenty-three, Andreas Riis traveled over one thousand kilometers from his home in a small rural community in southern Denmark to Basel, Switzerland, to apply to the Evangelical Mission Society. Both of Riis's parents had died, and after finishing a glazier apprenticeship under his older brother, Riis felt an increasing "desire to offer himself for the ministry of the Lord in the cause of mission." His deep religious conviction and Pietist ethics had connected with the stories that he had heard about missionaries who "left everything out of love for their savior to win souls for him."[1] Enrolling in the Basel Mission Theological Institute in 1828, Riis was exposed to its intense curriculum and its emphases on order, punctuality, diligence, humility, and personal spirituality under the leadership of Christian Gottlieb Blumhardt.[2] Following the Napoleonic Wars, the Evangelical Mission Society had founded a seminary for the education of overseas evangelists in 1815 in Basel. The Basel Mission became known for its evangelical, ecumenical, and international character.[3] At first, it trained missionaries for other mission organizations, but by 1821 it determined that it needed to establish its own overseas outposts "in order to bring the distinctive Pietist worldview to regions that were still laboring in 'unchristian darkness.'"[4] The Pietists in Basel believed that the end of the world was imminent and that it was the responsibility of anyone with means to help change the world before that happened.[5]

The goals of the Basel Mission in Africa were twofold: to create and sustain a Pietist Christian presence; and to bear witness against both the ravages of the European slave trade and the economic exploitation that accompanied and followed that trade.[6] The work of the Basel Mission in West Africa began in Liberia, but this effort failed when all the missionaries died. Soon thereafter the Danish government invited the Basel Mission to the Gold Coast (present-day Ghana) to pursue evangelism. The first four Basel missionaries arrived in 1828. Shortly after arriving, three of them died of sickness; the fourth would die before replacements arrived.

After his four years of training at the Basel Institute, Andreas Riis was chosen along with two others to continue the work of that mission in the Gold Coast. Within four months of their arrival in March 1832, Riis's two companions (one of whom was a physician) died from tropical sicknesses. Riis himself fell quite ill and was aided by an African doctor, who Riis referred to as a "Neger-Doctor" (Negro-doctor), who bathed him with soap and lemon and prescribed numerous cold baths that Riis found "not only pleasant and invigorating, but also worked upon the illness extremely quickly."[7] Given the choice in January 1833 by the Home Committee to abandon the mission and return home, Riis instead chose to become a preacher as the castle chaplain in Christianborg in the Gold Coast. His main responsibility was to train the European and mulatto children there. While serving as a chaplain, Riis continually kept his broader evangelistic mission in mind.

Two years later, Riis moved several miles inland, up to the hills, away from the mosquitoes, the diseases of the coast, the meddling of colonial officials, and the hedonistic, sinful behavior of his fellow Europeans. He chose to settle in Akropong, in the Akwapim hills, where a Danish surgeon, Dr. Paul Isert, had attempted to establish an agricultural colony in the late 1780s as an economic alternative to the slave trade.[8] The paramount chief (the highest-level political leader in the area), Nana Addo Dankwa I, and his elders warmly accepted Riis. Riis set about building a home (his nickname in the local language, Twi, was "Osiadan," meaning "house builder" or "architect"). After four years in Akropong (and seven years total in the Gold Coast), Riis could not report any converts to Christianity. Then Nana Dankwa said, "When God created the world he made books for the White Man and fetishes for the Black Man. But if you can show us some Black Men who can read the White Man's books, then we will surely follow you."[9] When Riis returned to Europe for a furlough in 1840, he shared Nana Dankwa's comments with the Basel Mission, which then made the decision to recruit missionaries from Jamaica to send to Akropong. In 1842, Riis traveled to the West Indies with George Thompson, an African Christian from Liberia, to recruit among the Moravian Christians.[10] The next year, after a two-month passage back to Africa, twenty-four new missionaries arrived at Christianborg. For Christians in Ghana today, the arrival and work of these English-speaking former slaves can hardly be overstated: "It was their presence that changed the face of the mission work in Akropong and for that matter the country as a whole."[11] The rural background of the Jamaican freed slaves made them a good fit for the agricultural work among the people in Akropong.

Riis was motivated by the perceived decay in morals of his fellow Europeans and the perceived ignorance of God of the people of West Africa. His concern about European secularization—understood as a decline in religious (i.e., Christian) belief and especially practice—intersected with the even then intensifying globalization, especially more rapid transportation and communication, that allowed him to hear the stories of missionaries to Africa and other lands. Through his stubborn and uncompromising personality, Riis persevered and is credited with bringing Christianity to Ghana.[12]

Yet there was another piece to his story: Riis was recalled to Basel in 1845 after it was discovered that he was trading in guns and gunpowder and running a mission plantation with eight slaves who were guaranteed their freedom on the day of their baptism.[13] Complicating this clear abuse of political, economic, and religious power is that the key moment in the entire missionary project in the Gold Coast was when Riis realized that he needed to recruit missionaries from Jamaica. As the Nigerian historian Ogbu Kalu has noted, "By 1840, it became obvious in the Gold Coast that only West Indians could save the efforts of the Methodists and Basel missions."[14] Though the colony of West Indians did not immediately serve the Basel Mission's evangelistic aims, some of their descendants did, and their cultural contributions, especially coffee plantations and mango trees, were significant.[15]

The enduring legacy of the Basel Mission was threefold: first, the translation of the Bible into the vernacular Twi by Johann Gottlieb Christaller, including a Twi dictionary; second, the focus on the education of both boys and girls; and third, the Presbyterian Church of Ghana (PCG).[16] World War I interrupted the work of the Basel Mission as the British authorities in the Gold Coast removed anyone with any connection to Germany.[17] The Presbyterians of the United Free Church of Scotland replaced the Basel Mission, leading to the fascinating pastiche that is the PCG today—a denomination rooted in traditional African religions, started by Swiss German Pietists, and organized by Scottish Presbyterians.[18] In 2012, the PCG had more than 565,600 members in almost 2,200 congregations and was one of the largest denominations of the historic mission churches in Ghana along with the Methodists and Roman Catholics.[19] Akropong-Akuapem became the center of the Presbyterian Church of Ghana—the denomination that ordained Bediako—and later the site of the Akrofi-Christaller Institute for Theology, Mission, and Culture that Bediako founded in 1987 with his wife, Dr. Gillian Mary Bediako.[20] When Bediako gave tours of the Old Mission neighborhood in Akropong called Hanover (named after the home parish of the freed slaves in the northwest corner of Jamaica) it was "always full of emotion, this history, this Hanover." For him, the coming of the Jamaicans as missionaries demonstrated to the Akan "that in becoming Christians they are still Africans."[21]

Bediako and the Basel Mission

Bediako routinely expressed his appreciation of the Basel Mission work in Ghana. The beliefs and practices of the Basel Mission contributed to his understanding of the Christian faith and the possibilities for the encounter between the gospel and African culture. For example, when giving a lecture on the future of education in Ghana, he appealed to the founding principles of the Basel Mission.

The instructions to the first missionaries sent by the Basel Mission to Ghana (then Gold Coast) in 1827 struck a similar note. The first Director of the Basel Mission, Christian Blumhardt, told them that [the] mission was to make 'reparation for injustice committed by Europeans, so that to some extent the thousand bleeding wounds could be healed which were caused by the Europeans since centuries through their most dirty greediness and most cruel deceitfulness.' Such expressed motivations by no means excuse the attitude of European cultural superiority which even some missionaries would demonstrate. Nevertheless, they help to explain some of the distinctive elements of the Christian ideal and content of education as practised on the Gold Coast.[22]

The Basel Mission sought to offer a version of Christianity not based on colonial exploitation but in reaction to it and in response to the theology of German Pietism. The Mission's goal was to engage in the work of the kingdom of God through the power of the resurrection for and with the Africans of the Gold Coast. Christian Blumhardt's hope was that this "better" Christianity could serve as "reparation" for past wounds. This revised understanding of Christianity offered an alternative in nineteenth-century European Protestantism. Blumhardt's intent was reflected in concrete differences in missionary practice in Africa. At the same time, Bediako was not naive, noting that the Basel Mission, including Andreas Riis, did not escape the colonial mind-set. Any "better" Christianity seeking "reparation" needs to address changes to material life.

The Basel Mission's affirmation of African languages and cultural concepts was unusual among late nineteenth-century Protestants. In the areas of Ghana influenced by the Basel Mission, schools placed a strong emphasis on education in African mother tongues.[23] This emphasis included teaching the grammar of mother tongues, not simply the use of the languages, in contrast to the mission-led schools founded by the Methodists (such as the Mfantsipim School, founded in 1876, that Bediako attended). The Basel Mission's dedication to encouraging the use of mother tongues was demonstrated by their commissioning in 1853 of Johannes Gottlieb Christaller (1827–95) from Winnenden in southwestern Germany "to devote himself solely to the Twi language, the most widely-spoken in the Gold Coast."[24] Christaller translated the entire Bible into Twi by 1862. He published his translation in 1870–71, a comprehensive grammar in 1875, and a monumental dictionary in 1881.[25] Christaller embodied the spirit of the Mission and has been widely revered for his work by both Europeans and Ghanaians[26] (*CiA*, 78–81). Christaller's work formed the basis for the first modern Twi Bible, produced by the Ghanaian Clement A. Akrofi (1901–67) in 1965. The convictions of nineteenth-century German Pietism allowed the Akan people to "bring their indigenous contribution to the spiritual achievements" of humankind.[27] When the Bediakos founded their research institute in Akropong-Akuapem, they named it the Akrofi-Christaller Mission Centre in tribute to these two scholars of the Twi language, Bible translators—one German, one Ghanaian—and pioneer figures in the cultural witness of the church in Ghana.

Bediako, an indigenous African theologian, is a direct heir of these pioneering efforts of the Basel Mission in the Gold Coast. He constructed his African Christian theology on the foundation of Christaller's and Akrofi's work of translating the Bible into an African mother tongue, Twi. Bediako's underlying theological conviction, the infinite translatability of the gospel of Jesus Christ, arises from the translation of the Christian scriptures into African languages and vernacular theological concepts. In this way, he continued the Blumhardts' legacy and the work of the Basel Mission.

Bediako's life and work was indelibly marked by the colonial legacy. His grandfather was a catechist with the Basel Mission, his education in middle and high school was in a missionary-founded school begun by the Methodists, his academic subjects considered the histories of *other* peoples, of civilizations outside Africa, as he learned Latin, Greek, and French.[28] His scholarly talents were consistently applied to mastering Western intellectual traditions. His university honors degree was rewarded with a scholarship to the metropole. Bediako was prepared—groomed, even—to function and succeed in the Western European world. And in his early life Bediako conformed to the expectations placed on him even in his atheistic religious beliefs. In short, Bediako was a recipient of globalization through colonialism.

Deeply influenced by the négritude movement during his graduate work for his first doctorate, Bediako abandoned what Frantz Fanon called the "Church in the colonies [that] is a white man's Church, a foreigners' Church. It does not call the colonized to the ways of God, but to the ways of the white man, to the ways of the master, the ways of the oppressor."[29] If God was responsible for colonization and its horrors, including slavery, who would want to believe in God? While rejecting the "religion of the white man," Bediako may have sensed that pursuing higher education—in France of all places—might lead to a way out of the colonial dichotomies that Fanon identified, such as Christian/pagan, civilized/savage, chosen/ rejected, saved/damned, redeemed/guilty, rich/poor, white/black.[30] An education in French African literature and the cultural resistance movement known as négritude could possibly give future generations of Ghanaians the tools to shape a post-colonial national identity, he thought. Yet in fact Bediako's graduate work in France began to demonstrate the cracks in his conformity to Western thought patterns and his assertion of his African identity. His decision to research the poetry of Tchicaya U Tam'si, a Congolese poet living in Paris who wrestled with issues of colonialism, faith, and identity, allowed Bediako to undertake similar questioning.

Later, in his theological work, Bediako sought the remaking of Christian theology. He viewed Africa as an ideal laboratory for that work. Theological insights gained in Africa could then be exported to the rest of the world—for their benefit. Once a passive recipient of globalization, Bediako later took advantage of the opportunities it provided. He traveled widely, speaking on every continent, building relationships with other theologians from what was then called the Third World, and raising funds for the work of the theological institute he and his wife founded in Ghana. The object of much of his theological writing was the secularism of the West, which, for him, led to the recession of the Christian church in Europe and North America. He spent much of his early writings focused on the relationship between theology and identity (his terms for gospel and culture). Much of his later work focused on the importance of connecting theologically with the spiritual world, including what he called the "primal imagination." Through it all, he asserted the legitimacy of African Christianity—at times even its superiority to Western Christianity.

As for Bediako, so for me, this is a welcome shift of authority in Christian theological reflection from the Global North to centers around the world. Bediako was constantly seeking to describe and understand how God in Jesus Christ relates to Africans, the connection between African culture and the Christian faith, and how understanding Christianity as a *non-Western* religion can reshape understandings of Christianity itself. For Bediako, as for most Africans, Christianity has always existed in religiously pluralistic environments—alongside Islam and African traditional religions. His understanding of the Christian faith sought to offer "faithful contextualization"[31] of the gospel of Jesus Christ that offers "relevance without syncretism" (*CiA*, 85). For him, Africa was a laboratory for Christian theology to understand and articulate God's revelation that is both faithful to the scriptures and relevant to culture.

Barth and the Blumhardts

While Bediako received the impact of Christian Blumhardt's ideas indirectly through colonial missionary structures and individuals who had been influenced by him, Barth knew the Blumhardt family directly. As Barth sought to navigate his personal theological crisis in 1914, following his teachers' support of the Kaiser's warmongering, he traveled to Bad Boll in southern Germany to meet with the Pietist theologian Christoph Friedrich Blumhardt (1842–1919). C. F. Blumhardt is the great-nephew of Christian Blumhardt (1779–1838) and the son of the pastor-theologian Johann Christoph Blumhardt (1805–80).[32] This dual connection to the influence of the Blumhardt family highlights the two sides of the colonial divide that Bediako and Barth inhabited.

As the year turned to 1915, Barth continued to suffer from a "hopeless confusion"[33] over how his German teachers could completely change religion and scholarship "into intellectual 42 cm cannons"[34] through their endorsement of the Kaiser's warmongering (see ch. 1). His friend, Eduard Thurneysen, first introduced Barth to the writings of J. C. Blumhardt and C. F. Blumhardt and then to Christoph Blumhardt himself. Barth took the opportunity to spend five days with the younger Blumhardt in Bad Boll on his way home from his brother's wedding in Marburg in April 1915.[35] Those eight months had been very challenging for Barth as he sought a new theological understanding. He had written to his longtime school friend Wilhelm Spoendlin in January 1915 describing his dismay as being "like the twilight of the gods," noting that "what we need is something beyond all morality and politics and ethics."[36] Barth had been reading leading socialist thinkers and was politically active in the Socialist Party in Safenwil, but his discouragement remained.[37]

Barth "was now ripe for a fundamental change of direction in his thinking."[38] His encounter with Christoph Blumhardt offered content to this new direction and was a decisive moment in Barth's theological development. "The most immediate consequence of this new starting-point in thought," wrote Bruce McCormack, "was the fact that criticism of religion moved to the centre of Barth's concerns."[39] McCormack named this shift "critically realistic."[40] Barth was immediately aware of the impact of the visit on his thinking, as he reflected a year later in his writings, "Blumhardt always begins right away with God's presence, might, and purpose: he starts out from God; he does not begin by climbing upwards to Him by means of contemplation and deliberation. God is the end, and because we already know Him as the beginning, we may await His consummating acts."[41]

On two occasions, Barth tied together the connection between his disappointment with his "liberal" teachers and the future that the Blumhardts provided. Looking back in 1927, he wrote, "In the midst of this hopeless confusion [at the beginning of the war in 1914], it was the message of the two Blumhardts with its orientation on Christian hope which above all began to make sense to me."[42] The Blumhardts offered hope amid the "black day" when his teachers endorsed Germany's war efforts. The second mention of the connection came at the very end of his life, in the "Concluding Unscientific Postscript" appended to his *Theology of Schleiermacher*. Barth wrote, "From Blumhardt I learned just as simply (at least at the beginning) what it meant to speak of Christian hope. . . . [T]hen the First World War broke out and brought something which for me was almost even worse than the violation of Belgian neutrality—the horrible manifesto of the ninety-three German intellectuals who identified themselves before all the world with the war policy of Kaiser Wilhelm II and Chancellor Bethmann-Hollweg."[43] The realization that almost all his German teachers (with the exception of Martin Rade) were signatories greatly dismayed Barth. He reflected, "An entire world of theological exegesis, ethics, dogmatics, and preaching, which up to that point I had accepted as basically credible, was thereby shaken to the foundations, and with it everything which flowed at that time from the pens of the German theologians."[44] The hope that Christoph Blumhardt taught offered succor to Barth and his theological reflection. Instead of following his teachers and placing his hope in the German war machine, Barth followed the Blumhardts by placing his hope in Jesus Christ alone; a hope grounded in the resurrection.

Although Barth would later identify the moment of his break with theological liberalism as a "sudden" realization in August 1914, McCormack's assertion that it was more of a process is closer to reality: "The ethos of the liberal world had become alien to him at a much earlier point in time.... Expressed positively: if Barth's disappointment over the ethical failure of his theological teachers was the impetus which sent him in search of a *new theology*, his search for a *new world* had been set in motion much earlier."[45] Barth's search led him to find the hope offered by the Blumhardts amid the confusion and dismay of the Great War. The impact that Christoph Blumhardt and his father Johann Blumhardt made on Barth's theological development lasted well beyond 1915.

Eberhard Jüngel noted the ongoing impact of the Blumhardts for the rest of Barth's career.[46] He wrote, "By the time Barth began to stray from his teachers' theology, he had read not only Overbeck, but also the two Blumhardts and Friedrich Zündel. And Barth remained theologically close to the two Blumhardts for the rest of his life. He knew that he was in their debt."[47] Jüngel then cites from *The Christian Life*, §78.3, where Barth lauds the Blumhardts in his last student lectures. More recently, Christian Collins Winn has offered a more expansive account of the Blumhardts' influence: "Their persistent presence as theological interlocutors makes plausible the presupposition that the Blumhardts' life and thought influenced Barth both in the deeper structures of his thought as well as in some of its thematics."[48] This seems correct. The implications of Barth's new starting point lasted the rest of his life. Barth's understandings of the resurrection, the Holy Spirit, and the present and coming kingdom of God, in particular, are all indebted to the influence of the Blumhardts (IV/3, 168–71; *TCL*, 256–57).

The question then is to clarify more precisely *how* these diverse contextual issues—the support of the Kaiser's warmongering by Barth's teachers, Barth's disillusionment with "liberal theology," and his meeting with Christoph Blumhardt—influenced Barth's thought. For Timothy Gorringe, "The impact of the Blumhardts on Barth can hardly be overestimated."[49] McCormack writes, "From now on [August 1915], knowl-

edge of God—the a priori of all true representation of the kingdom—
would be *the* central question in Karl Barth's new theology."[50] In his later
work, Barth commented on the Blumhardts' insight, "Jesus is Victor": "In
content, far from having the character of a new revelation, it merely sums
up and succinctly formulates many New Testament sayings behind which
there may be seen either directly or indirectly the central witness of the
whole of the New Testament" (IV/3, 168).[51] Barth's appropriation of
metaphors and themes from the Blumhardts, then, was "not a repristina-
tion, but was rather constructive and creative."[52] The work of the Blumhardts significantly influenced Barth's Christological approach and his
understanding of the victory of Christ in the resurrection and Christ's
ongoing activity in and through the kingdom of God, as well as the interrelationship between the resurrection and the kingdom of God. Barth
employed the Blumhardts' language "Jesus is Victor" in §69.3 and "Thy
Kingdom Come" in §78.3 to affirm the primacy of the resurrection to
Christ's reconciling and prophetic work.

Barth saw his other teachers as choosing the appearance of cultural
relevance over faithfulness to the gospel. Broadly speaking, Barth understood himself to be rejecting the same nineteenth-century European theology that Bediako rejected. In these ways, Bediako and Barth are oppos-
ing the same complex: Christendom is colonialist at its core.

Juxtaposing Bediako and Barth

As these accounts demonstrate, there is more to connect Barth's Basel and
Bediako's Akropong than one might initially expect. The most direct connection is through the Basel Mission, which sent missionaries to the Gold
Coast in the nineteenth century, thereby influencing the expressions of the
Christian faith to which Bediako was exposed as a child and in which he
participated as an adult. Further, the Basel Mission was started by the
Blumhardt family. From radically different religious backgrounds, cultural
locations, and historical moments, Bediako and Barth reflected theologically about the nature and scope of divine revelation. In the remainder of
this chapter, I identify and explore theological resources for contemporary
theological reflection through the juxtaposition of the theologies of Bediako and Barth.

Juxtaposition is a common practice in postmodern reflection, a practice that involves "the method of both making and recognizing juxtapositions of contingently related texts or practical situations before proceeding to more systematic theory-making."[53] For Larry Bouchard, "A juxtaposing of fragments demarcates a particular space and time. Between what is juxtaposed, there is set aside time and space to enter."[54] The engagement of Barth and Bediako in this book performs a similar juxtaposition. By reading Bediako and Barth together, side by side, engaging similar themes while each reader considers his or her own context, a new space is created that we can enter. Bouchard describes the process this way: "It is not only a matter of enjoying the new meanings or resonances that the coinciding works occasion. . . . It is also a matter of the opportunities for sustained reflection that their coming together offers. We enter the space and time they set apart."[55] Juxtaposition encourages new thinking and new perspectives on seemingly fixed or intractable situations. By juxtaposing the theologies of these two disparate theologians who are both responding to the colonial-Christendom complex, insights will be gained for the task of theological reflection in contexts that are increasingly affected by globalization and secularization.

Shared Inheritances

The influence of nineteenth-century European Christianity on both Bediako and Barth has given them a common inheritance. Both theologians were products of their historical-cultural contexts: Barth in early twentieth-century Germany and Switzerland and Bediako in mid-twentieth-century West Africa. Juxtaposing these theologians explores two distinct, yet overlapping approaches to Protestant thought in the twentieth century, for Bediako and Barth share a number of inheritances that inform their work. Bediako's education shared many common sources and influences with Barth's training in European liberal Protestantism. Most generally, as two theologians working within the Reformed tradition, their writings featured the themes of the sixteenth-century European reformations: *sola scriptura, sola gratia, sola fides,* and *solus Christus.* The *solae* of scripture alone, grace alone, faith alone, and Christ alone played a prominent role in both authors' theologies. And hidden connections in their common theological "ancestors"—as Bediako would put it—become evident when comparing their shared sources for dialogue partners.

Both authors stress God's movement toward humanity in Jesus Christ and faith as a free gift of grace that cannot be earned. Bediako did so in his widely read text, "Jesus in African Culture: A Ghanaian Perspective" (hereafter JAC). Barth is known for his unwavering focus on Jesus Christ in his *Church Dogmatics*. Their shared commitment to scripture is also evident in the numerous citations of biblical texts and their in-depth engagement with significant passages. Although making different points and using different language to do so, Bediako and Barth engaged in a shared conversation about the future of Christian theology. Each responded to the failings of nineteenth-century European Protestantism. Bediako received this legacy through colonialism and offered a post-colonial theology in response. Barth received this legacy through his "liberal" teachers steeped in modernism and offered an initial "postmodern" theology. In spite of these common inheritances, I must acknowledge that each man would have been skeptical of the other and of his theological contributions.

Mutual Suspicion

Many colonial missionaries leveled chauvinistic criticisms against Africans. At the World Missionary Conference in Edinburgh in 1910, traditional African religions were talked about as figments of the imagination and expressions of the work of the devil.[56] The vast majority of European missionaries to Africa in the late nineteenth and early twentieth century viewed it as the "dark continent," devoid of religious goodness. Such a dualistic style of thought that typified the entire colonial project—one that oppressed Africans through the use of dichotomies—proved deeply damaging for both the colonized and the colonizers.[57] Fanon describes the dualistic structures of colonialism as a Manichaean world: "First and foremost, stating the principle 'It's them or us' is not a paradox, since colonialism, as we have seen, is precisely the organization of a Manichaean world, of a compartmentalized world."[58] The colonial mind-set that viewed Africans as unintelligent, irreligious objects of colonial missions, including its manifestations in theological circles, led, in part, to many Africans' suspicions of Europeans and European thought.

Bediako was no exception. Bediako was extremely familiar with Western thought; Adrian Hastings, a renowned historian of the Christian church in Africa, referred to Bediako as "intellectually a Scot, as well as an Akan" following Bediako's years of study at the University of Aberdeen.[59]

Bediako's work was in large part a justification of African Christianity to Westerners. For him, the mistrust of Western theology ran very deep. Much of his antipathy to Western thought stems from two sources: the colonial legacy and French existentialism. Although Bediako was grateful to European missionaries for translating the Bible into African languages and bringing the name of Jesus Christ to Africa (*CiA*, 185, 203), in his own experience Europe also brought atheism to him through his exposure to existentialists such as Jean-Paul Sartre. Bediako understood his conversion to Christianity as a return to his Africanness and a turn away from Europe. While Bediako's work does not especially evidence anger toward Europe, he was well read in the authors of négritude—particularly Léopold Senghor and Aimé Césaire—whose writings harshly rejected colonial rule and European hegemony while articulating a vision of "blackness." Bediako, an African whose ancestors had not been taken as slaves, found Senghor's vision of a recovery of the black African past more compelling than Césaire's longing for a history that had been cut off in the Middle Passage. Bediako's work was a post-colonial project articulating an African Christian identity through the recovery of the precolonial African religious past.

As Africans began to convert to Christianity, the African versions of their Christian practices, especially worship practices, were never pure enough for many Westerners. African Christians have been often criticized as syncretists—for combining the gospel with African cultural forms. These same critics ignored, or better yet, were blind to, evidence of syncretism in the West. Bediako's work demonstrated awareness that the concept of a "pure gospel" was a Western cultural myth that has detrimental effects—both on Africans and on Westerners.

Bediako viewed any theology that he believed to be based on the imperializing and totalizing claims of Christendom as flawed; Barth's theology, by his reckoning, fit this description for being captive to Western assumptions and categories. Bediako did study some of Barth's writings while at London Bible College (now the London School of Theology). In a course on modern theology taught by Richard Sturch in 1975–76, Bediako read excerpts from *Church Dogmatics* I and II.[60] (There is no evidence that Bediako ever read any of Barth's Doctrine of Reconciliation, *Church Dogmatics* IV.) When asked why Bediako did not read Barth, his widow, Gillian Mary Bediako, replied tautologically, "Western theology is

Western theology."[61] Bediako's view of Barth fit within the well-rehearsed critique of Barth's theology as too transcendent and otherworldly, with no points of connection to everyday human life, particularly the lives of Africans. Gillian Mary Bediako reported that her late husband understood Barth as interested in "addressing the particular and peculiar phenomenon of a West that was departing increasingly from its primal rooting and Christian heritage."[62] Kwame Bediako believed, more basically, that all Christian theology needed to be remade; Western theology was too deeply flawed to be rescued.

One significant flaw in Western theology was its perceptions about race, particularly nonwhite peoples. While working on his doctorate in Aberdeen, if not before, Bediako became familiar with Barth's comments about the Ghanaian theologian C. G. Baëta.[63] After Barth met Baëta and his wife in 1951, he had described them in a letter to his son as "both coal black, but I got on with them very well."[64] While not necessarily a racist term, Barth's use of the descriptor "coal black" (and the conjunction "but") displays an obvious cultural insensitivity. This comment, when Bediako read it, was enough for him to cast Barth's writings into the same heap as the rest of Western theology.[65] Instead, Bediako focused on the theological and spiritual needs of his fellow Africans, an interest that Barth did not share.

Vocationally, both men served as pastors at the beginning of their careers. Both were Protestants and in the Reformed tradition—though the precise understanding of what it meant to be "Reformed" was different for each. Neither set out to be a theologian. Bediako only felt compelled to pursue a vocation in theological education after his conversion. Barth jumped at the offer of a professorship after the acclaim for his groundbreaking theological commentary, *The Epistle to the Romans*,[66] though he did not have a doctorate. On the other hand, Bediako earned two doctorates (one in Francophone literature and one in Patristic theology). Barth wrote prolifically—including his twelve-volume *Church Dogmatics* of over eight thousand pages; Bediako wrote only two monographs but over seventy-five articles and book chapters. Bediako founded and administered a research institute and school, the Akrofi-Christaller Institute for Theology, Ministry, and Culture in Akropong-Akuapem, Ghana.[67] Barth did not hold any administrative positions and eschewed the possibility of founding a school of thought, as some nineteenth-century theologians—Albrecht Ritschl and others—had done.

Barth concludes his 1953 preface to *Church Dogmatics* IV/1 with gratitude for the freedom he enjoyed to devote himself to his writing, without the added burdens of overseeing a movement or an institution. He wrote, at age sixty-seven, "I am still in good heart, and—without having to carry the dignity and responsibility of being head of a school—I can devote myself to this great task surrounded with as much consideration and loyalty."[68] Barth's prolific and prodigious writing career—which spanned more than five decades—was fueled by the discipline of preparing lectures and engagement with students without being inhibited by other responsibilities. Bediako, by contrast, poured his energies into establishing the Akrofi-Christaller Institute (through administration and fund-raising), the first theological institution in Ghana that could grant doctoral degrees. He squeezed his writing into the margins of his hectic schedule, usually in preparation for a conference or a public lecture, frequently reusing material from one occasion to another.

For many Western theologians, Bediako is considered to be an *African* theologian who wrote *African* theology. Perhaps non-Africans might want to read Bediako's writings, but—this line of thinking continues—those writings would not have any immediate claim on non-African readers, though non-Africans may try to appropriate some insights for their own purposes. The opposite claim is made for Barth.

Barth's theology is viewed as universal, applicable to all, Westerners and non-Westerners alike. Everyone, so we are admonished, should read Barth because of the power and impact of his writings. Even when one disagrees with Barth, the disagreement must be carefully reasoned, for Barth cannot be ignored or quickly disregarded. Upon Barth's death, he received a front-page obituary in the *New York Times* that quoted the American Protestant theologian Robert McAfee Brown: "One can responsibly disagree with Barth; one cannot responsibly ignore him."[69] In contrast, when Bediako died his tributes were more circumscribed. On the website of *Christianity Today* the by-line for the notice that called Bediako "a brilliant scholar" noted that he was "a key player in the African theology movement."[70] Iwan Russell Jones commented that Bediako was a "leading African theologian."[71] Even his colleague and former student, Kwabena Asamoah-Gyadu, referred to him as an "outstanding and accomplished theologian of Africa."[72] Each time a qualifier, African or of Africa, was added to the praise of his intellect and charismatic personality. Indeed, Jones also referred to Bediako as "a giant of the Christian church," and Asamoah-Gyadu called Bediako "a colossus, indeed an icon of a scholar in the field of African Christianity," adding, "his combination of academic rigor with a deep personal evangelical faith, devotional interest in the Bible and pastoral heart were rare gifts."[73] In short, though many obituaries tend toward hagiography, Bediako's tributes still do not compare to Brown's assessment of Barth and its promotion by the *New York Times*.

Until the 1970s, Barth tended to be read as if his theological contributions were timeless, atemporal, and arose out of a vacuum. In 1972, however, Friedrich-Wilhelm Marquardt in his *Theologie und Sozialismus* insisted that Barth's theology "was always directed to a particular situation and really had no intention of being 'timeless.'"[74] My book takes Marquardt's claim seriously while eschewing his reductive analysis of Barth's thought. I read Barth with attention to his context, thinking with-and-beyond Barth with an eye toward the constructive possibilities present in his thought for engaging twenty-first-century questions. Accordingly, this section presents a brief account of the shift in Barth's early theological thinking that informed his lifelong understanding of his work as a theologian to be one of witness, that is, pointing to Jesus Christ regardless of the circumstances he encountered in twentieth-century Europe.

For many reasons related to the colonial mind-set, the Western perspective has been privileged over the non-Western. Bediako's theology has been marginalized (and dismissed) as particular to his sociocultural circumstances without reflection on the implications of his claims for other contexts. Western theology cannot be assumed to be universally applicable to every time and place. This chapter counters both myopic views by reading Bediako as a theologian whose ideas are applicable to non-African contexts and by reading Barth as a theologian-in-context.

Remaking a Non-Western Religion

For Bediako, two of Christendom's main problems were the attempt to minimize religious pluralism and the concurrent equation of Christianity with culture. Instead, he understood Christianity as a non-Western religion: "This is not to say that Christianity has ceased to exist in the West, but simply that the faith and its expression are no longer determined by dominant Western cultural and social norms."[75] For nearly seventeen hundred years, Western Christianity has operated as if it was the center of worldwide Christianity. Not only is there "no *one* centre from which Christianity radiates," Bediako claims, but "it was never intended to be so" (*CiA*, 164). There has therefore been a shift from the perceived center of Christianity in Europe to multiple centers, a development Bediako calls "the emergence of a positive polycentrism, in which the many centres have an opportunity to learn from each [other]."[76]

The theme of multiple centers leading to multiple "Christianities" was present in Bediako's work from his earliest writings to his last major lecture. In 1984, Bediako noted that in the twentieth century "the missionaries were completely unaware that there could be other 'Christianities' than the form they knew. This problem persists right up to our day."[77] Thus, not only were the missionaries mistaken in presuming that their understanding of Christianity was the only possibility, but Western Christianity has not learned any different in the ensuing hundred years. Even when he was a graduate student in Aberdeen, Bediako concluded that "the sheer number of African Christians makes it difficult to ignore what African theologians say and write."[78] Yet his real concern lay with the future of the church worldwide as a result of "the increasing intellectual stiffening of African Christian conviction."[79]

As the Christian faith came to be understood more and more as a non-Western religion, Bediako understood and appreciated that a number of tangible changes would be vital. Foremost among these changes was the "considerable . . . intellectual adjustment" required to consider the extent that Christianity "has now ceased to be shaped primarily by the events and processes at work in Western culture."[80] The intellectual adjustment then "requires nothing less than the complete rethinking of the Church history syllabus" (*CiA*, 207).[81] Here Bediako was quoting Andrew Walls and perhaps thinking of John Mbiti's famous quotation (cited in ch. 1) that Western Christians know more about the heretics of the second and third centuries than about contemporary Christians living in the developing world. Africa and other parts of the developing world ought no longer to be seen as destinations for missionaries. Rather, the Christians in these lands are potential teachers and collaborators in the work of the kingdom of God.

Bediako perceived "the significant cultural crossings of the Christian gospel" that are taking place today in the churches of the Global South and in Africa in particular.[82] These crossings allowed for three observations regarding "the reorientation that is needed for embracing the task of theology afresh in our time[:] . . . first, a recovery of the religious dimension to theology which can provide a confident basis for courageous Christian witness amid religious pluralism; second, the recognition of the critical importance of the living church for doing theology; and third, a recovery of spirituality in theology."[83] By attending to religious pluralism, the critical importance of the living church, and a recovery of spirituality in theology, African Christian theology can help to provide answers to the questions that are being asked in Western contexts but that the West has not recently considered. Thus, in "the remaking of theology in our time, the Christian churches and scholars of Africa, and also of the other Christian heartlands in Latin America, Asia and the Pacific, are called upon to lead the way."[84]

The change in role for African Christian theologians—from the earliest stages of seeking an African Christian identity to leading the way for the remaking of Christian theology worldwide—transformed Bediako's understanding of the African theologian's task. African Christian theological scholarship "is no longer merely for Africa. It is for the world," he wrote.[85] Africa now becomes a source of inspiration for the theological task and African theological scholarship becomes part of the heritage of the whole church, speaking to all peoples—not just Africans—from the perspective of African Christians.

The shift to a non-Western Christianity also leads to "a reverse process to the prevailing Western-driven globalization[,] . . . a process of globalization 'from below.'"[86] These mutually reinforcing processes—as the former theological centers in the West and the emerging centers in the developing world both produce theological contributions—establish that a monolithic cultural expression of Christianity is not possible and that in fact it never was. The growth of African Christianity and the concurrent process of globalization (and reverse globalization) have offered a new role to Africans within the worldwide Christian community. For the next stage, African theologians will lead and others will follow.

Transcultural Theological Reflection

Twenty-first-century theological reflection cannot take place in isolated silos. Because the richness of God cannot be captured within a single cultural framework, current and future theological work in fact needs to be *transcultural*. Fernando Ortiz coined this neologism to describe "the highly varied phenomena that have come about . . . as a result of the extremely complex transmutations of culture."[87] For Ortiz, transculturation "better expresses the different phases of the process of transition from one culture to another" because the process "does not consist merely in acquiring another culture, which is what the English word *acculturation* really implies, but . . . also necessarily involves the loss or uprooting of a previous culture, which could be defined as a deculturation."[88] Further, the process of transculturation includes "the consequent creation of new cultural phenomena"[89] that results from every union of cultures. This new creation always has something from both prior cultures but is different from each of them. Though Ortiz is focused on the history of Cuba—and the "intense, complex, unbroken process of transculturation of human groups [there], all in a state of transition,"[90] his insights can be applied more broadly to the constructive work of theology today. Today's rapid technological changes—both in transportation and in information—create more dynamic cultural environments than Barth, Bediako, or Ortiz experienced or envisioned. These changing cultural contexts are constantly creating new questions to be addressed by new theologies—that is, fresh interpretations of the Christian scriptures, tradition, and practices in rapidly evolving and constantly changing cultural and religious environments.

Juxtaposing "Shards of a Broken Cultural Order"

I explored the changing context for contemporary theological reflection in chapter 1 and noted that we live in a world shaped by increasing secularization and intensifying globalization. Thinking about these developments together—from a theological perspective—enables us to consider the shape and content of theological reflection today. Chapter 2 brings together two twentieth-century theologians from different geographic and cultural backgrounds for a juxtaposition of their thought. The end of Christendom has left much contemporary theology with the "shards of a broken cultural order."[91] Instead of lamenting the decline, or recession, of the Christian church in Europe and parts of North America, the task of this book is to examine some of these shards "in isolation and in new juxtapositions."[92] The hope then is to "illuminate reality by an oddly refracted light."[93] Bouchard noted that "such arrangements are contingent and temporary. They do not compel us to synthesize what is juxtaposed, but invite us to hold them tentatively as fragments, and think with them and between them, perhaps as we have not thought before."[94] This book is an invitation to reflect on the task of theological reflection after colonial Christendom. Our guides, Kwame Bediako of Ghana and Karl Barth of Switzerland, will lead us down a path with five markers of contemporary theological reflection. For them, as well as for us, contemporary theological reflection is to be Christological, contextual, cultural, constructive, and collaborative.

These five markers chart our progress through the book as the content of the remaining five chapters. Three themes will also be interspersed within the narrative: revelation, religion, and culture. They were the major emphases of Bediako's corpus, and Barth addressed them in close proximity in his mature Christology in *Church Dogmatics* IV/3, §69. The compelling nature of this juxtaposition is the way that these two authors from different starting points use similar theological assumptions to address the same themes. In addition to modeling a possible path for contemporary theological reflection, this juxtaposition offers insight into the complex character of contemporary theological reflection and the vexed issues of world Christianity(-ies) and religious pluralism today.

Bouchard does not promise that juxtaposing "shards of a broken cultural order" will produce new or better insights. Instead, he cautions us to proceed slowly and to hold our assumptions loosely. He writes, "We may have to simply wait—to wait for other fragments and juxtapositions [and] ... for better ideas than our own. They will probably come, but juxtaposed with other, perhaps devastating ideas as well."[95] Together, Bediako and Barth have better ideas than either one alone or than any other single theologian. The power of their combined insights lies in their juxtaposition. The discourse of this book is intentionally performative. I am seeking to demonstrate what I am describing. In doing so, I hope to model how contemporary theological reflection can be Christological, contextual, cultural, constructive, and collaborative.

But be warned: reading on may confirm some assumptions about contemporary theological reflection, yet will likely challenge others and raise new thoughts and questions for consideration.

The next section offers an overview of the three themes that cut across the juxtaposition, followed by chapter summaries for each of the five chapters in part 2.

Three Themes: Revelation, Religion, and Culture

Questions about revelation animated the work of both theologians as they considered in what ways God has spoken to humanity in the past and how God continues to reveal who God is today. Bediako's work sought to counter two misconceptions of European missionaries: first, that Europeans brought God to Africa; and second, that there was nothing good in traditional African religions. Barth's work sought to counter what he took to be the misleading impact of cultural Protestantism on the task of theology. This reorientation of Barth's thought began with his study of the Bible, particularly *The Epistle to the Romans*; his opposition to cultural Protestantism was then demonstrated in particular moments of protest, including against theologians who endorsed Kaiser Wilhelm II's war effort and the German Christians' cooperation with Adolf Hitler and the Nazi Party. Such instances disturbed Barth due to their claims that asserted human reasoning over against God's self-revelation. These movements in Germany shared with colonial officials in Africa overconfidence in the human interpretation and application of revelation over against, or in addition to, God's self-revelation in Jesus Christ.

This shared focus on the person and work of Jesus Christ also led both theologians to ask questions about the nature of religion: What is true religion, and in what ways can Christianity be a "true religion"? For Bediako, Christianity can be the true religion when the Christian faith is separated from Western cultural interpretations and focused on Jesus Christ. This expression of the Christian faith is indigenous to Africa and is authentic to the African context. For Barth, the Christian faith consists in living in correspondence with the work of God in Jesus Christ that has already been completed and accomplished on behalf of all humanity. Christianity, then, cannot be based on abstract principles, or merely the name of Jesus Christ, but only on the concrete history of the person of Jesus Christ.

The expression of God in human flesh, the incarnation of the second person of the Trinity in Jesus Christ, is deeply significant for both authors. In the incarnation, God's revelation takes human, bodily, cultural form. God uses materiality for the purpose of God's self-revelation. In short, for both authors, culture matters. That is, culture—understood both as material culture (i.e. created things) and nonmaterial culture (i.e., stories, myths, religions)—can be and is used by God to reveal to humanity who God is.

For Bediako, the incarnation is the theological foundation for the translation of the gospel into human cultures through the use of vernacular and mother tongue African languages. Translatability becomes, in Bediako's words, "the hermeneutical key" for interpreting scripture (*TI*, xvi, 426). For Barth, the incarnation is the material content of volume 4 of *Church Dogmatics: The Doctrine of Reconciliation*, specifically, "The Way of the Son of God in the Far Country," §59.1 in IV/1, and "The Homecoming of the Son of Man," §64.2 in IV/2. The incarnation is the constituting event of the God-man himself whose glory as mediator and significance as prophet are explored in IV/3, §69. This shared emphasis on Jesus Christ leads to the first marker of contemporary theological reflection: Christological. As I do with the other four, I explore this marker in the present-day context of increasing secularization and intensifying globalization.

Chapter 3: Christological Reflection

The trends identified as secularization and globalization have altered the location of authority in theological reflection. No longer is the authority for theological reflection mediated by and through the institutional church (secularization), nor is there a single center (or even a finite number of centers) of theological authority. Questions about the sources and norms of theological reflection are staples in the prolegomena of doctrinal theology and in introductory theology courses. The so-called Wesleyan quadrilateral can be used to talk about scripture, reason, tradition, and experience as sources of theological reflection. While for John Wesley the four sources were not all equivalent—scripture is given pride of place—Bediako and Barth would agree that there is only one authoritative source for theological reflection: Jesus Christ.

Barth sought to overcome the conflation of culture and revelation by the Nazis and of religion and revelation by the German Christians. While the institutions of the state and the church both retained power and influence in 1930s Germany, Barth's critique was that both had lost touch with the ground of the gospel, that is, Jesus Christ. Both presented a false gospel as true. Much of Barth's theological output criticized the conflation of gospel and culture or religion. Near the end of his *Church Dogmatics*, Barth presented his understanding of Jesus Christ as prophet in IV/3, §69. Here Barth argued that Jesus is the true revelation of God, that

Christ's reconciling acts *are* revelation. Barth's understanding of Christ as prophet is a combination of history, narrative, and action. To make his argument, Barth developed the imagery of Jesus Christ as the Light of Life whose enlightening presence kindles understanding through the revelation of God in Jesus Christ. In this entire section, Barth was seeking to overcome the "dark shadow" that was Christendom with the ongoing self-revelation of God to all people. For Barth, the only possible source of theological reflection was Jesus Christ, the revelation of God incarnate.

Bediako's strong objection to the European attempt to export Christian theology to Africa led to his articulation of his understanding of the "infinite translatability of the gospel of Jesus Christ."[96] Christian theological terms and concepts that had been developed in Europe could not, he said, simply be transported to the African context and forced to take root. Instead, Bediako asserted that the Christian faith was indigenous to Africa, not imported. In this way, Christianity is a non-Western religion whose God is able to communicate to everyone in their mother tongue.

Chapter 4: Contextual Reflection

Chapter 4 argues that not only must the message of the gospel be translated into vernacular languages and concepts, but the process of translation often changes the understanding of what that message is. This conviction—for which Bediako in particular advocates—claims that the gospel of Jesus Christ has to make sense in *this* time and *this* place. There is not one message for all times and all places. The gospel must be contextualized; both Bediako and Barth are to be read as contextual theologians—theologians whose work and interests have been indelibly marked by their social, cultural, ethnic, political, geographic, and economic experiences *and* whose work addressed particular audiences. Neither Bediako nor Barth is to be read as offering the authoritative interpretation for all times and places. In short, the Christian faith cannot be packaged for export; the Christian faith and all contemporary theological reflection based on it is to be contextual.

The work of faithful contextualization can occur organically, from the grassroots, or intentionally, through reflection on cultural concepts. Bediako focused on indigenous theological reflection, whereas Barth sought to untangle conflations between gospel and culture. Both were well educated and considered economically privileged. One area where their concerns overlapped was the category of religion. Both Bediako and Barth opposed any conflation of divine revelation in Jesus Christ with human culture, either in the form of myth or that of projection. By learning how both theologians navigated the difficult questions of gospel and culture (as well as the place of religion in theological reflection), we can shape our own understandings of contextual theology that are relevant to culture without becoming synonymous with culture. While this chapter considers context broadly construed, the next chapter engages culture as one aspect of any given context.

Chapter 5: Cultural Reflection

Chapter 5 continues the dialogue by pursuing further the question of expressions of the gospel of Jesus Christ that are contextual and cultural. On the one hand, there is no such thing as a "pure gospel." Revelation is mediated *through* culture. Yet is the gospel revealed *by* or *in* culture? This chapter engages Bediako's understanding of the African primal imagination as the substructure of African Christian thought in juxtaposition to Barth's understanding of true words of revelation coming through cultural media that he names "parables of the kingdom." Bediako understood the Christian faith to be in continuity with African culture and traditional religions. Instead of the European understanding of Africans as a tabula rasa religiously and spiritually, Bediako believed that traditional African cultures and religions served as *praeparatio evangelica* (evangelical preparation) for the Christian faith. As the Christian faith engages African culture, Bediako asserted an understanding of continuity. Since God has been active among Africans for millennia, they have worshipped the same God as Christians. When the missionaries came they brought the Bible and the name of Jesus Christ but not the presence or activity of God.

In contrast, Barth understands Jesus Christ to be prophetically proclaiming a message of good news that opposes many (Western) cultural assumptions. Barth used the office of Christ as prophet to "think together" (*zugleich denken*) about the person of Christ, as divine and human, and the work of Christ in justification and sanctification—while simultaneously revisiting, and perhaps revising, his understanding of God's self-revelation. I read Barth's view that "Reconciliation is also revelation"

(IV/3, 38) as enabling him to hear Christ's "true words" through contemporary "parables of the Kingdom" in such a way as to, quite unintentionally, anticipate postcolonial concerns by rejecting binaries, destabilizing religious power structures, and expanding the possibilities for theological reflection. Christ's prophecy proclaims the reconciliation that his work has achieved. Barth's articulation of Jesus as Prophet in §69, particularly his "*universal* prophecy" (IV/3, 50), presents a more robust understanding of God's self-revelation while maintaining a consistent understanding of religion. Christ not only speaks to all people universally, but he can also speak in any and all ways. Barth's discussion of "parables of the Kingdom" offers the surety that Christ's "voice will also be heard without" the church or the Bible (IV/3, 117). The self-communication of God is not limited by scope or means. Through the presence of Christ, "true words" are spoken to the Christian community through a variety of media. Thus, Barth's understanding of the "Light of Life" (Barth's "*christologized* epistemology of IV/3")[97] serves to desacralize the Christian community and the biblical scriptures and collapses the categories "sacred" and "profane." Eliminating this binary categorization opens up the possibility of affirming traditional African religions as media of revelation.

Chapter 6: Constructive Reflection

Chapter 6 demonstrates how contemporary theological reflection is to be constructive. Interpretations of divine revelation in one time and place will likely not be sufficient to address contemporary questions and concerns in rapidly changing societies. Bediako and Barth demonstrate how theological reflection today is to be imaginative and prophetic. There is a deep need to break free of colonial paradigms, both for descendants of the former colonizers (genetically and/or theologically) and for the former colonized. The work of theology today is not simply to respond to earlier trends in ways that are still captive to old categories, but is truly new work. This chapter engages Bediako's theology of ancestors as a demonstration of the interrelation of revelation, religion, and culture. The chapter further identifies the pervasiveness and near-inevitability of syncretism in theological reflection as gospel and culture are mixed together in and through divine revelation. The varying methods of exegesis of the two theologians is juxtaposed in relation to the opening chapter of two of their favorite texts:

the Gospel according to John and the Epistle to the Hebrews. Their imaginative and prophetic readings model the constructive nature of contemporary theological reflection.

Chapter 7: Collaborative Reflection

Chapter 7 concludes the book by naming what has been performed. The juxtaposition of Bediako and Barth has allowed a conversation between the two on which we have eavesdropped and in response to which we can reflect on the task of contemporary theological reflection. Such reflection cannot take place in isolated silos where only like-minded theologians gather or only those with certain political or theological views are admitted. Particularly for theologians from privileged backgrounds, the task is to listen, not to talk, to learn, not to teach. Anyone seeking to reflect theologically today needs to seek diverse collaborative partners across race, class, gender, and even geographic boundaries.

Transitional Theological Interlude

The Argument Thus Far

Chapter 1 demonstrates how the rise of secularization and increasing globalization correspond to the decline of Christendom. As Barth noted, just when the church started to collapse within Europe, Europe, as both a political and a religious entity, started to expand to the continents we now call Africa and the Americas. From the fifteenth to the nineteenth century, these parallel processes intensified. In Europe, the Christian church was steadily losing its long-held cultural and political hegemony. In Africa and the Americas, the church was seen as pioneering and necessary for civilization—and, indeed, for commerce as well. Chapter 2 notes the impact of nineteenth-century European Protestant theology on two representative twentieth-century theologians. At home, if you will, the Swiss Karl Barth's whole theological project can be seen as a response to the failings that he identified in nineteenth-century theology. As Barth put it, "For me at least, nineteenth-century theology no longer held any future."[1] Abroad, the Ghanaian theologian Kwame Bediako inherited the legacy of nineteenth-century European Protestantism through the work of missionaries. Bediako's theological quest then became a process of trying to "understand what had happened to [him]"[2]—as an African and as a Christian.

In these ways Bediako and Barth share an inheritance: both of their theological journeys were shaped in reaction to what they identified as the failings of nineteenth-century European Protestantism. Both the circumstances and the content of their theological journeys are deeply important for the work of contemporary theological reflection. Through an exploration of Bediako's corpus and Barth's late Christology, five themes emerge that are essential for contemporary theological reflection. The juxtaposition of Bediako from Africa and Barth from Europe demonstrates that contemporary theological reflection must be Christological, contextual, cultural, constructive, and collaborative. The next chapter offers fuller descriptions of the life and times of each theologian, so that we may better understand how and why both men found the theology of nineteenth-century European Protestantism of limited usefulness. In doing so, the importance of interpreting one's context theologically is shown.

Toward Part II

Part I has established the significance of learning from Bediako and Barth as they responded to globalization and secularization. In many twenty-first-century local contexts, the task of theological reflection is shaped by a combination of secularization and globalization. The understanding of the Christian faith that many people—worldwide—inherited from their parents or first understood does not sufficiently address the questions and issues of our changing world without some modifications. Part II seeks to learn from the insights of Bediako and Barth by shaping a fivefold approach to contemporary theological reflection. As Bediako and Barth share the insights they each gleaned from interpreting scripture in their own times and places, patterns will emerge for the present.

PART II

Rethinking Divine Revelation

THREE

Christological Reflection

Revelation in Jesus Christ

On the afternoon of May 16, 1934, in Frankfurt, "fortified by strong coffee and one or two Brazilian cigars,"[1] Karl Barth revised the six theses of what would become known as the Barmen Declaration while his two Lutheran colleagues took a three-hour nap.[2] These finishing touches were the culmination of over a year of theological reflection on the ascension to power of Adolf Hitler and the National Socialist Party and the appointment of Ludwig Müller as *Reichsbischof* over all church affairs. A year earlier, Barth had composed *Theologische Existenz heute* (*Theological Existence Today*), "virtually at a sitting," and sent a copy of the pamphlet directly to the Führer.[3] In it, he criticized the church reforms, the question of a national bishop, and especially the cooperation of the *Deutsche Christen* (German Christians) with the Nazi regime. He asserted the revelation of God in Jesus Christ as the sole theological authority, writing, "[If] under the stormy influence of certain 'principalities, powers, and rulers of this world's darkness' [Ephesians 6:12] we seek God elsewhere than in his Word, and his Word elsewhere than in Jesus Christ, and Jesus Christ elsewhere than in the Holy Scriptures of the Old and New Testament, and thereby [we] are actually they who do not seek God at all."[4] Over 37,000 copies of *Theological Existence*

Gospel ? Scripture

Today were printed before it was banned and confiscated by the Nazis in late July 1934. Barth later referred to the pamphlet as "the first trumpet blast of the Confessing Church."[5] Barth's emphasis on the centrality of Jesus Christ to all theological reflection—particularly in the present time of crisis—launched the Confessing Church movement that led to the Barmen Declaration. The first thesis of the declaration reads:

> Jesus Christ, as he is attested for us in Holy Scripture, is the one Word of God which we have to hear and which we have to trust and obey in life and in death.
>
> We reject the false doctrine, as though the church could and would have to acknowledge as a source of its proclamation, apart from and besides this one Word of God, still other events and powers, figures and truths, as God's revelation.[6]

Barth explicitly concentrated his theological efforts on the person and work of Jesus Christ throughout his work.

This Christocentric focus led to someone asking him an insightful question following the final session of his 1962 Warfield lectures at Princeton Theological Seminary: "In what specific way, Professor Barth, does your theology avoid being Christomonistic?" Barth replied:

> Sound theology can only be "unionistic," uniting God and man. . . . Christomonism would mean that Christ alone is real and that all other men are only apparently real. But that would be in contradiction with what the name of Jesus Christ means, namely, union between God and man. . . . Christomonism is excluded by the very meaning and goal of God's and man's union in Jesus Christ.[7]

Barth thereby rejected Christomonism as an abstraction (an "ism") that distorted both the divine-human unity in Jesus Christ and the true humanity of all human beings. He states his point succinctly: "Just as there can be no anthropomonism, so also can there really be no Christomonism."[8] Barth was quite clear that his theological approach was Christocentric (focused on Christ) without being Christomonistic (focused on Christ as the *sole* reality).[9] Repeatedly, Barth emphasized the Trinity to mitigate against critiques of Christomonism. His understanding of God's self-revelation is that the fullness of the Godhead—in three modes of being, Father, Son, and Holy Spirit—is revealed in the person of Jesus Christ.

Because of their diverse contextual circumstances, Bediako encountered different challenges and questions. Specifically, he was never forced to consider the differences between Christocentrism and Christomonism. Bediako's concern was to articulate his focus on Jesus Christ in contrast to movements he viewed as syncretistic, such as Afrikania (*CiA*, 17–38), or non-Christian, such as Islam or African traditional religions.[10]

Bediako understood a singular focus on Jesus Christ as an evangelical badge of honor, not as a possible source of error. His widow, Gillian Mary Bediako, captured this stance well in response to a question about her late husband's remarkable consistency in his thought throughout his career: "Of course. His focus was on Jesus Christ and he never strayed."[11] The assumption was that such a focus on Christ inherently provided Bediako with appropriate boundaries and direction in his work. As much as his approach might be viewed as unreflective or uncritical, it is certainly unapologetic and unswerving.

Maintaining a Christological focus was at the core of Bediako's entire theological project. As an African, Bediako sought to resist the hegemonic attempts of European colonialism to define African identity and the Christian faith. Bediako's first book, *Theology and Identity*, asserted that one could be Christian and (remain) African. African Christians had a twin heritage: first, African traditional religions and culture; and, second, the Christian faith. Underneath his claim about African Christian identity lay his conviction that Christianity is a non-Western religion that is indigenous to Africa. He made this point succinctly in the title of a 2006 lecture, borrowing from the Kenyan theologian John S. Mbiti: "Missionaries did not bring Christ to Africa—Christ brought them."[12] While Bediako often expressed gratitude to European missionaries for their courageous and important work in Africa, he was also very clear: missionaries brought the Bible and the name of Jesus Christ; they did not bring the presence or activity of God. God had been active as long as humans had lived on the continent—and even before.

Through their writings, Bediako and Barth each demonstrated a similar assumption: a determined and dogged concentration on the person of Jesus Christ. More than an abstract notion of God in general or of God as Father or God as Spirit, the second person of the Godhead, Jesus Christ—Immanuel, God-with-us—offered the basis and the content for their theological reflection. Both theologians also turned to the scriptures of the Old and New Testaments as their authority for learning who Jesus Christ is, what Christ has done, and how to interpret events in the contemporary world. Bediako's first major scholarly publication, "Biblical Christologies in the Two-Thirds World," was deeply Christological and laid out the significant themes of his life's work.[13] Barth's *Epistle to the Romans* accomplished a similar task. This common Christological beginning defined their respective understandings of divine revelation, which they maintained throughout their engagements with religion and culture.

Both Bediako and Barth understood themselves as offering a Christocentric approach to theological reflection. Both theologians responded to their fellow Christians who believed that they and they alone were speaking on God's behalf. For Bediako, the problem was white Europeans telling black Africans what God was saying. For Barth, the problem centered on the conflation in the early twentieth century of German culture, the Christian religion, and divine revelation—first with his theological teachers in 1914 and then with the *Deutsche Christen* in 1933–34. Both critiqued claims of human cultures for masquerading as God's revelation. Both proposed Jesus Christ as the true revelation of God, not human constructs.

This chapter employs insights from Bediako and Barth in order to articulate why and how contemporary theological reflection should be Christological. The argument proceeds in five sections. First, the gospel of Jesus Christ is both indigenous and prophetic. The Word of God speaks in mother tongues, yet remains a Word from outside, a call for more. The prophetic nature of the gospel seeks to prevent and overcome human meddling with the message. Second, all revelation is God's self-revelation. Jesus Christ is the sole incarnation of God. The indigenous nature of the gospel of Jesus Christ demonstrates, third, that revelation is for all people. The good news of Jesus Christ is infinitely translatable into the languages and concepts native to any and all human cultures. This infinite translatability is possible because Jesus Christ is the light of life shining into all places. Therefore, fourth, revelation is ongoing. The proclaiming work of

Christ as prophet is not confined to a bygone era. Jesus Christ continues to reveal who God is in new and fresh ways. Bediako demonstrates this general theological conviction in his articulation of the twin heritage of African Christianity as a product of the gospel of Jesus Christ and traditional African religions and cultures. And fifth, Bediako's and Barth's differing understandings of the universality of Jesus Christ retain a Christological focus and give each of them the theological grounding to practice contemporary theological reflection contextually (as ch. 4 shows).

Indigeneity of Christianity in Africa

The engagement between gospel and culture is possible, says Bediako, because Christianity is indigenous to Africa. That is, Christianity arose from within African culture, not foreign imposition from without. Recall Bediako's claim that missionaries brought the Bible and the name of Jesus Christ, but they did not bring the presence or activity of God. God in Jesus Christ is not a new arrival to Africa; God is indigenous to Africa. Therefore, the Christian faith is indigenous to Africa. Bediako understood much of African theology as describing how God has been active amid African culture. He described this theological approach as "indigenization, a rooting of Christianity in African life by claiming for it a past in the spiritual harvests of the African pre-Christian religious heritage" (*CiA*, 76). The movement of the gospel in Africa is from the inside out. The process is called indigenization because the gospel does not have to be imported to Africa; instead the gospel has to be discovered within Africa and named as such. God has always been at work in Africa with Africans. Thus Bediako prefers the term "indigenization" to other labels such as adaptation, contextualization, or inculturation (*CiA*, 76). The work of the African theologian is to uncover the workings of God within African cultures and peoples, not to translate God or understandings of God for the African context. God does the translating; humans do not. Bediako's work articulates the twin heritage of African Christianity, the precolonial African past and the pre-Christendom Christian past, to demonstrate how the Christian faith arose within Africa rather than being contextualized or inculturated from outside of Africa. As such, African Christianity responds to and critiques the colonial-Christendom complex.

Bediako connected translation to indigeneity through his understanding of the incarnation. He appealed to John's gospel to make his claim. He wrote, "For the Word who took flesh and dwelt among us, not only exegetes (and so translates) God (John 1:18), but also exegetes the human predicament (John 4:29), bringing the two together in a mutually intelligible communication" (*CiA*, 122). Bediako did not leave translation in the past, however. He understood a vital connection between translatability and indigeneity: "If it is translatability which produces indigeneity, then a truly indigenous church should also be a translating church, reaching continually to the heart of the culture of its context and incarnating the translating Word" (*CiA*, 122). The translation of the gospel into cultural forms is "mutually intelligible communication" that grounds indigeneity in translatability. Because the Word took flesh and dwelled among us, the culture receiving the gospel is valued, not denigrated. The gospel of Jesus Christ—as understood through the translation of Christian scriptures into African mother tongues—is therefore local and aptly expressed in African concepts and cultural terms. The gospel assimilates—without overcoming—indigenous culture. This process is ongoing and mutually enlightening; it teaches about culture and goes hand in hand with an appreciation of the God who reveals. The incarnation of Jesus Christ, particularly John's description in John 1:18, is central to Barth's understanding of revelation, culture, and the sending of the church in the world.

A comparative perspective is useful at this point. Two of the authors that Bediako analyzed in *Theology and Identity*, the Nigerian Bolaji Idowu and the Kenyan John Mbiti, take opposite positions on the question of indigeneity. Both asserted the continuity of ATRs with African Christianity, yet while Idowu believed that Christianity could be made to take African cultural forms, he maintained that the Christian gospel was foreign to Africa.[14] By contrast, Mbiti believed that the Christian faith is indigenous to Africa.[15] Idowu advanced the claim that all African primal religions are monotheistic to demonstrate continuity between ATRs and the foreign religion of Christianity. To oversimplify, Idowu argued that since ATRs worshipped one God and Christianity worshipped one God they must have been worshipping the same God. According to Bediako, "Idowu remained haunted by the 'foreignness' of Christianity, and having started from that foreignness, was never able to arrive at indigeneity" (*CiA*, 116). The logic of Idowu's argument necessitated postulating monotheism as the continuity, even though his claim could not be proven based on the empirical evidence. Idowu understood the multiplicity of "spirits" or "divinities" venerated in traditional religious practices as manifestations of "a single God."[16]

Although Bediako identified the claim of continuity as "one of Idowu's most valuable theological insights into African religious tradition" (*TI*, 288), he took a different track on the question of monotheism. In *Theology and Identity*, Bediako had reluctantly agreed with Idowu that ATRs are inherently monotheistic. Later he backed off this claim and instead proposed the Trinity as a way to understand multiple African divinities so that the one-in-the-many conception of divinity present in African religions can continue.[17]

Mbiti, in contrast to Idowu, understood the Christian gospel as indigenous to Africa and believed that the gospel should be appropriated in African terms. Like Bediako, because Mbiti viewed ATRs as *praeparatio evangelica* for Christianity, Christianity could be understood as originally a non-Western religion.[18] Thus "Mbiti rejected the very idea of the quest for indigenization of Christianity or of theology in Africa" (*CiA*, 117). Since Christianity was always and already present in African culture, Mbiti objected to Idowu's claim that Christianity was external or foreign to Africa. Bediako shared this objection and further interpreted Mbiti, claiming, "for theology is always indigenous, resulting from the effort to articulate the meaning of the Gospel in a particular cultural milieu in response to the realities of that milieu" (*TI*, 306). Christian theology, not just in Africa, is inherently indigenous—local, authentic, contextual—and cannot be indigenized. Since God in Jesus Christ was active in Africa before missionaries arrived on the continent, the seeds of the Christian faith were already, inherently, in African culture.

The work of African theology, then, "has been about the redemption of African culture" (*CiA*, 177). Developments within African Christianity and African theology were therefore authentic expressions of the gospel of Jesus Christ, not primarily the result of missionary or ecclesial actions. I repeat this claim because Western Christians (Europeans and North Americans) have had difficulty comprehending this point. For Bediako, the ongoing translatability of the gospel was propelled by the activity of God.

Bediako wrote that "indigeneity . . . is presumed within the very translatability of the Christian religion. Indigeneity is as much a matter of recognition within the Gospel as it is an achievement of actual Christian witness. Thus, universality, translatability, incarnation and indigeneity belong in a continuum and are integral to the warp and woof of the Christian religion" (*CiA*, 123). By this he meant that the gospel is applicable to all people (universality), can be communicated in vernacular languages and concepts (translatability), is based on God assuming human flesh in Jesus Christ (incarnation), and is authentically present in human cultures (indigeneity).[19]

The Office of Jesus Christ as Prophet

By the 1900s in Germany, Barth's teacher, Adolf von Harnack, described how the church had lost its position in society. In *What Is Christianity?* Harnack sought to demonstrate "the leading changes which the Christian idea has undergone in the course of its history."[20] Harnack's image for these changes is that of husks that hold the kernel of the Christian faith in different eras.[21] Ironically, given their disagreements in the 1920s, Harnack and Barth both sought a return to the kernel of the Christian faith that has become deeply hidden in the culture of European Protestantism (*Kulturprotestantismus*)—though Barth would not use such language. As Barth saw it, the European church in the twentieth century faced a difficult choice. It "might try to fight for the maintenance or restoration of its vanishing respect and influence," or it might "retreat to the reservations of a self-satisfying religiosity," or "it might accept the increasing secularism on an optimistic interpretation" (IV/3, 19–20). Barth chose the third option, intending his *Dogmatics* "to offer to the adult world a suitably adult form of Christianity" (IV/3, 19–20).[22] Dietrich Bonhoeffer later developed Barth's understanding of "a suitably adult form of Christianity" in dialogue with the world-come-of-age in his *Letters and Papers from Prison*.

Barth noted two ironies presented by the church's choice. First, in the sixteenth century, as the church turned *toward* the world, the world turned *away* from the church (IV/3, 37). Second, as Christianity regressed in Europe, following the Reformation, there began "an age of unparalleled Christian missions[;] . . . modern Christianity, externally attacked and constricted[,] . . . engaged in an original and spontaneous outward movement" (IV/3, 23). The external pressures marginalizing the influence of the church in Europe led to an internal compulsion among Christians to expand the reach of their faith to the "newly discovered" lands of Africa and the Americas. Barth praises the work of organizations like the Basel Mission (IV/3, 25) while indicating that colonialism offered "vexatious hindrance instead of help" to the colonized peoples and to the spread of the gospel of Jesus Christ (IV/3, 26).

Barth used the first article of the Barmen Declaration twenty-five years later as the thesis of IV/3, §69, "The Glory of the Mediator": "Jesus Christ as attested to us in Holy Scripture is the one Word of God whom we must hear and whom we must trust and obey in life and in death" (IV/3, 3).[23] Immediately here he displays a number of themes of this part volume. The theme of revelation pertains to how one hears and knows what God is saying or showing; the theme of culture pertains to the context in which hearing, trusting, and obeying occurs; and the theme of religion pertains to the corporate "we" as a reminder that hearing, trusting, and obeying do not take place alone but in relation to others. These are the elements that constitute an adult form of Christianity that might confront a church that has lost its connection to its origins.

Barth used the imagery of Christ as prophet to present his Christology of the God-man in *Church Dogmatics*, IV/3.[24] Earlier, he had used the imagery of Christ as priest in IV/1 and Christ as king in IV/2. Barth suspected that there was something wrapped up with the prophetic office that "a modern theology cannot ignore because it is inescapably presented to it in the destinies, happenings and forms of the modern Church" (IV/3, 18). He understood the rediscovery of the prophetic office of Christ at the time of the Reformation as being no accident or coincidence (IV/3, 38).[25] The church reoriented itself outward (IV/3, 35), just as the world turned from the church (IV/3, 37). At this point, the boundary between the sacred (the church) and the secular (everything else) blurred. In the opening subsection of §69, Barth described how increased secularization in Europe demonstrated the rupture present between contemporary Christian communities and the God-man Jesus Christ (IV/3, 20–21). European churches had turned inward to fortify themselves against what many perceived to be a hostile outside world. These communities seemingly lacked the ability, interest, and theological rationale to engage the world around them. Their only outward focus involved supporting foreign missions to *other* people who needed to know of Jesus Christ. Barth, however, was unwilling to abandon educated Europeans. In IV/3, he turned to Calvin's rediscovery and codification of the *munus triplex* (Christ's threefold office) and used the motif of prophecy to present a reconsideration and renegotiation of the frontiers of church/world and sacred/secular (IV/3, 35).[26] He argued specifically that Christians ought to understand the prophetic office of Christ that shines the light that gives life to all people as an occasion to consider revelation in an expansive way. In the best-known portion of §69, Barth presented his view of "parables of the Kingdom," which at times are forged by God to proclaim true words outside the church or the Bible (IV/3, 114–35). Barth refused to offer any examples of these true words (or parables of the kingdom), yet emphatically stated that true words do happen (IV/3, 135). His affirmation of extraecclesial words challenged long-held assumptions by claiming a higher authority than the religious establishment and its leaders. Barth did not want people to have intractable criteria that could be used to imprison a biblical text and evade the reality of God;[27] he wanted to acclaim God's freedom to communicate with humankind—now "in many and various ways" (Hebrews 1:1).

Before progressing further, let us pause to define these three terms— "revelation," "religion," and "culture"—as Barth understood them. Barth is most explicit in his *Church Dogmatics* in offering definitions of revelation and religion, less so of culture. For Barth, revelation is Jesus Christ, specifically the *actions* of Christ that are *narrated* in a *history* recorded in the Old and New Testaments (IV/3, 165–66). Barth explicitly addressed religion in I/2, §17, "The Revelation of God as the Sublimation of Religion." In the thesis statement of that paragraph, Barth defined religion as "the realm of attempts by man to justify and sanctify himself before a willfully and arbitrarily devised image of God" (I/2, 280; 33).[28] Barth's definition of culture must be inferred from scattered mentions. It seems, as Jessica DeCou aptly put it, that Barth had an "allergy to [a] 'theology of culture' [that] was influenced by his aversion to modern theological trends toward the deification of human achievements that, in his view, led theology to be uncritical of (and eventually absorbed by) the larger culture."[29] I read Barth with Kathryn Tanner's *Theories of Culture* in mind. Tanner views culture as a "consensus-building feature of group living . . . [that] forms the basis for conflict as much as it forms the basis for shared beliefs and sentiments."[30] Culture then does not create agreement but rather "culture binds people together as a common focus for *engagement*. . . . Participants are bound together by a common attachment to or investment in such cultural items, and not necessarily by any common understanding of what they mean."[31] Therefore, for Tanner, as for Barth,[32] "theology is something that human beings produce . . . as a part of culture, as a form of cultural activity."[33] Such a definition allowed Barth to separate revelation (as outside of culture) from religion (a product of culture) while allowing cultural forms to serve as the media of God's self-revelation. In doing so, Barth suggests a Christological response to the colonialist-Christendom complex. Bediako responded with the infinite translatability of the gospel of Jesus Christ. For Barth, Christ as prophet addresses the complex.

Prophecy, History, and Narrative

In IV/3, the double movement, downward and upward, of Christ's humiliation and exaltation, in his life, death, resurrection, and ascension, was proclaimed in the *outward* movement of Christ as prophet. In volume IV of his *Church Dogmatics*, Barth used the threefold office of Jesus Christ, the *munus triplex*, to organize his Doctrine of Reconciliation.[34] In IV/3, Barth proceeded to "think together" (I/2, 160) the person of Christ—as human and divine—with the work of Christ—in justification and sanctification—as the God-man, "The True Witness: Jesus Christ, the Mediator." The description of the acts of Christ described in IV/1 and IV/2 remains incomplete without the account of proclamation in IV/3.[35] In late 1955, just after completing work on IV/2, Barth responded to a student's question about the significance of his architectural arrangement of the *Church Dogmatics* with regard to Calvin's ordering (prophet, king, priest) and Schleiermacher's (prophet, priest, king) by saying, "To speak the truth I have to begin with this reality. Christ's priestly and kingly offices are the subject-matter, the content of His prophetic office, because He reveals Himself."[36] The priestly and kingly offices must be treated first, he said, because they are the material content of the proclamation of the third, prophetic office. If theology communicates truth about God, then the truth of the reconciliation of humanity in Jesus Christ is proclaimed in

Christ's ongoing prophetic activity. In IV/3, §69, Barth's exposition of the ongoing prophetic activity of Jesus Christ articulated his understanding of reconciliation as revelation: the work of Christ as prophet proclaimed the justifying and sanctifying work of Christ as Priest and King.

In Barth's response to the student's question he stated that in order to proclaim Christ prophetically one must first know who Christ is and what Christ does (has done, is doing, and will do).[37] In seeking to know who Jesus Christ is and what he does, Barth rooted his understanding of revelation in God's concrete actions in the world. The work of the prophet is to proclaim what the priest and the king have accomplished. This proclamation often disturbs the status quo within and outside the theological academy and local congregations.

Barth always views God in Jesus Christ as a single subject, the unified God-man. There are not separate parts of Christ that perform these different roles. As such, the threefold office is *one* office of Jesus Christ that is described in three ways. The priestly and kingly work demonstrates that reconciliation for all humanity had been accomplished in Christ's atonement. In the opening words of the Christological paragraph in IV/1, Barth described his understanding of the atonement and its connection to history, succinctly: "The atonement is history [*Geschichte*]. . . . The atonement is the most particular history of God with humanity, the most particular history of humanity with God" (IV/1, 157 rev.). Atonement is history; it is achieved in human history, in the history of the God-man, and cannot be known apart from that history. Importantly, Barth used the German word *Geschichte* to describe the type of history that best describes the atonement.

Barth intentionally used *Geschichte*, translated above (and throughout his *Dogmatics*) as "history," because it has a broad meaning that encompasses both "history"—a cluster of events in time and space—and "story"—a retelling of events that draws attention to their coherence and meaning.[38] Through the use of *Geschichte*, Barth demonstrated that for him, theology—and more broadly the divine-human relationship—is not about truth propositions or abstract concepts but the story (history) of God's pursuit of humanity. (In this way, Barth's narrative theology anticipates postmodern critiques of propositional truth claims.) The work of reconciliation of humanity by God in Jesus Christ is known as atonement. Barth's understanding of atonement as story/history was rooted in the actual events of Jesus Christ's life, death, resurrection, and ascension as witnessed to in the Bible. According to Barth, Jesus Christ, the Son of God, fully God and fully human, lived a life without sin (as God intends for all humanity), died as a common criminal (receiving the punishment that human disobedience deserves), and was raised from the dead (and by overcoming death itself accomplished eternal life with God for all humans). This story, the Christ event—which is actualized in concrete, historical moments—brings reconciliation between God and all humanity.

The history of Jesus Christ as the history of reconciliation means, further, that Jesus Christ is the saving fulfillment of the covenant. Barth played with this meaning of *Geschichte* throughout §69. He claimed that it is in and through the history of Jesus Christ that humans know God: "Whoever says Jesus necessarily says: history (*Geschichte*)—his history— the history in which he is who he is and does what he does. In his history, we know God" (IV/3, 179 rev.). God reveals who God is (God is what God does), and humanity knows God through God's reconciling actions toward humanity. This is what Barth means by "reconciliation is revelation." Reconciliation is history (IV/3, 181), and the history of reconciliation is revelation. There is no private sphere, nowhere that Christ's prophetic activity is not known or felt, even if there are many places where it is not recognized as such (IV/3, 182). The office of Christ as prophet is to proclaim the reconciliation that has been accomplished through Christ's priestly and kingly work.

Although the event of reconciliation is complete (and in one sense "finished"), it also continues. In Barth's words, Christ's "history has been, but it has not passed. . . . As history, it begins with history. But although this history of Jesus Christ took place once, in its very singularity it really takes place, and therefore shines and speaks, for all times and in many other times" (IV/3, 224). For sure, the history of Jesus Christ is bound to the gospel narratives. Yet, because the event of reconciliation includes Christ's resurrection from the dead, Jesus Christ continues to act today. While his time on earth in human flesh has passed, he and his *Geschichte* (history/story) live on.[39] Through the power of the resurrection, specifically, Jesus Christ keeps on acting, not as a principle, but as a person who bears his past and present into the future. The living Jesus Christ "is not something but Someone who lives[,] . . . [not] He has lived or . . . He will live" (IV/3, 40, 44). The living presence of Jesus Christ among us recasts concerns about increasing secularization and intensifying globalization.

With characteristic objectivism, Barth declared "that the life of Jesus Christ speaks for itself" (IV/3, 45). In this self-speaking, Christ is "His own authentic witness . . . [and] the light of life[,] . . . the light which life itself radiates because it is itself light" (IV/3, 46). The sum and substance of this prophetic message recalls the tetragrammaton and encapsulates the fourth gospel: "I am" (IV/3, 181); Barth's emphasis on Jesus Christ as a living person defined the content of §69. He wrote, "As Jesus Christ lives, He also shines out, not with an alien light which falls upon Him from without and illuminates Him, but with His own light proceeding from Himself" (IV/3, 46). This light that is shining out from Jesus Christ to all is God's self-revelation to humanity.

The glory of the mediator is then who Christ is, what Christ has done, and Christ's ongoing prophetic activity. Christ is revealed, by himself and as he reveals himself, as the one he is, in what he does. His being is in his action (IV/3, 275). Barth conjoined the person of Christ with the office of prophet in order to show that God is revealed in Christ, as the light of life (§69.2), and that Christ reveals himself, shining as the Light (§69.3). Paragraph 69.4 transitions to the remaining paragraphs of IV/3 as the focus turns from the purely Christological to the outworking of these Christological claims about the ongoing prophetic activity of Jesus Christ to the realms of sin, soteriology, pneumatology, and ecclesiology. Barth continually reinforced the idea that Christ's threefold office is indivisible and notes repeatedly that the priestly and kingly offices require the third (the prophetic) to describe "the outreaching, embracing, and comprehensive character" of the atonement (IV/3, 279). Indeed, one can even say that the priestly and the kingly require the prophetic, just as the salvific power of Christ's life and death requires the resurrection (IV/3, 296–97). The ongoing movement of prophetic activity that took place even in Christ's ascension to the living God continues toward all humanity and the world (IV/3, 356).

The resurrection as prophetic proclamation receives Barth's particularly close attention, for this is the medium in which Christ reveals himself in the present and future. Because of the resurrection, reconciliation can be communicated in diverse ways. "Without this event," Barth wrote, "it would have lacked the glory and revelation and therefore the prophetic character of His being and action. His life would still have been the life of the whole world, but it would not have been light shining in this world and illuminating it" (IV/3, 282). The resurrection announces to the world that Jesus Christ is no ordinary human being; death could not contain him. The prophetic proclamation of Christ's identity in the resurrection not only declares humanity's reconciliation with God; the resurrection publishes the fact of reconciliation, and in so doing *applies* reconciliation to individuals and communities. "Without this event beyond His life and death which destroys His death," Barth wrote, "He could not be the One who comes to us as He who has lived and died for us, but only the One who in His death has gone infinitely far from us like anyone else who dies" (IV/3, 283).

In response to the impact of the resurrection on Christ's ongoing prophetic activity, Barth called the third subsection of §69, "Jesus Is Victor" (IV/3, 165–274). Barth took this title from an encounter that the German Pietist Lutheran pastor J. C. Blumhardt had with a young woman, Gottliebin Dittus, who claimed that she was possessed by a demon in 1843. As Blumhardt was working to cast out the demon, he heard Dittus cry out, "Jesus is victor!," in the moments just before the demon left her (IV/3, 168–71). Barth was quite struck by this story and chose the phrase as the title of this subsection "for the simple reason that this statement, which is really to be heard and read as a challenge, is the sign under which a presentation and therefore a narration of the prophetic work of Jesus Christ must always stand. . . . "Jesus is Victor," is the first and last and decisive word to be said in this respect" (IV/3, 168). The resurrection was a narrative historical event for Barth. The resurrection happened in space and time, but it also rewrote the very human history (story) of Dittus; it intervened, reframing this woman's life. The power of God shown in the resurrection is not confined to the past but remains active in the world even today. This very power—the power of the resurrection—set Dittus free from demon possession.

The poignancy of Barth's choice of title clearly comes through in the excursus in which he responded to G. C. Berkouwer's characterization of his theological progress as "the triumph of grace."[40] Berkouwer sought to find a single, unifying principle in Barth's work and articulated it as grace overcoming all. The thrust of Barth's strong reply was that "Jesus is Victor" is a better characterization than "the Triumph of Grace," because he was not concerned with the "principle" of Grace but instead with the living person of Jesus Christ (IV/3, 173).

In sum, the resurrection certainly expressed this grace and the phrase, "Jesus is Victor!," described the accomplishment of the reconciliation of all humanity (IV/3, 191). The ongoing prophetic activity of Jesus Christ offers fresh possibilities for theological reflection by continually presenting God in Jesus Christ to humanity in particular contexts.

All Revelation Is Self-Revelation

The self-revelation of Jesus Christ occurs in and through the reconciliation of humanity to God. Barth based his understanding of revelation in §69 on the ongoing prophetic activity of Jesus Christ. This ongoing activity is made possible through Christ's resurrection, as the risen Christ raises up witnesses to himself. Barth's explication of revelation in §69 has three distinctive elements. First, all revelation is self-revelation; there is no possibility of revelation apart from God's self-revelation. Specifically, Jesus Christ, and Jesus Christ alone, is the full revelation of God as Son. Jesus Christ fully reveals who God the Son is in relation to the Father and the Son; there is no "God" hiding behind the God who is revealed in Christ. Through the reconciling acts of Christ's life, death, resurrection, and ascension, the character of God is revealed to humanity.

Second, revelation is not just for Christians or the Christian community, but for *all* people at all times and places. Revelation is also universal in as much as it coincides with the universal reconciliation of all humanity to God in Jesus Christ. The content of revelation is the person of Jesus Christ, not any principles or concepts derived from the Bible or elsewhere.

Third, revelation is ongoing in and through the prophetic activity of Jesus Christ. Through the work of Christ and the Holy Spirit, God continues to reveal who God is in new times and places. Although who God is does not change, the mediums of communication do change from one sociohistorical context to another and human interpretations of God's revelation result in different understandings of who God is.

Barth's account of revelation as the self-revelation of God in Jesus Christ, decentered "religion" from a position of power and authority as the controller of information or of access to the divine. Indeed, as God reveals who God is in unexpected places, the Christian community is called to live in correspondence to God's prophetic revelation and to live in humble service to others.

Through the ongoing prophetic activity of Jesus Christ, "the light of life shines in the darkness, the world and all men come within the reach of its beams, but as it shines in the darkness, the world and all men are still in the sphere of darkness" (IV/3, 191). This light penetrates the darkness but does not eliminate the darkness: "That reconciliation is also revelation means that in its accomplishment, which establishes, orders and guarantees peace between God and man, it also reveals and proclaims itself as divine-human truth" (IV/3, 165). The person of Jesus Christ shines light on all calcified doctrines and ways of thinking.

Imagery of Light

For Barth, revelation is the *how* of the *what* of reconciliation; revelation makes clear and proclaims the work of Jesus Christ. Barth understood "that, as reconciliation takes place, it also declares itself" (IV/3, 10). Indeed, revelation "takes place as reconciliation takes place; as it has its origin, content and subject; as reconciliation is revealed and reveals itself in it" (IV/3, 9). Thus revelation is coextensive with the ongoing prophetic activity of Jesus Christ.

Just as the life of the Son of God has been engaged in the event of reconciliation from the beginning of time, revelation has been the proclamation of reconciliation since the beginning. Barth appealed to the prologue of the Gospel of John to defend his claim. John 1:1 reads, "In the beginning was the Word (Logos) and the Word was with God and the Word was God." Barth used this verse to place Jesus Christ (the Logos) at the beginning as one with God. In his exegesis of John 1:4, Barth yoked revelation and reconciliation: "In him was life; and the life was the light of all men. And the light shineth in darkness" (IV/3, 9). By connecting Jesus Christ with life and light, in contrast to darkness, John 1:4 served as the theme verse for Barth's exposition in §69.

The event of reconciliation in Jesus Christ "is outgoing and self-communicative, announcing, displaying and glorifying itself. It is not merely light but the source of light" (IV/3, 10). The imagery of glory introduced here is closely tied to light for Barth, as discussed below. In contrast to the Christological paragraphs in IV/1 and IV/2 that focused on the *downward* movement of Jesus Christ toward humanity (§59) and the *upward* movement of Jesus Christ with humanity toward God (§64), in §69, Barth now emphasizes the *outward* movement of reconciliation. By connecting the imagery of glory to light, Barth insists that reconciliation is not simply a past event, but a continued source of light that shines and announces God's work in Jesus Christ. Christians are then called to follow the light of Jesus Christ into the world, not remain in cozy colonial-Christendom-era institutions.

Barth reaffirmed his Christocentric approach to theology here, much as he had practiced throughout his *Church Dogmatics*. His method was to speak first of God in Christ, then of humanity as such, *then* of human knowledge of Jesus Christ. Therefore, the person and work of Christ are the primary (and inseparable) means by which humanity comes to know who God is (and who they are) through the acts of Jesus Christ as recorded in the biblical witness. Specifically, Barth uses the office of prophet where, as in the Old Testament, the message and the messenger were inextricably intertwined. Jonah's reluctance to go to Nineveh to call for repentance landed him inside a whale. Hosea was instructed to marry a prostitute as an example of Israel's unfaithfulness. Jesus as the true Prophet, the fulfillment of the type, proclaims the message of the kingdom of God with his very body in his actions. Jesus's life, death, resurrection, and ascension proclaim to all the reconciliation between humanity and God. For Barth, then, "reconciliation is indeed revelation. But revelation in itself and as such, if we can conceive of such a thing, could not be reconciliation" (IV/3, 8). If there were words that could be uttered, true words even, that reveal who God is, these words would not, in and of themselves, bring reconciliation of humankind. Yet the acts of Jesus Christ not only perform the reconciliation of humanity to God, but they proclaim it as well. In this way, "that reconciliation is also revelation," is for Barth, understood as an event in Jesus Christ "who is its Mediator and Accomplisher in His own person" (IV/3, 38). The person of Christ and the work of Christ are held together in Barth's understanding of the ongoing prophetic activity of Jesus Christ. Revelation is for Barth the act of reconciliation as it confronts human beings.

Barth's understanding of how revelation occurs is consistent with his memorable articulation of God's sovereignty in the opening part-volume of his *Church Dogmatics*: "If the question what God can do forces theology to be humble, the question what is commanded of us forces it to concrete obedience. God may speak to us through Russian Communism, a flute concerto, a blossoming shrub, or a dead dog. We do well to listen to Him if He really does" (I/1, 55). The point in I/1 is repeated in §69.2: God's self-revelation can, in principle, take any form. God's sovereignty is such that God has the power to speak through anything at all. Most important, God is the one who speaks; humanity's role is to listen. Yet in §69 Barth fills in the content of revelation more fully than in I/1.

The content of God's self-revelation is *always* Jesus Christ. Barth hinted in this direction when he wrote, "The equation of God's Word and God's Son makes it radically impossible to say anything doctrinaire in understanding the Word of God. . . . The only system in Holy Scripture and proclamation is revelation, i.e., Jesus Christ. Now the converse is also true, of course, namely that God's Son is God's Word" (I/1, 137). For sure, late in I/1, Barth begins to make the argumentative moves that he will develop in §69. There are anticipations in I/1 of Barth's moves in §69, but they are *only* anticipations. In I/1, §11, he writes, "If they are to be authentic revelations and reconciliations, they can only be identical with the revelation and reconciliation through the Son of God. Jesus Christ will have to be recognized as living and acting in them. The one revelation and reconciliation will not be one among others" (I/1, 425).[41] Yet, while maintaining the uniqueness of reconciliation in Jesus Christ, at this point Barth only anticipated what will come later in describing how Christ will be recognized and how revelation and reconciliation are related. More forcefully than before, Barth defined in §69 the "matter of reconciliation as revelation" (IV/3, 38).[42]

In his second part-volume on the Word of God, Barth did discuss prophecy in the Old Testament (I/2, 84)[43] and the threefold office of prophet, priest, and king (I/2, 254). Again, there are hints in I/2 demonstrating a continuity of thought with §69, though the earlier presentation lacks the fullness of the later exposition.[44] The focus on Jesus Christ as the subject of revelation initiates an examination of the incarnation. Both the necessity of God taking human form and the distinctiveness of Jesus Christ's incarnation are of interest to Barth. He wrote:

He would not be revelation if He were not man. . . . It is here that we find ourselves at the point at which the biblical doctrine of the incarnation of the Word and the familiar parallels in the history of religions part company. There are also incarnations of Isis and Osiris; there is an incarnation in Buddha and in Zoroaster. But it is only the New Testament that says "he hath made him to be sin" and "he became a curse for us." Only here do we have so strict a concept of Emmanuel, of revelation and reconciliation. (I/2, 152)

The revelation of God in Jesus Christ does not merely take human form, but human *flesh*—fallen flesh, capable of sin.[45] Christ assumed human flesh in order to redeem humanity from the curse of sin. That God-in-the-flesh takes on the polluting and defiling sin of humankind differentiates Jesus Christ from the central figures in other world religions.

Barth uses the prologue of John's gospel for his Christology here in I/2 to propose that the way to understand the incarnation is to "think together . . . both the ὁ λόγος [the Word] and the ἐγένετο with the strict simultaneity with which they are given us in Scripture" (I/2, 160; John 1:14). This "strict simultaneity" that Barth proposes here in the Christological paragraph in I/2, §15, serves as the inspiration for §69, as the divine nature of Christ (most directly articulated in IV/1, §59) and the human nature of Christ (most directly articulated in IV/2, §64) are "thought together" in the ongoing prophetic activity of Jesus Christ as mediator and revealer in IV/3, §69.[46]

As Barth filled in his understanding of revelation between I/1 and IV/3, he appropriated the imagery of light to describe God's self-communication.[47] By II/2, Barth had moved closer to the position he asserted in §69, including adopting the imagery of light. He wrote, "Jesus was the life which was light, the revelation of God, the saying, or address, or communication in which God declares Himself to us. But as this revelation He was not something other outside and alongside God. He was God Himself within the revelation. . . . He was *revelation in its complete and absolute form*" (II/2, 97; emphasis added). Here Barth directly equated the *life* of Jesus with the revelation of God in a more blunt way than in I/2. God has chosen to address humanity in and through the life of Jesus Christ. The life of Jesus is "revelation in its complete and absolute form" (II/2, 97). By looking at the life of Jesus Christ, humanity can come to know God. The life of Jesus is *light*. This light publicizes and proclaims the already accomplished work of Christ in justification and sanctification. The life shines, and that shining is light. There is not another light separate from the life of Jesus Christ. The light shines freely on all peoples, displaying the work of Christ on their behalf.

The use of the imagery of light dominates §69, most notably in the title of §69.2: "The Light of Life." Yet the use of light to describe the life of Jesus Christ is not new in IV/3. In §69, Barth tied Jesus Christ as the "Word of life" in 1 John 1:1 and the "light of life" to the biblical concept of glory and to his earlier discussion of "glory" in II/1 (IV/3, 47). In his presentation on "The Perfections of God" in II/1, Barth discussed "The Eternity and Glory of God" in §31.3 (II/1, 640–77). Barth reflected on the significance of the Hebrew word for "glory" in the Old Testament, *Kabod*, as light, meaning both source and radiance. This glory or honor "is the worth which God Himself creates for Himself (in contrast to what He is not) simply by revealing Himself, just as light needs only itself and has only to be light in the midst of darkness to be bright and to spread brightness in contrast to all the darkness of heaven and earth." This is what it means that God is glorious. "Only God is light in this sense." Barth continued, "All other light and also all other glory (especially all the glory of men) can only copy Him" (II/1, 642). Christ in his full divinity shines and reveals who God is. In fact, Barth foreshadows the outshining of the Light of Life (in §69.2) here in II/1. The glory of God is self-revealing; it displays who God is without effort or decision. Since the glory of God "is the self-revealing sum of all divine perfections" (II/1, 643), its revelatory acts are perfect and complete. God is a being "which declares itself" (II/1, 643). In §69, Barth specifically names the glory of God. Jesus is "the authentic image of the glory of God.... His *doxa*, His power of revelation is a concrete event" (IV/3, 48). The concrete actions of the actual human being Jesus Christ reveal who God is.

In distinction from all the prophets of the Old Testament, Jesus Christ's "prophecy is universal prophecy" (IV/3, 50). His prophecy is not for Israel alone, but it is light shining on and for the whole world. Christ's prophecy is unique (IV/3, 49–52), yet it is consistent with the prophetic history of Israel (IV/3, 53–65).[48] Barth wrote, "The history of Israel says earlier what that of Jesus Christ says later" (IV/3, 66). There is only one prophet, one revelation, one light, and one word, one "biblical and Christian theology"

(IV/3, 71). There is only one Prophet of one covenant who was first concealed (in Israel), then revealed (in Jesus Christ). The self-revelation occurs through the life of Jesus Christ, the Light of Life. This revealing light shines on all people; revelation is no longer restricted to one people.

Ivor Davidson articulated this connection between the doctrine of God and divine luminosity: "The triune God really does shine forth, dispelling creaturely darkness by the sheer potency of his inner splendor, reaching us as he really is . . . [by making] visible for creatures something of what is eternally visible to God himself."[49] In God's eternal freedom, God chooses to shine light into the world. The out-shining of the light expresses who God is in God's innermost being. The light shines because of "the freedom of God's will" in choosing to make things visible. God freely shines the light of life on all people because God's eternal decision has been to be in relationship with humanity. God freely gives the light, but in giving himself, God does not give himself away. The concept of light does not encapsulate the being of God. Instead, God *is* light. Light is not something apart from the being of God. There is no other God than the one who shines out, no light force behind the triune God. As the light shines, it calls forth a response from those it reaches. Thus, even in the shining of the light, God remains sovereign.

From Davidson's perspective, Barth's discussion of light is quite unusual among twentieth- and twenty-first-century theologians. "A fair bit of theology," he writes, "modern and postmodern, might be said to have proceeded pretty much as if God were not light at all. . . . [On the contrary,] Barth's dogmatics offers a sustained endeavor to grapple with what it is to confess that the God who is all-glorious in himself invades and dispels our darkness."[50] Davidson has put his finger on the distinctive outward movement of the ongoing prophetic activity of Jesus Christ. For Barth, God is not withdrawn or isolated from humanity. Neither is God simply a projection of human yearnings in the way that Barth critiqued European Protestant culture. Instead, God is living, active, and, as evidenced in the incarnation, "on the loose" among humanity. God is not content to leave humanity to our own devices. The light of God publicizes and proclaims the reconciling work of the life of Jesus Christ.

There are other lights, what Barth refers to as lesser lights, but these other lights only shine because of the light of Jesus Christ (IV/3, 97). The life of the living God-man Jesus Christ is self-disclosing and self-revealing in ways that all can hear (eloquent) and see (radiant). "Because it is the life of grace," Barth wrote, "it is this eloquent and radiant life" (IV/3, 81). There are also "true words" that may be spoken outside the walls of the church; they too communicate the one Word of God, Jesus Christ (IV/3, 110). The life of Jesus Christ as the Light of Life bears witness to the being of God through its ongoing prophetic activity that revealed who God is in the life, death, resurrection, and ascension of Jesus Christ and *continues* to bear witness through the shining of true light and the proclamation of true words to all people. This light shines freely—both within and outside ecclesial structures. In contrast, for Bediako, revelation primarily occurs because of "the infinite translatability of the gospel of Jesus Christ."[51] Translatability, then, makes possible an authentic African Christian identity.

The Infinite Translatability of the Gospel

Though he borrowed the phrase from Andrew Walls,[52] Bediako built his entire theology on the insight that "the translatability of the Christian religion signifies its fundamental relevance and accessibility to persons in any culture within which the Christian faith is transmitted and assimilated" (*CiA*, 109). As such, the Christian faith is relevant and accessible to anyone in any culture on earth. The translatability of the Christian faith is what defines its uniqueness and its universality.[53] The phrase, "translatability is another way of saying universality," is well loved and often repeated by Bediako (*CiA*, 109).[54] He believed both in the translatability of the Christian scriptures and in the translatability of the gospel itself,[55] by which he meant the person, life, and work of Christ that is expressed in the scriptures.[56] And both translations are possible because of the initial act of translation: God taking human form in the person of Jesus Christ. Bediako wrote, "Underlying the translatability of the Christian Scriptures lies the prior act of divine translation, the Incarnation, for the divine 'Word became flesh and dwelt among us' (John 1:14)."[57] Or as Bediako puts it, the "Christian claim is that in Jesus Christ 'Divinity became translated into humanity.'"[58]

The basis for his claim of translatability is John 1:14: "The Word became flesh and dwelt among us" (*CiA*, 110).[59] Because of the incarnation, "translatability . . . may be said to be in-built into the nature of the Christian religion and capable of subverting any cultural possessiveness of the Faith in the process of its transmission" (*CiA*, 110). Translatability is an inherent characteristic of the Christian faith. It undergirds "the true character of continuing Christian witness and enhance[s] the genuine development of new indigenous traditions of Christian thought" (*CiA*, 110). Moreover, the process of translation must occur anew in every distinct culture. Transporting one cultural translation of the gospel to a different culture without allowing the gospel to be translated anew can have harmful consequences.[60]

While Bediako's understanding of the gospel is universal in application, theological reflection is necessarily provisional. This is because "all theology, wherever it is produced, is contextual and therefore provisional rather than universal, and that theology itself is always a struggle with culturally-related questions" (*CiA*, 129). Understandings of the gospel, or simply put, theologies, are culturally bound and subject to error and misinterpretation. As such, "theology can be authentic only in context."[61] It follows, for Bediako, that any attempt at a universal theology, that is, an a-contextual theology, creates a false gospel. In fact, the consequences of misplaced cultural confidence in such a "false gospel" are devastating in Bediako's view. He wrote, "The price that is paid by converts to such a truncated Gospel is incalculable."[62] Bediako had in mind here the damaging erasure of African cultural and religious memory by colonial missions. This deep concern—that the scriptural witness of the gospel is corrupted by the blind adaptation of cultural assumptions—drives his work.

Bediako's fundamental critique of Western Christianity was its implicit and uncritical embrace of Western culture as inseparable from the gospel. He frequently criticized Western formulations of the gospel for assuming they were pure and untranslated. European missionaries failed by assuming that the translation process was complete, once and for all, when the gospel was translated into Western culture. Instead of bringing "the gospel" to Africa, as many naively assumed, the missionaries brought a bastardized version of Christianity—a hybrid of the gospel of the Christian faith and Western culture—that they passed on as the pure, unadulterated, unencultured gospel. This approach prevented Africans from developing indigenous understandings of the Christian faith; they were simply asked to receive Western Christianity as "the gospel." The missionaries' practice of imparting their Western understanding of Christianity perpetuated the notion that Christianity was foreign to Africa and that the gospel did not need to be translated.

Bediako was charitably understanding of the missionaries and particularly grateful to them for bringing the Bible to Africa and translating it into so many African mother tongues (*CiA*, 185, 203). Yet he saw the encounter of Western Christianity with African culture not as invalidating Christianity but as unmasking Western Christianity for what it is. Bediako wrote, "Not only in demographic terms, but in some other respects too, Christianity has become a non-Western religion. . . . It is not that Western Christianity has become irrelevant, but rather that Christianity may now be seen for what it truly is, a universal religion, infinitely culturally translatable—capable of being at home everywhere without loss to its essential nature."[63] Through the infinite translatability of the gospel, Bediako asserted that "Christianity . . . [is] capable of being at home everywhere without loss to its essential nature."[64] Therefore, in Africa, and given the colonial history, seemingly *even* in Africa, the gospel of Jesus Christ (the "essential nature" of Christianity) can take an authentic form. Bediako pressed his point further: "Accordingly, the popular notion of Christianity as 'the white man's religion' or Western religion, is effectively set aside, for African Christianity is no less Christian for being mediated through African languages, whilst Western Christianity does not enshrine universal standards. On the contrary, the very possibility of Scripture translation, as well as the elements that come into play through it, demonstrates that an African 'incarnation' of the Faith is valid too" (*CiA*, 121). Bediako understood the revelation of the gospel in Africa to have begun in and through African traditional religions and to have continued to completion in African Christianity.

The Light of Life

Barth's understanding of the ongoing prophetic activity of Jesus Christ helps to counter two commonly held misconceptions. Some evangelicals, particularly (but not only) in the United States, criticize Barth for his understanding of scripture. Specifically, they critique Barth's understanding that Jesus Christ is *the* Word of God and that the Bible contains the Word of God—as Jesus Christ revealed in the written words of the scriptural text.[65] Their critique more specifically is that Barth offers a "relativistic" understanding of scripture. Because the biblical texts are not *objectively* the Word of God (as it taught under the heading of a restrictive account of biblical inerrancy), then anyone can interpret the Bible in any way.[66] In contrast, postcolonial theologians, among others, accuse Barth of portraying God as too distant and aloof.[67] This God is insufficiently relational and imminent and fails to adequately enter into the pain, suffering, and difficulties that humans experience in their everyday lives.

The reasons informing these interpretations are twofold. First, many of Barth's critics have only read selections of *Church Dogmatics* I/1. This selective reading offers only a partial view of Barth's theology (as occurred for Bediako, who was only exposed to excerpts of *Church Dogmatics* volumes I and II in his Modern Theology course at London Bible College). Contributing to this partial reading for English-language readers was the initial lag and order of publication of *Church Dogmatics* in English. After volume I/1 appeared in English in 1936, twenty years passed before an additional volume appeared. In 1956, volumes I/2 and IV/1 were published in English; by 1961, all eleven completed part-volumes had been translated and published in English.

Barth's insights in §69, over seven thousand pages and twenty-five years later than his initial thoughts in I/1, offered a presentation of the ongoing prophetic activity of Jesus Christ that addressed both concerns in interesting ways. For some evangelicals, whose broader theological concerns were of interest to Bediako, Barth's consistent and explicit Christological exposition based in detailed arguments of biblical exegesis might go some way to assuaging the worries about scripture. Further, the *ongoing* prophetic *activity* of Christ presented the underlying thrust for the sending of the Christian community in §72 that offered a profound theological rationale for mission and evangelism.[68]

For postcolonial theologians and others with similar concerns, the *prophetic* nature of Christ's ongoing activity and the universality of divine-human reconciliation and revelation that Barth articulates in §69 might be deemed significant and helpful resources. The witness of Christ that counters human claims to power and relativizes all worldviews results from Christ's ongoing prophetic activity. God in Jesus Christ is at work in the world, especially on behalf of those on the underside of power.

Barth clearly established that the biblical understanding of Christ as prophet undermined and critiqued the practices of European coloniza-tion and missionary activity. Barth wrote, "He [Jesus Christ] would have contradicted them, showing to the world and men only the kind of lop-sided favor which European nations used to exercise without consulting them to the peoples of their colonies" (IV/3, 333). Indeed, at one point Barth asserted that Jesus Christ was on the side of the colonized, not the colonizers. Barth's understanding applies not only to the past errors of formal colonization in the nineteenth and twentieth centuries but also to the practices of theological reflection in the present day. He wrote, "The debate about whether the aim of the mission should be to represent a European-American Christianity or to found an autochthonous African or Asian Christianity could not remove the hidden problem that either way it was still a matter of the 'glory' of one Christianity or the other in its relation to the needs and postulates of man" (I/2, 336, 97). From this early expression in I/2, §17, of his views of the failure of Christianity as a reli-gion, Barth sketched his hopeful understanding of the possibilities that could result as "the grace of Jesus Christ . . . [would continue] to speak, shine forth, and assert itself" (I/2, 336, 97). Barth's exposition of the on-going prophetic activity of Jesus Christ in IV/3, §69, expanded and filled out these nascent thoughts by reformulating Barth's understanding of revelation, religion, culture, and their interrelationship.

Revelation Is for *All* People: History/Worldview

For Barth, as one who was not interested in theological theories or ab-stractions in and of themselves, the key to every theological locus is the person of Jesus Christ. Thus, in terms of revelation, in his prophetic office Jesus Christ is the sole and sufficient revelation of God. In the opening of volume IV of his *Church Dogmatics*, Barth wrote that Jesus Christ is the "epistemological principle" (IV/1, 21). Yet Barth was quick to add that no one could claim to grasp fully who Christ is because that would entail constructing a system and trying to live "by its own light" (IV/1, 21). Barth named such a self-justified and self-sufficient system "a myth" (IV/1, 21). The only place to look for true knowledge of God is in the person of Jesus Christ. (Here, Barth is criticizing Roman Catholicism, certain aspects of

Pietism, and German cultural Protestantism.) Theories about Jesus Christ are not sufficient. Only Jesus Christ himself fully and sufficiently reveals who God is. The self-revelation of God in Jesus Christ occurs in the event of reconciliation.

For Barth, light shines on everyone, whether they seek the light or hide from it. As the sun shines, rays of its light fall on all people. "The reconciling work of Jesus Christ is not just accomplished, but has gone out into the reconciled world as a shining light comparable with the leaven hid among three measures of meal (Matt. 13:33). This means that the leavening of the whole ... is not merely possible but actual and in process of fulfillment" (IV/3, 301). Reconciliation, for Barth, is not a static past event but continues as a dynamic "shining light." This light is like yeast leavening bread—yet not just the "bread" of Christians but also "the whole." Through the life, death, resurrection, and ascension of Jesus Christ, true humanity is shown its full capabilities and possibilities. The impact of the event of reconciliation is so powerful and so pervasive that "the determination given the world and man in this event is a universal one" (IV/3, 303). The event of reconciliation changes our understanding of what it means to be human. The eternal determination is "total" and results in the reconciliation of the world—not just satisfaction of the little flock or solely the Christian community (IV/3, 301). The shining of divine light publicizes the standing of humanity before God. This reconciliation of all humanity with God does not necessarily result in universal salvation, though that is Barth's hope. He believes that the biblical witness teaches universal reconciliation but stops short of teaching universal salvation.[69] The impact of Barth's understanding of revelation has an impact on how knowledge is established, how history is understood, and which worldviews are possible.

Just as revelation establishes knowledge because "Christian knowledge [is] established, awakened, and fashioned by the revelation, manifestation, and prophecy of Jesus Christ" (IV/3, 211), so Christ's prophecy "creates history" (IV/3, 212). Without the telling of the story, none other than the participants in the event ever know that it occurred. As the primary actor in the event of reconciliation, "Jesus Christ did not become a Witness and Revealer. He was from the very first" (IV/3, 232).[70] Barth's understandings of history and of Christ's activity in reconciliation allowed him to assert that Christ was active in reconciliation both at its inception and in its future. Even the event of reconciliation "did not only take place then. It has not become past" (IV/3, 223).

The presence of the living Christ within history—both then and now—is what Barth is trying to convey in his title for the subsection of §69.3, "Jesus is Victor." All of Christian faith and theology is a response not only to the written scriptures and the life and death of Jesus Christ but also to the ongoing self-revelation of Jesus Christ both within and outside the walls of the church. Further, since the prophetic activity of Christ is ongoing, it cannot be domesticated into principles or abstractions. This emphasis on Christ's ongoing prophetic activity fuels Barth's critique of worldviews, since "no world-views can find any place for Jesus Christ" (IV/3, 257). Abstract notions of "God," "man," "a supposed historical Jesus," or a "Christ-idea" can be fit into a worldview, wrote Barth, "but not for the living Lord, for the High-priest, the King and especially the Prophet Jesus Christ. This Jesus Christ is of no value for the purposes of a world-view. He would not be who He is if He were" (IV/3, 257).

Why is this so? Worldviews are too static, too abstract, and, most important, too disconnected from the person of Jesus Christ. They are a human means of trying to understand and contain an idea or concept. For Barth, this is no different from the role that religion (or another type of philosophical perspective) attempts to play with Jesus Christ. Humans cannot gain mastery or power over God. The ongoing prophetic activity of Christ cannot be contained or predicted. Any worldview that attempts to do so would be false, unprofitable, and unable to accept the revelatory potential of Christ's ongoing activity.

Revelation Is Ongoing

While Barth believed that the primary vehicle of God's self-revelation occurred in the witness of the scriptures of the Old and New Testaments, he did not believe that revelation is over or finished. Instead, through the ongoing prophetic activity of the risen and ascended God-man Jesus Christ, God's self-revelation continued through cultural forms that Christ takes hold of. The reason for this is that the resurrection is not simply the triumphant completion of Jesus Christ's life on earth and the final demonstration of his victory over death. It also marks the beginning of a new phase in Christ's prophetic activity. Even in the resurrection, Barth kept the movement of prophetic activity moving forward and outward. Barth's use of the threefold office in reference to soteriology offers helpful interpretive insights here. The event of the cross actualized and disclosed God's humiliation and confirmed Christ's priestly work of justification. The event of the resurrection enacted humanity's exaltation and confirmed Christ's kingly work of sanctification. The event of the ascension actualized and disclosed Christ's prophetic vocation. These events are theologically inseparable in a perichoretic relationship.

Even as the resurrection is a once-and-for-all event, the resurrection is followed by the ascension to confirm its prophetic character (IV/3, 282). Christ's resurrection and ascension (as described in §69.4) proclaimed Jesus to be alive, living onward in and through his prophetic activity. Barth began §69.2, "The Light of Life," with the claim, "Jesus lives." This is the importance of Easter, more than Christmas or Good Friday, that Jesus lives (IV/3, 284). Jesus lives, and his light can never be extinguished (IV/3, 291). The reconciling work of Jesus Christ, in his life, death, resurrection, and ascension, is not just accomplished, but has *gone out* and is continuing to go out as a shining light, as a fire (IV/3, 301). Christ's light, the light of life, is a *radiating* light (IV/3, 305). This light radiates and spreads to all places, peoples, and cultures without regard for whether or not it is received.

The Twin Heritage of African Christianity

Even after Western influences had stopped overtly trying to impose that light of Western Christianity on Africa, truly African theology had not been welcomed within Western theological circles. Thus for Bediako, "The overall goal of African theology was to show that there were genuinely and specifically *African* contributions . . . to be made to the theology of the universal Church."[71] Through his act of theological négritude, the identification of the "twin heritage of African Christianity" in African primal tradition and the African experience of the Christian gospel,[72] Bediako searched for and found a history for African Christians, recovering a cultural and religious memory as the basis for an African Christian identity.

Bediako performed the task of connecting twentieth-century African Christianity with its Christian past primarily in his first book, *Theology and*

Identity: The Impact of Culture on Christian Thought in the Second Century and Modern Africa.[73] He clearly articulated his goal in the introduction: "Whilst the book seeks to make a contribution to the understanding of modern African Christianity, it seeks to do so by situating twentieth-century African theology within the organic tradition of Christian theology as a whole" (*TI*, xii). Bediako understood African Christianity as an organic aspect of Christian theology, not a foreign element that needed to be grafted on later. As such, Bediako connected twentieth-century African Christianity to its precolonial Christian past, freeing African Christianity from its "historical limbo[,] . . . caught between African 'non-Christian' beliefs and values on the one hand, and Western 'Christian' ideas on the other" (*TI*, xii).

For Bediako, a direct line can be drawn (akin to the red thread of history from Barth's *Epistle to the Romans*)[74] from the earliest Christian theologians directly to modern African theologians—without having to go through European mediators. The result connected the African present to its Christian past and also enabled African Christians to articulate their own understanding of the gospel in their own (religiously pluralistic) contexts. Put summarily: Bediako suggests that African Christians can construct local theologies within a religiously pluralistic modern world in a way that Western theologies based in a worldview shaped by Christendom and the Enlightenment may be incapable of doing.

In the second-century apologist Justin Martyr, Bediako found an early example of such continuity between a pre-Christian past and a Christian present. Justin claimed that there were "Christians" before Christ and "that he and the Christians of his own day had a common cause with those of the past" (*TI*, 150). For Justin, as later for Bediako, "the truth of the Christian Gospel is the truth of the person rather than of the religious tradition to which one belongs" (*TI*, 156). The person of Jesus Christ, "the Word Himself" (*TI*, 152), was the source of Christian knowledge and the conduit for participation in God. In Justin, he saw an apologist who while "interpreting the past . . . is also explicating the present" (*TI*, 149). Bediako did not study the early fathers merely for their roles in the development of Christian doctrine but rather saw them as making a valuable contribution to contemporary discussions of Christian identity.

Bediako argued that Clement of Alexandria subsequently built on the continuity that Justin had articulated. He saw here a "universalizing of

'salvation-history'... [that] involves the Christianising not only of Hellenistic tradition, but the Jewish also; 'holy pagans' and Jewish saints become 'Christians before Christ,' on the same terms; and the Old Testament, by virtue of Christ foreshadowed therein, becomes a Christian
book" (*TI*, 160). Bediako latched onto the universalizing approach of
Clement. For Clement, "the Christian account of reality . . . supersedes
the entire history of intellectual and philosophical speculation in Hellenistic tradition . . . by absorbing it" (*TI*, 80). The superiority of the Christian understanding enabled it to absorb the Hellenistic tradition. And yet,
whereas the process of absorption of the Jewish and Hellenistic religious
traditions by Christianity is acceptable to Bediako, the absorption of primal African religious traditions to Christianity is somewhat problematic.
Bediako considered African religions a freestanding substructure of
Christianity; he considered Hellenism to be the beginning of the Western tradition that departs from primal religious understandings and, in
the long run, distorts the Christian faith.

Though one could use Bediako's approach to postulate a Hellenistic substructure of Western Christianity by rereading the Hellenistic tradition as a
distinctive preparation for Christianity (akin to the apostle Paul's Mars Hill
speech in Acts 17), Bediako did not do so.[75] In this way, while Bediako's
(and Clement's) Christianity would still be universalizing, it would not be
totalizing. The absorption of Hellenistic religiosity would be complemented
by the preservation of African religiosity. Bediako hinted in this direction
in his concluding comments on Clement: "Advancing beyond Justin,
Clement even postulated a tradition in Hellenistic culture which bore witness to an apprehension of the divine truth in the Hellenistic past" (*TI*,
207). Bediako sought a similar presence of divine truth in the African past.
The advantage of Clement's views, according to Bediako, was that they
connected Christians as part of an ancient nation through the Old Testament "with laws and traditions which entitled them to a place in the common history of mankind, a right that was being denied them by Graeco-
Roman traditionalists" (*TI*, 203–4). All told, Clement's task was "integrating
Christian faith with culture" (*TI*, 207), and Bediako understood himself to
be doing the same as a modern-day apologist for Christianity in Africa
with implications for Christianity itself and the wider world.[76]

While the core of Bediako's work built on the view of history and the
universalizing role of the Christian faith that Justin Martyr and Clement

of Alexandria espoused, the deeper connection still is with the person of Jesus Christ revealed in the scriptures of the Old and New Testaments. Bediako's underlying theological conviction was that Africans are fully human, created by God, and that Christ's governance of history encompassed Africa as well as the West. He wrote, "The fact of the matter is, if Jesus Christ is not in the cultural heritage of African peoples, then Africans as human beings would not have been created in and through Jesus Christ, the Word of God, Agent of creation, and the Second Adam and New Man."[77] Put a bit differently: because God created Africans as human beings in the image of God, Jesus Christ is the cultural heritage of Africans just as much as of Europeans.

Whether in the midst of the German church conflict under Nazism or in the cities and bush of Ghana, according to Karl Barth and Kwame Bediako, the starting point for theological reflection is Jesus Christ. Contemporary theological reflection, then, is also to start from Jesus Christ as the colonial-Christendom complex collapses in the face of increasing secularization and intensifying globalization. Bediako and Barth—from their different socioeconomic, political, and cultural contexts—both point to Jesus Christ who, as infinite translator and prophet, speaks anew into the present historical moment. The impact of each theologian's context on his thought is the subject of the next chapter.

FOUR

Contextual Reflection

Revelation, not Religion

Every cat's politics comes from what he sees when he wakes up in the morning.
The liberals see Central Park and we see sharecropper shacks.
> —Stokely Carmichael, African American civil rights activist,
> quoted in Jack Newfield, *A Prophetic Minority*

What could Karl Barth possibly mean for black students who had come from
the cotton fields of Arkansas, Louisiana and Mississippi, seeking to change the
structures of their lives in a society that had defined *black* as nonbeing?
> —James Cone, African American theologian, *God of the Oppressed*

Christiana Afua Gyan (1900–1987), better known as Afua Kuma, was an
oral poet, yam farmer, and village midwife from Asempaneye in the hills
of eastern Ghana who was also a member of the Church of Pentecost.[1]
She expressed her prayers and praises to God in Jesus Christ contextually,
in the vernacular Twi language through images and concepts that were

familiar to her. She had received no formal schooling and did not read or write. Her hymns were tape-recorded, transcribed into Twi, and then translated into English as *Jesus of the Deep Forest*.[2] Her words demonstrate an embodied, contextual theology. She expressed her beliefs in indigenous forms using the culture that she knew. She sang songs of praise to Jesus Christ, such as the following:

O great and powerful Jesus, incomparable Diviner,
The sun and moon are your *batakari* [long flowing robe].
It sparkles like the morning star.
Sɛkyerɛ Buruku [local divinity associated with this mountain],
     the tall mountain,
all the nations see your glory.

You weave the streams like plaited hair;
with fountains you tie a knot.
Magician who walks on the sea:
he arrives at the middle,
plunges his hand into the deep and takes out a whale![3]

Her lyrics announced Jesus Christ's many titles. She refers to Jesus as "Hero," "the Python," the "great Rock," "the big Tree," "Wonderworker," "the untiring Porter," "the Chief of Police," "the Elephant Hunter," and "the Bravest of Muscle-Men." Much of the imagery she employed is agricultural and focused on praising Jesus for his roles as provider and protector. Madam Kuma also clearly asserted the continuity between Onyankopɔn, a traditional Akan name for God, and God-in-Jesus-Christ. She sang:

Our ancestors didn't know of *Onyankopɔn*: The great God.
They served lesser gods and spirits, and became tired.
But as for us, we have seen holy men, and prophets.
We have gone to tell the angels
how Jehovah helped us reach this place.
Jehovah has helped us come this far;
with great gratitude we come before Jesus,
the one who gives everlasting life.[4]

This is what Bediako called contextual theology. This is what he meant by saying God was always in Africa; Western missionaries did not bring God to Africa: "the 'Jesus of the deep forest' is also the Jesus of the Gospels."[5] Jesus feeds, Jesus heals, Jesus saves.

Bediako understood that by ascribing ancestral and royal titles to Jesus, Afua Kuma was demonstrating that "the biblical world is felt to be so close to the African world, that biblical realities take on a remarkable immediacy."[6] Kuma was practicing contemporary theological reflection in the context familiar to her. Bediako cited the following stanza by Kuma to support his observation.

Jesus! we have taken you out
and nailed you to a cross.
On a cross we have nailed You.
The cross is your fishing net;
you cast it in the stream and catch men.

The cross is the bridge we cross over
to search for the well of His blood.
The blood-pool is there.
If it were not for the cross
we would never have the chance to wash in that blood;
the cross is the Christian's precious inheritance;
it brings us to eternal life.[7]

In addition to the significance of calling Afua Kuma's poetry "grassroots theology,"[8] Bediako was careful to note "that the christology of these texts is very elevated and stands as a significant illustration of an African response to Jesus marked by authentic African Christian religious experience and meditation."[9] For Bediako, *Jesus in the Deep Forest* was yet more "clear evidence that Christianity in Africa is a truly African experience."[10] While certainly influenced by non-Africans (indirectly if not directly), Afua Kuma's understanding of her faith in Jesus Christ is thoroughly local. She understood who Jesus is in light of her own particular circumstances and context. Her confidence in who she knew Jesus to be, combined with her freedom from doctrinal constraints, allowed her to sing, "Jesus! You are the Mother whom we will return to," "the elephant Hunter," and "the brightest of Lanterns."[11] Afua Kuma's mother-tongue theology demonstrated that African theology did not need to be held captive by normative European formulations.[12] Instead, her faith was a lived African experience that engaged her surroundings, a true contextual lived theology. Whereas articulating indigenous interpretations of the Christian faith in non-Western images and categories has a history of being condemned as syncretistic, African theologians such as Bediako and Mercy Amba Oduyoye praised Afua Kuma.[13] They lifted up her process as a model for others, though they do not expect that all theological reflection in a single context will produce identical theological convictions or express them in the same ways. Afua Kuma's Christology of the jungle demonstrates the potential and possibilities of contextual theological reflection.

All encounters between gospel and culture must occur in a *place*. Eugene Peterson's paraphrase of John 1:14 in *The Message* captures this engagement: "The Word became flesh and blood, and moved into the neighborhood."[14] The inhabitants of a place develop their understandings of culture and identity within that place.[15] The questions asked and the theological responses given are inextricably linked to the site of each particular encounter between gospel and culture. The interaction between place, culture, politics, language, identity, faith, and theology is also full of possibility (and, some would say, peril). In these encounters, issues of revelation, religion, and culture become intertwined and not easily separated. Bediako and Barth were both cognizant of the very particular contextual details in each engagement between the gospel and culture. This bifocal engagement with two contextual theologians models how contemporary theological reflection can be undertaken amid increasing secularization and intensifying globalization.

Unfortunately, all too often Western theologians are read out of context, or perhaps more precisely, as if they had no context.[16] This error has frequently been applied to Barth's thought. In part, Barth himself is to blame for this. And in part, this mistake is the fault of Barth's interpreters. While one can often see the effects of Barth's context (whether Nazi Germany, or the Cold War, or other circumstances) in his writing, rarely do social or political events explicitly appear in his dogmatic works, giving his theology an atemporal quality. When Barth is read, this seeming timelessness also allows interpreters to dislocate the text from the setting of its original composition. While *Church Dogmatics* originated as student lectures, their underlying intent was to understand the meaning of the gospel of Jesus Christ (full stop)—in any and every time and place.

Reading Barth in Context

Karl Barth is a contextual theologian in the sense that he was deeply influenced by the people and events surrounding him and that his work often addressed particular situations.[17] As Barth reflected in 1957, "My thinking, writing and speaking developed from reacting to people, events and circumstances with which I was involved, with their questions and their riddles."[18] Yet to be contextual for Barth meant reading contemporary circumstances as always subordinate to God's self-revelation in Jesus Christ. Context was never king. Thus in an article about his retirement from teaching, Barth recalled advising young theologians, "Take your Bible and take your newspaper, and read both. But interpret newspapers from your Bible."[19] For Barth, theological reflection (as an expression of biblical interpretation) occurred in a context but should not be driven by, or bound to, that context.

Barth's last assistant and biographer, Eberhard Busch, described Barth's thought process and approach to doing theology when Barth was working on his *Church Dogmatics*: "He was outwardly pressured by many external responsibilities on which he adopted pointed, fearless, and often offensive positions. Undoubtedly the two lines of activity, the internal and the external, were related. What took place outwardly was a kind of commentary on that to which he was devoting himself at the inner level."[20] While commenting on current events, authors, and circumstances, Barth always understood his work as a theologian to be one of a witness—to be following in the legacy of John the Baptist—as one always pointing to Jesus Christ, and the hope Christ offers, as the one who said, "He must increase, but I must decrease" (John 3:30). Above the desk where he wrote, Barth hung a haunting picture of Matthias Grünewald's *Crucifixion*—from the Isenheimer Altarpiece—with the bony hand of John the Baptist pointing to Christ on the cross.[21] Barth understood the Bible, and by extension, his work, as pointing-as-witness in a similar manner.[22]

Busch offers this helpful imagery in describing Barth's posture: "In addressing its temporal context, his theology was more like the needle of a compass than a weather vane. Reflecting on the eternal truth of God, it spoke not from the rocking chair but from the trenches of the church militant."[23] In the liberal theology of his teachers, Barth saw a weather vane, blown by the shifting winds of the era and pointing to where the wind originated. In contrast, Barth understood his role as a witness—as John the Baptist before him—as one that required pointing to the fixed point of God in Jesus Christ. The needle will move as one's position or context changes, but the needle will always point true North, to Jesus Christ.

Barth most vividly displayed his commitment to witness by pointing to Jesus Christ amid trying circumstances during the German church struggle in the 1930s. Barth was teaching in Bonn when Hitler came to power. He joined the Confessing Church movement and was the primary author of the Barmen Declaration in 1934 (see ch. 3). Barth's refusal to salute Hitler before lecturing in Bonn led to his expulsion from Germany in 1935. He was immediately offered a chair in systematic theology at the University of Basel, where he remained for the rest of his career. Each page of *Church Dogmatics* began as a student lecture in Basel that was then revised for publication. After retiring, Barth found the act of writing more strenuous without the constant, repeated, and energizing act of lecturing to students.

Although the circumstances in early twentieth-century Europe were in dynamic flux, Barth's context remained distinctly European. Significantly, Barth did not travel outside of Europe before his trip to the United States in 1962 when he was seventy-five years old and had finished teaching and generating new material for his *Church Dogmatics*. Much earlier, his younger contemporary, Dietrich Bonhoeffer, commented on Barth's relatively insular existence. In his diary on March 10, 1928, after spending a month in Barcelona at the age of twenty-two, Bonhoeffer wrote, "My theology is beginning to become humanistic; what does that mean? I wonder if Barth ever lived abroad?"[24] Though Barth had lived in Geneva as the assistant pastor of a German Reformed congregation for two years, from 1909 to 1911, traveled to France in 1934, and traveled extensively in Europe in 1938, including in the United Kingdom, during the lead-up to World War II, Bonhoeffer's instincts were correct:[25] Barth's theology indeed had been shaped within Europe, predominantly within Swiss

German culture. In contrast, Bediako had traveled around Africa, Western Europe, Egypt, India, the United States, Mexico, and Thailand before his fiftieth birthday. Unlike Bediako's thought, then, Barth's theology emerged largely from within a particular cultural worldview that was not challenged by direct encounters with other cultures. In addition, Barth's writings do not demonstrate much explicit consciousness of race, class, or gender.

Yet Barth's world was by no means static. Central Europe in the early twentieth century, and Germany in particular, experienced tumultuous change. Barth's career and writing were defined and shaped by the social and cultural challenges of German ambition, the harsh terms of the Versailles Treaty, the economic deprivations of the 1920s, the rise of National Socialism in the 1930s, the events of World War II, including the Holocaust, and the ensuing Cold War. Barth's break with Protestant liberalism, his public expression of opposition to the theological endorsement of the Great War, and his subsequent criticisms of the German Christians all demonstrate the possibility of a contestation of cultural assumptions in view of God's self-revelation in Jesus Christ.

Bediako and Barth thus embodied contrasting approaches to contextual theological reflection. In Barth's understanding, theology addressed context. As circumstances change, theology must respond to the changes in order to remain contextual. Theology appears as an extension of revelation and thus must always remain separate. Theology speaks into a context; the movement of revelation is unidimensional—from outside in.

Bediako's engagement of Afua Kuma's *Jesus of the Deep Forest* described an alternative process. By describing Madam Kuma's work as "grassroots theology," Bediako emphasized a process of contemporary theological reflection that moved from within a context. Certainly for Bediako, Afua Kuma's insights are given to her by God through the Holy Spirit, yet her theology was not fully formed until she processed who Jesus Christ is through the lenses of her own experiences and cultural context. In this way, Bediako believed that Afua Kuma demonstrated that the "African experience of the Christian faith can be seen to be fully coherent with the religious quests in African life" (*CiA*, 60). Through repeated emphasis on the infinite translatability of the gospel of Jesus Christ in his corpus, Bediako advanced an understanding of revelation that accentuated the direct communication of the gospel to Africans and claimed that Christian faith is continuous with traditional African religious practices.

This contrast—which can be oversimplified as revelation coming solely from outside of human cultures and contexts, for Barth, or God working in and through human cultures and contexts to reveal Jesus Christ, for Bediako—is important to remember as we engage an unexpected convergence in their thought: a similar approach to religion.

"We all wear cultural blinkers"

The category of religion often functions for Bediako as a description of the "cultural blinkers," or blinders, that humans bring to their understanding of God. His writings are a call "to dissociate the Christian Gospel from the trappings of western culture."[26] He was deeply aware that "the interrelation of Gospel and human culture is a complex one; the Gospel can only be perceived by us in some cultural form or other—a pure Gospel devoid of cultural embodiment is simply imaginary."[27] In short, there is no gospel apart from its cultural context. Any and all attempts to articulate a theology for all peoples in all places are deeply flawed. Theology cannot be exported. Yet Bediako's claim that there is no "pure Gospel" goes further. Instead of solely pointing his critical finger at Western Christians, he acknowledged the fingers pointing back at himself and other African Christians when he wrote, "The trouble is that we all wear cultural blinkers, and whilst we may affirm an absolute Gospel and accept the relativity of our diverse cultures, each of us fails to perceive some important facets of the one Gospel."[28] The cultural blinders that shape how every human being perceives the world determine how we understand the gospel of Jesus Christ as well. Faithful theological reflection can only take place when one has acknowledged the cultural blinders that one inevitably wears.

The deep historical problem that Bediako criticized was that Western Christian theology acted as if it was not wearing any cultural blinders. In particular, the legacy of colonialism demonstrated the Western overconfidence in revelation that he saw as all too synonymous with Western culture. At the same time, African traditional religions, in Bediako's view, also could blind adherents to God's complete revelation that comes through the name of Jesus Christ and the scriptures of the Old and New Testaments. The remarkably consistent argument of Bediako's work was that Africans must recover their history, as Christians and as Africans, in order to shape and articulate an African Christian identity. In doing so, Bediako believed, Africa may save Christianity itself through the remaking of Christian theology.

Religion: Projection and Myth

The engagement of Bediako and Barth with the category of religion produces one of the unexpected convergences between their thought: both authors criticized religion as projection. For Bediako, the death and resurrection of Jesus revealed that the ancestors are a myth. He wrote, "The potency of the cult of ancestors is not the potency of ancestors themselves; the potency of the cult is the potency of myth" (JAC, 30). By "myth," Bediako meant that the ancestors do not possess independent power of their own. Belief in the cultural and religious traditions gave the ancestors the appearance of power; intrinsically, lineage ancestors are merely the memories of dead human beings and are thereby powerless. In his death and resurrection, Jesus Christ surpassed the ancestors and replaced the cult of ancestors for African Christians. Only Christ has the power and ability to bestow the benefits believed to be given by lineage ancestors (JAC, 30). Just as each ancestor was believed to remain the spirit of a formerly living human being with his own personality and life experiences, so also for Bediako Jesus retained his personal identity while in the spiritual realm. In this way, Bediako insisted on holding together the person and the work of Jesus Christ—just as he would for any ancestor.

While Bediako was not the first Christian theologian to offer a theology of ancestors, aspects of his approach are innovative and they are particularly instructive for a consideration of the possibilities (and limits) of culture for Christian theological reflection. Bediako presented a Christological reading of the role of the ancestors in African culture that simultaneously declared Jesus to be the Supreme Ancestor and denied any real existence to other ancestors. For Bediako, Jesus is alive while the other so-called ancestors are dead and gone. Only the (significant) memories of these deceased elders remain.

Bediako argued that the death and resurrection of Jesus exposed the ancestors for what they really were: "the death of Jesus is also the defeat of Satan and of all the elemental demonic terrors which masquerade behind the presumed activity of ancestors."[29] Ancestors did not have any real power over the living. Only God in Jesus Christ had the power and re-sources to support and affect life. "If Jesus has gone to the realm of the 'spirits and the gods,' so to speak," Bediako wrote, "he has gone there as Lord over them in the same way that he is Lord over us. He is Lord over the living and the dead, and over the 'living-dead,' as ancestors are also called" (JAC, 27). The ancestors, if they are ontological beings at all, are squarely under the authority and reign of God. Jesus the Ancestor has conquered death and displaced any powers of terror and misfortune that had abided in the afterlife. Bediako's ancestor Christology displaced the traditional understanding of the ancestors. Bediako asked: "Are not an-cestors in effect a projection into the transcendent realm of the social values and spiritual expectations of the living community?" Then, he con-tinued, the "ancestors have no existence independent of the community that produces them. . . . Strictly speaking, the cult of ancestors, from the intellectual point of view, belongs to the category of myth, ancestors being the product of the myth-making imagination of the community" (JAC, 30). Jesus Christ holds spiritual power over all (lesser) spiritual forces. The dead-yet-risen one, Jesus Christ, has power; the dead ancestors do not.

Indeed, for Bediako, the entire cult of ancestors is a myth—albeit a very significant myth in the lives of Africans. Bediako's point of view is shared by most African Christians but rejected by practitioners of ATRs.[30] One of the primary distinctions separating Christians from non-Christians in Africa is precisely this question of whether or not the ancestors have power. If an individual or community believes that the ancestors do have power, then they cannot be Christian, many Africans think. And this distinction is what enables some Christians to label Afri-can Independent, or Initiated, Churches (AICs) as syncretistic. The logic runs as follows: while AICs incorporate many Christian elements, since they believe in the power of ancestors and venerate them, they cannot be Christian, because the Ten Commandments state that there should be no gods other than God in Jesus Christ.

Bediako's understanding of ancestors as "a myth" was part and parcel of his belief that ATRs were a shadow of the full revelation of God in Jesus Christ. The traditions and practices of ATRs point to truths about who God is but only partially and incompletely. Bediako's understand-ing of ATRs was not all that different from many Western Christian understandings of the incompleteness of Judaism.[31] Bediako clearly and explicitly stated that ATRs are fulfilled with the name of Christ and the Christian scriptures. He also repeatedly asserted that Western Christianity is a religion that is actually a flawed worldview, a distortion of the true Christian faith. After all, "it is not Christianity that saves, but Christ" (*TI*, 244). On this point, Bediako followed the fairly typical evangelical Protestant perspective that Christianity is a relationship, not a religion.[32] What, then, does this mean for African Christianity? As the subtitle of Bediako's second book, *Christianity in Africa: The Renewal of a Non-Western Religion*, indicates, Bediako saw positive possibilities for religion once it was stripped of its cultural baggage. He walked a fine line as he sought to peel away the layers of false cultural interpretation imposed on the Christian faith while simultaneously affirming that Christianity must be translated into cultural forms. Indeed, it often appears that, for Bediako, no form of the Christian faith in the Western world can be sufficiently separated from Western culture to be authentically Christian. But if there is no such thing as a pure Christianity and the Christian faith must take cultural forms, then how can "relevance without syncretism" (*CiA*, 85) be achieved? Before addressing this question, let us explore Barth's views on religion as projection.

Real Revelation versus Projection

Barth adapted Ludwig Feuerbach's critique of religion as projection. Barth did not understand the Christian religion, or even any Christian rituals, to contain or offer any divine power. In religious rituals, and in religion more generally, Barth was seeking the person of Jesus Christ behind the human projections. Barth believed that Christianity can be the true religion *if* Christians worship the one true God in Jesus Christ (see I/2, §17.3). On this reckoning, no non-Christian religion can be true, although other religious traditions may have truth in them.[33] Barth believed that his treatment of Christ as prophet was sufficiently grounded in the actual events of Christ's life to address any critiques by Feuerbach. Barth wrote, "The good confession of the prophecy of Jesus Christ is both legitimate and obligatory for us. We can venture it without embarrassment, and need to be afraid of no Feuerbach" (IV/3, 85).

For both authors, the name of Jesus Christ is of the utmost importance. In *Church Dogmatics* I/2, §17.3, Barth insisted that the *name* Jesus

Christ set Christianity apart from all the other religions of the world as the true religion. Barth then filled out the meaning of the name throughout the rest of the *Dogmatics*, particularly in volume IV. Intriguingly, for Bediako, the *name* Jesus Christ is one of the two things that the European missionaries brought to Africa that Africans did not have (the other is the Bible). For both authors, there was something about that name that was important and significant that uniquely distinguishes the Christian faith from other religious traditions. As I discuss below, Bediako and Barth differ on how they understand the specifics of Christ's— indisputably central—role in salvation because of their disparate understandings of universal revelation and universal reconciliation.

Barth was aware of the possibility that his claim about Christ's prophetic work might not be revelation but rather human projection onto the divine. He is, in other words, deeply aware that the critiques of Feuerbach must be addressed. Aptly, then, after two pages of comments on Feuerbach in §17 (I/2, 290–91), Barth presented his most sustained treatment of Feuerbach in §69.2 (IV/3, 72–85).[34] Fundamentally, Barth claimed that "immunity against the type of answer given by Feuerbach to his own questions begins with the recognition that these are not our questions and we are quite unfitted to play the role of questioners" (IV/3, 73). Barth's initial reply to Feuerbach involved an intense focus on the person of Jesus Christ, not on any principles of the Christian faith. The single focus on the *name* Jesus Christ that Barth often emphasized was characteristic of his understanding of religion in §17. Yet, from the perspective of §69, the concentration on the name almost seems like a principle, such as Barth was trying to avoid in his Christological presentations of the Light of Life (§69.2) and Jesus is Victor (§69.3). The focus on the name serves as a placeholder in §17 for the more thorough and fuller exposition in §69. For Barth, Jesus Christ is "self-disclosing life . . . eternally repeated and confirmed in the act of His existence as the living God" (IV/3, 80). Reading Feuerbach and Barth together converges with the question of religious knowledge.[35]

Feuerbach insisted that humans must look *inward* for God since one's understanding of God is the product of human projection and desire. Barth, on the other hand, insisted that humans must look *outward* for God since one's understanding of God can only come from God's self-revelation in Jesus Christ. In his earliest writing on Feuerbach, part of a 1926 lecture on the history of modern theology given at Muenster,[36]

Barth therefore portrayed Feuerbach "as an enemy of theology who is the friend of religion."[37] However, Barth believed (1) that Feuerbach "is entirely right in his interpretation of religion . . . [as, quoting Feuerbach,] 'Theology long ago became anthropology'"; and (2) that "Feuerbach's intention is positive," since his desire is to "'make God real and human' by asserting that the object of religion is 'nothing but the essence of man.'"[38] Further, he sincerely applauded Feuerbach's understanding of religion "whose query does nothing less than locate the Achilles heel of modern theology."[39] In sum, Barth was deeply grateful for Feuerbach's penetrating analysis of the "deep shadow" into which Christianity had fallen. Yet he also saw Feuerbach as the final marker in the "sad story" of Protestant theology in the nineteenth century where in the end theology was "no longer taking itself seriously as theology" (I/2, 290, 291; 44, 45).

After appealing to Feuerbach to bolster his critique of religion in §17, Barth offered a deeper engagement in §69. He paused in the midst of his presentation of the Light of Life in §69.2 to ask, "Hitherto we have presupposed and maintained that the life of Jesus Christ as such is light, that His being is also name, His reality truth, His history revelation, His act Word or Logos. We have simply ascribed to Him what the Bible calls glory and therefore His prophetic office. On what ground and with what right may we do this?" (IV/3, 72). Barth had Feuerbach in mind here, as he was conscious of the possibility that all that is claimed as revelation may not come from God but from humans themselves. He was acutely aware that "we must be very careful how we state and try to answer" this question, lest "[we fall] victim to Feuerbach in our very attempt to resist him" (IV/3, 72). Barth's worry, one might say, was that Christians will answer the question, "On what ground and with what right may we do this?," with appeals to human reasoning or to qualities or characteristics in the Christian religion instead of the "self-witness which precedes and transcends all our self-witness and by which all our self-witness must be orientated" (IV/3, 73). Responding to the question he posed and his fears surrounding possible answers, Barth then sought to change the question itself. If a theologian intends to remain true to her calling as a Christian theologian, then "there can be no possible answer in the spirit and along the lines of Feuerbach" (IV/3, 78). Feuerbach's questions were primarily about the nature of humanity, while, for Barth, theology begins from a position of having been encountered by God in God's self-revelation. Feuerbach reversed the process; Barth aimed to reverse the reversal.

The only possible ground to maintain "that the life of Jesus Christ as such is light, that His being is also name, His reality truth, His history revelation, His act Word or Logos" (IV/3, 72) is the self-witness of God in the prophetic activity of Jesus Christ. If revelation is the starting point, and indeed the sole "point of contact" for all theological and religious reflection, including the Christian religion itself, then "questions like that of Feuerbach will not be even remotely possible. Considering and taking seriously the fact that God is present and active, we have renounced all such questioning from the very outset" (IV/3, 80). Barth was appealing to a God in Jesus Christ who is neither silent nor mute but eloquent, neither withdrawn nor dull but radiant. In the end, for Barth, "the good confession of the prophecy of Jesus Christ is both legitimate and obligatory for us. We can venture it without embarrassment, and need to be afraid of no Feuerbach" (IV/3, 85). Thus Barth saw the dangers and the appeal of basing theological reflection on the human apprehension of revelation, not God's self-revelation itself.

Person versus Principle: Reading I/2, §17, in Light of IV/3, §69

For Barth, the work of Jesus Christ accomplished in the event of reconciliation is self-revealing and also established knowledge, that is, "Easter knowledge" (IV/3, 283). On this basis, as Barth foreshadowed in his exegesis of Genesis 3:4–5 in I/2, §17, knowledge of God cannot come from within a person or religion. Barth contrasted the serpent's advice for humanity to come of age by asserting independence from God (IV/1, 435) to his hope that humanity—as individuals and as the Christian community—will practice dependence on God and God's self-revelation, that they will "come of age in relation to God and the world, i.e., the mature Christian and mature Christianity, its thought, speech and action in responsibility to God, in living hope in Him, in service to the world, in free confession and in unceasing prayer" (IV/4, preface). These more personal words demonstrated Barth's concern from the beginning: the external revelation of God in Jesus Christ is the only sufficient basis for the Christian life and a Christian religion. Knowledge of God can only come from God's self-revelation. So, as "atonement takes place . . . it is also revelation establishing knowledge. . . . [This] Christian knowledge [is] established, awakened, and fashioned by the revelation, manifestation, and prophecy of Jesus Christ" (IV/3, 211). All knowledge of reconciliation is grounded in the event of revelation (IV/3, 213). As opposed to the static "name of Jesus Christ" from §17, "the living Lord Jesus, is the theme and basis and content of Christian knowledge" (IV/3, 212). The content of this knowledge narrates a "present history" (IV/3, 233) because "Jesus Christ exists" (IV/3, 236) in the present through Christ's ongoing prophetic activity.[40]

In *Church Dogmatics* I/2, §17, we read that the story of the church's relationship with empire can only be told alongside the "sad story" (I/2, 291) of the gradual emergence of religion as "an independent known quantity alongside revelation" until at last "religion is not to be understood from the point of view of revelation, but rather revelation from that of religion" (I/2, 291; 44–45). The reversal of the proper ordering of religion and revelation results in the theological task losing its object. Instead of studying and reflecting on revelation, this history of Christianity "maturing" or "coming-of-age" is one of theology trading revelation for religion, to its detriment. Theology's "catastrophe" was "that it lost its object, revelation, in its particularity and with it the mustard seed of faith by which it could have moved mountains, even the mountain of humanistic culture. That it really lost revelation is shown by the very fact that it was possible for it to exchange revelation, and thereby its own birthright, for the concept of religion" (I/2, 293; 49). Barth appealed to the Genesis account of Esau exchanging his birthright as the firstborn for a bowl of stew. The language of birthright—that revelation is theology's own birthright—is significant. This birthright is what offers the possibility of Christianity as the true religion. Only through attending to God's self-revelation in Jesus Christ is a true religion possible. Barth affirmed this view in the concluding sentence of §17.1: "Remembering the Christological doctrine of the incarnation, and applying it logically, we speak of revelation as the sublimation of religion" (I/2, 297; 52). Barth offered primarily a *theological* understanding of religion, not a *sociological* one. These definitions were held constant in §69, where each of Barth's claims, about Jesus Christ, the Word of God, and Christianity as a religion, has "really nothing whatever to do with the arbitrary exaltation and self-glorification of the Christian in relation to other men, of the Church in relation to other institutions, or of Christianity in relation to other conceptions" (IV/3, 91). Barth's interest is in Jesus Christ, the one Word of God.

Barth's understanding of religion was shaped by his understanding of Jesus Christ. Here Garrett Green's translation of *Aufhebung* as "sublimation," not "abolition," is helpful. The coming of Jesus Christ, said Barth, did not abolish or eliminate religion. Barth understood the necessity of true religion as the human expression of the body of Christ on earth. The coming of the Son of God in human flesh did not leave religion untouched. In fact, all human religion is subject to God's judgment. Barth wrote, "In the sphere of reverence before God, the reverence before human greatness must always have its place; it is subject to God's judgment, not ours" (I/2, 301; 56). Green noted that this "aspect of Barth's theory of religion is especially important for religious studies, since it clearly precludes the frequent tendency to dismiss Barth as a detractor of religion or as a Christian imperialist passing lofty judgments against other religions."[41] As §17 makes clear, all religion is under God's judgment as human attempts at greatness. Only when revelation is not contained in religion is true religion possible. True insight, wisdom, and power cannot come from within a human or humankind. Instead, Barth wrote, "only from a place outside the magic circle of religion, along with its place of origin—that is, only from a place outside of man—could this real crisis of religion break in" (I/2, 324; 83).

This is the sense in which Barth's comment on the opening page of §17.3, "The True Religion," is to be understood. When Barth wrote, "No religion *is* true. A religion can only *become* true" (I/2, 325; 85; original emphasis), he is reaffirming the external validation for a religion and the impossibility of a religion justifying itself. For Barth, a parallel to a religion's attempt at self-justification is a human's, a sinner's, attempt at the same. Just as a sinner cannot justify himself, neither can a religion. Further, as a sinner can never stop being a sinner, so too a religion can never get outside of God's judgment. For Barth, since "religion is never and nowhere true as such and in itself," talking about "true religion" can only be done in the sense of a justified sinner (I/2, 325, §85). For Barth, neither of these pairings is an oxymoron; instead, they are theological realities. In "the linchpin of his theological theory of religion,"[42] Barth elucidates the meaning of his analogy: "There is a true religion: just as there is a justified sinner. . . . [W]e must not hesitate to state that *the Christian religion is the true religion* (I/2, 326; 85; original emphasis). This true religion, in other words, is predicated on God's self-revelation—though Barth is, of course, quick to point out that God's freedom in revelation was in no way hindered because the religion of Christianity was based on it. Thus, "the religion of revelation is indeed bound to God's revelation, but God's revelation is not bound to the religion of revelation" (I/2, 329; 88–89). All other religions "appeal to this or that truth inherent in themselves. . . . [While] Christianity can take part in this struggle . . . it has then renounced its very birthright, the unique power accruing to it as the religion of revelation" (I/2, 333; 93). Barth again used the language of "birthright" to describe Christianity's unique relationship to revelation.

Barth chose an Asian religion to further his point about the uniqueness of Christianity as the true religion. In a five-page excursus (I/2, 340–44), Barth described Pure Land Buddhism as "the most exact, comprehensive, and plausible 'pagan' parallel to Christianity" (I/2, 340; 101). Yet this excursus had more to do with the uniqueness of Christianity through the name Jesus Christ than that of Buddhism or any other religion. The bottom line for Barth was that while Pure Land Buddhism may have grace, it does not have Jesus Christ, so it is not true religion (I/2, 343; 105). He wrote, "The name Jesus Christ creates the Christian religion, and without it it would not exist" (I/2, 346; 109). In §69, insisting on the mere presence of the name of Christ is treated as a principle that insufficiently captures the story/history of Jesus Christ. Barth also employed the imagery of light that will be further developed in §69, but he did not hint at how the twofold office in §17 (I/2, 360; 124) was expanded to the threefold office in §69. The priestly justification and the kingly sanctification did not yet have the prophetic vocation to call them forward. As a result, in §17, Barth operated with a less dynamic understanding of revelation than he would later employ in §69.

In §17, "truth" operated as an abstract category that was connected to the name Jesus Christ. In §69, the notion of truth was embodied in the history of the Son of God—the Word of God from the beginning—who brings life to all. The "reconciling work of Jesus Christ, was not just accomplished, but has gone out into the reconciled world as a shining light[,] . . . a fire" (IV/3, 301). The insight that reconciliation *is* revelation in §69 points to a dynamic understanding of the role of Christ in reconciliation; the gospel is continually outgoing and out-shining. The work of reconciliation did not stop on Golgotha. While the life, death, resurrection, and ascension of Jesus Christ is sufficient for humanity to be reconciled to God, the work of reconciliation continues in and through the ongoing prophetic activity of Jesus Christ. Succinctly, "reconciliation carries with it a call to advance!" (IV/3, 315 rev.). This call forward points to the dynamic character of revelation that gives life and meaning to true religion.

Thus in contrast to the very exclusive language about true religion at the end of §17, where Barth connected Christ's name to revelation as "the revealed fact of God in the *name Jesus Christ*," the defining characteristic of a true religion (I/2, 355; 118), Barth is now making inclusive statements about how "the real goal and end of the resurrection of Jesus . . . was the reconciliation of the world and not just the satisfaction of the little flock of believers" (IV/3, 303).

Yet two observations are in order. First, Barth's change in focus from religion to reconciliation may account for the change from exclusive to inclusive claims. After Barth's placement of the doctrine of election within the doctrine of God in *Church Dogmatics* II/2, Barth's dogmatics proclaimed universal reconciliation for all in Jesus Christ—something that religion alone could not achieve. Second, Barth's understanding of reconciliation was totalizing: all peoples in all times and places are reconciled to God in Jesus Christ. His view is inclusive, yes, but perhaps too forceful. He wrote, "The determination given the world and man in this event is a total one[,] . . . a universal one" (IV/3, 301, 303).

While some may find Barth's understanding of universal reconciliation comforting and generous and others may find it a violation of human agency, Barth sought to preempt all such concerns. For him, Jesus Christ and Jesus Christ alone defined humanity. And living in correspondence with one's reconciled humanity is what it means to be human. Just as "the Easter event is grounded in the necessity of Christian mission" (IV/3, 304), so, too, Christians and the Christian community are to follow Christ's "radiating light" (IV/3, 305) outward in service of others. In contrast to §17's exclusive claims to a privileged club, known as Christianity—the true religion—the outward, radiating movement of Christ's prophetic activity invites everyone to join the forward movement.

Universality of Christ: Revelation

For both Barth and Bediako, the revelation of God in Jesus Christ is available to all peoples through the universality of Christ. Yet the reasoning each theologian used to inform his understanding of Christ's universality is significant and revealing. The first section below considers Bediako's understanding of universality through Christ's divinity. The second section engages Barth's understanding of universality through Christ's resurrection.

For both authors, the name Jesus Christ identifies the second person of the Trinity, the Son of God incarnate. Both authors appealed, as has been shown, to the prologue to the Gospel of John as a starting point for their theological reflections about the activity of God in the world. Many of the themes of interest to Bediako and Barth appear in the first four verses: time; the relationship between God and the Word; the process of creation; and the connection between Jesus Christ, life, light, and all people. For Bediako, John 1:14 serves as the basis for his understanding of the infinite translatability of the gospel of Jesus Christ: that the Word "became and dwelt" in flesh demonstrates that God cannot be contained within the spiritual realm but decisively entered into the human, earthly realm. This transcendent boundary crossing that took place continues throughout recorded time and history in the continual engagement of the gospel and culture.

For Barth, the significance of verse 14 has already been discussed above. The more interesting verse, at least for the sake of this comparison, lies earlier in John's prologue, when Barth connects the Word and the words from John 1:4.[43] Very early in §69, Barth used this verse to connect the major themes of §69 (IV/3, 9). Note Barth's emphases in concluding his one-page excursus on the verse, "What is said in Jn. 1:4f is that this life in its determination as light, reconciliation in its character as revelation, is outgoing and self-communicative, so that, as it has taken place in the world, it breaks out and goes into the whole world, to every man (v. 9)" (IV/3, 9). The concepts that Barth draws from John 1:4—life, light, reconciliation, and revelation—fill his exposition of the third problem in the doctrine of reconciliation, Christ as Prophet, understood as the "Glory of the Mediator" and of his articulation of Jesus Christ as the Light of Life in particular. The ongoing prophetic activity of Jesus Christ brings life to all people by indiscriminately shining the light of reconciliation that reveals who God is.

If Bediako's driving question is, "What happened when God-in-the-flesh moved into the neighborhood of Africa?," how would Barth likely answer this same question? We begin with Bediako's process. For Bediako, "what happened?" unfolds in two steps. First, God has always been in Africa and did not need to "move in" after Africans already lived there. The identity of God-in-the-flesh, Jesus Christ, was "hidden" in sub-Saharan Africa prior to the arrival of the European missionaries. In these years, God was at work among God's (African) people, incompletely and imperfectly revealing aspects of who God is through African traditional religions and African culture. Second, as Europeans introduced the name Jesus Christ to Africans and, more important, first translated the texts of the Old and New Testaments into African mother tongues, so, too, African Christians have been seeking to translate the words, images, and concepts of the Bible into African terms and idioms. This process is ongoing as African realities change and Africans seek to better understand and appropriate the gospel of Jesus Christ.

Barth might reject the image of Christ coming to Africa as distinct from Christ coming to humanity as a whole. In God's primal decision to be a God-for-others, God chose for the second person of the Trinity to become a human being as Jesus Christ. Indeed, Jesus Christ is the true human, in whose image all other humans have been created. Humans who happened to live on the continent of Africa he understood to be made in the image of God and God has been present among them in ways that are hidden and veiled. One can also say, in light of IV/3, that God's sovereignty supports the claim that God could use any and all cultural forms to reveal who God is. Yet, in spite of the multitude of ways that God might be working, true knowledge of and relationship with God is only possible in Jesus Christ. And Barth is certainly not going to displace Judaism with ATRs as *praeparatio evangelica*. (Granting the important debates about Barth and supersessionism,[44] Barth sees an important and unique place for Israel and the Jews in his theology; a comparable affirmation cannot be made about Bediako.) Barth would presumably believe that the rays of Christ's light, the light of life, would shine on all Africans and seek to draw all people to live in correspondence with the command of God.

The shining of this "eloquent and radiant" light through "true words" and "parables of the kingdom" is a result of Christ's ongoing prophetic activity. The shining of this light is similar to Bediako's understanding of translatability, but Barth stresses the outgoing movement of Jesus Christ, the Light of Life, more than the human reception of the gospel in the encounter of the gospel with culture. Certainly, Bediako bases his understanding of translatability on the "first translation" of God into human flesh. But much of the rest of his work on translatability focuses on humans continuing, or mimicking, the work of that first translation, not on how God continues to "translate" Godself. A linguistic hint of this difference lies in Bediako's consistent use of "the gospel" (not Jesus Christ) as the object of translation, as in "the infinite translatability of the gospel." Barth does not allow this translation of God to take place apart from God's eternal divine decision, God's communicative and revelatory action, and God's occasional uses of parables of the kingdom and true words. Again, God *always* uses creaturely media; what is "occasional" is God's use of media that are not scripture and preaching.

In a sense, the difference between Bediako and Barth on translatability rests on two interpretive decisions. First, in exegeting John 1, what is meant by two phrases: "In the *beginning*" (v.1) and then "the Word *became* flesh" (v.14)? Is there a temporal gap between verses 1 and 14? Bediako seems to say yes; Barth says no. For Barth, the second person of the Trinity is always and forever Jesus Christ, the incarnate one;[45] Bediako offered no such specificity. Second, Barth chose to emphasize the being and movement of God at all times, prior to human action. Bediako resists any deemphasizing of human agency in translation, particularly because of how many Christian missionaries' attempts to translate the gospel have had detrimental effects on Africans and African culture.

Bediako: Universality through Christ's Divinity

Bediako writes, "The needs of the African world require a view of Christ that meets those needs" (JAC, 22). His claim, specifically, is that the New Testament makes clear the connection between Jesus Christ—as a non-African—and African peoples. Bediako's underlying assumption was that Jesus Christ is the "*Universal* Saviour" (JAC, 20; Bediako's emphasis). By "*Universal*," Bediako meant that Jesus Christ has value, relates to, and has significance for *all* peoples, including Africans. He was not differentiating here between Christ's person and work; instead he was suggesting that Africans can think differently about their relationship with a non-African claiming to be God. At the same time, there is a potential problem. While Bediako claimed that traditional African religions were continuous with Christianity (one God with different mother-tongue names, revealed in part through traditional religions and more fully in Jesus Christ) and while he connected Africans with the Father and the Spirit, Jesus's Jewishness seemed to complicate the relationship between scripture and African cosmology and religiosity.

The reason is as follows: African spiritual communities consist of one's family, clan, tribe, and nation—often based on linguistic groupings. As opposed to many contemporary Western individuals, many Africans, and certainly the Akan, consider themselves part of a community from their birth, a *spiritual* community. The religion of the Akan (the largest ethnic group in Ghana and Côte d'Ivoire) is particularly ethnocentric; the philosopher J. B. Danquah puts it bluntly: "In a word, Akan religion, in its highest expression, is the worship of the race."[46] How, then, can an Akan worship one who is not of his race? Bediako, an Akan himself (as is Danquah), worried about how to relate to the God-man Jesus of Nazareth who is most certainly *not* an Akan. How can Jesus Christ join in this "unity of the ultimate,"[47] as Danquah described it, if he is an outsider to Akan religion? Akan ancestors come from within the clan and are understood to intercede in the lives of individuals and the clan as a whole. Akan religious rituals implore the ancestors (who are also Akan) to work with Nyame (the Akan name for God) for the health and prosperity of the Akan people.

The challenge, as Bediako understood it, was to connect Jesus to Africans so that Africans could relate to God's Son who is not of their tribe. He wanted Christ to be the fulfillment of ATRs in the same way that he understands Christ to be the fulfillment of ancient Israelite religion and the Old Testament. To meet this challenge, Bediako emphasized Christ's divinity—his Spirit that has been present in Africa for thousands of years—over the humanity of Jesus's non-African flesh. Instead of identifying Africans as Gentiles, similar to Paul in Galatians, Bediako desired a more primal relationship with God—similar to the relationship that Jewish people have—which is to worship God as a member of their ethnic group. To make this move, Bediako downplayed Christ's Jewishness.[48]

Bediako's belief in Christ's universality led him to make this point explicitly: "Jesus Christ is not a stranger to our heritage" (JAC, 24). He overcame the gap between Christ and Africans by "starting with the universality of Jesus Christ rather than from his particularity as a Jew, and

[by] affirming that the Incarnation was the incarnation of the Saviour of all people, of all nations and of all times" (JAC, 24). Years later Bediako reaffirmed his view in an interview. Roar Fotland recounted Bediako's emphasis on Christ's divinity.

> Bediako thinks that it is the divinity of Jesus that is the point of contact with the universality of Jesus. Therefore, to start with his divinity is to make him universal. If I start with him as human, Bediako said, I have to see him as a Jew and will have problems accepting him as an Akan ancestor. Jesus needs to be human first in order to live, and die in order to become an ancestor, but as a universal ancestor he must communicate from the other side.[49]

The question for Bediako, then, was not merely theoretical but practical; that is, apologetic concerns motivated his theological inquiry.

The Priesthood of Christ in the Epistle to the Hebrews

The Epistle to the Hebrews explains how Jesus, a non-Levite, can be a high priest by asserting the priesthood of Jesus Christ "according to the order of Melchizedek" (Hebrews 5:10, 6:20, 7:1–17). Since Jesus was not a Levite but of the tribe of Judah, how could he be a priest? The fundamental question is analogous for early Jewish Christians and for contemporary Africans: how do you relate to one of a different tribe? Jesus became a priest not through Aaron but through Melchizedek. Aaron was a high priest of the tribe of Levi—the tribe that served in priestly roles on behalf of all twelve tribes of Israel. The ancestry of Jesus of Nazareth, as told in Matthew 1, is traced back not to Levi but to his brother Judah. Melchizedek is described in Genesis 14:18 as a "priest of God Most High." This is the only time in the Hebrew Bible that a non-Levite is referred to as a priest. The only other mention of Melchizedek in the Bible, outside of Hebrews and Genesis 14, occurs in Psalm 110:4, when David wrote that the Lord will not change his mind in regard to Melchizedek's priesthood. Based on the presence of Melchizedek, a non-Levite, as a priest of God and the application in Hebrews of Genesis 14 and Psalm 110 to Jesus of Nazareth, another non-Levite as a priest of God, Bediako concluded, "Therefore, the priesthood, mediation and hence the salvation that Jesus Christ brings to all people everywhere belong to an entirely different category from what people may claim for their clan, family, tribal and national priests and mediators" (JAC, 28). Put slightly differently: as a "high priest according to the order of Melchizedek" (Hebrews 5:10), all of Jesus's benefits (his priesthood, mediation, and salvation) are not limited only to Jews (his tribe), but are available to all of humanity, including the Akan and other Africans. (Bediako's interest in Melchizedek and the significance of Melchizedek for him is, incidentally, in stark contrast to Barth's mere four mentions of Melchizedek—all related to Genesis 14 and none to Hebrews—in the entire *Church Dogmatics*.)

Bediako's theological understanding of Jesus's universality applied to the spiritual realm that also encompassed the earthly realm. He wrote, "Who Jesus is in the African spiritual universe must not be separated from what he does and can do in that world. The way in which Jesus relates to the importance and function of the 'spirit fathers' or ancestors is crucial" (JAC, 22). Specifically, Jesus Christ, in the context of African ancestral understandings, was described in terms of "our Elder Brother" (JAC, 26). In turn, and more broadly, Bediako argued for Christ's "spiritual value in the religious worlds of other faiths . . . [and] his universal significance."[50] As "Universal Savior," Christ has spiritual value for *all* peoples: Africans and non-Africans, Christians and non-Christians.

Bediako's reading of Hebrews brings together his understandings of identity and history. On this point, he shares a close connection with Barth. Bruce McCormack noted how the themes of identity and history are at play in a theological reading of the Epistle to the Hebrews. He wrote, "What is true is that the writer never spells out in detail the ontology which holds the various christological elements together. His approach to treating their relationship is more indirect than direct. It lies in a focus on the *identity* of the subject of whom both things must be said. He narrates the identity of this subject in the form of a history—a history which begins in eternity-past and ends in eternity-future."[51] History as we know it, including the history of an individual human life, lies between these endpoints.

As Bediako considered the Christological elements of Hebrews, he certainly did not limit Jesus Christ to a particular spatiotemporal locale. Rather, he understood Christ as a spiritual being who was more powerful in an African cosmology than any earthly being. Even when, for Bediako, this being from before time becomes incarnate (as "the Word becomes flesh"; John 1:14), the identity of Jesus Christ remains inherently spiritual—emphasizing the divine over the human. For Bediako, Christ's spirit existed prior to the bodily presence of Christ on earth and continued to live following Christ's ascension. The spirit of Christ never dies. A key difference between Jesus Christ and other ancestors, however, is that Christ's spirit did not continue to return to earth inhabiting, or possessing, the bodies of others. For Bediako, Jesus Christ is a unique Spirit, the Greatest of the Ancestors, the only Son of God.

His hope, more broadly than the specifics of Christology, was that the vernacular terminology for Jesus would penetrate the spirituality of African Christianity, such as in the songs of Afua Kuma. In fact, Bediako hoped that the vernacular, the mother tongue, and a theology of ancestors could be blended. "In my experience in Ghana," Bediako wrote, "hardly anyone will pray in English to 'Ancestor Jesus' or 'Chief Jesus,' but many will pray in Akan to 'Nana Yesu.' 'Nana' means 'ancestor' and is the title for ancestors (and chiefs)."[52] The use of Nana Yesu allowed for the person and message of Jesus Christ to be internalized and contextualized *as an ancestor* within Akan culture.

The language of prayer is just one example of how traditional African religions are not the end of a conversation about African spirituality for Bediako but the beginning. African traditional religions served as the vital "substructure" for Christianity in Africa.[53] Bediako always stressed the continuity of the Christian faith with traditional African religious beliefs. Even when he did not endorse the specific religious practices themselves, he stressed the continuity of the human person, or human ontology. He believed that the "theological importance of such an ontological past consists in the fact that it belongs together with the profession of the Christian faith in giving account of the same entity, namely, the history of the religious consciousness of the African Christian."[54] So while chronologically the rites and traditions of traditional African religions are still present in Africa in ways that have remained substantially unaltered for hundreds and thousands of years, what it means to be human, or "the account of the same entity" in Bediako's language, has been irreversibly altered. The "religious consciousness" of the African Christian begins in traditional African spirituality and finds its fulfillment and completion in the Christian faith; African traditional religions are incomplete without Christ and serve in God's economy as preparation for Christianity. Through his divinity, Jesus Christ is revealed to all as the universal Savior.

Barth: Universality through Christ's Resurrection

Like Bediako, Barth believed in an unbreakable relationship between God and humanity; however, he understood the relationship as based not on the divine Christ's connection with the ancestors or with traditional cultural festivals but on Christ's resurrection: "the living Jesus Christ risen from the dead" (IV/3, 281). In the excursus that immediately followed this quotation, Barth cited Acts, 1 Peter, Colossians, Ephesians, and 1 Corinthians to support his claim that "the testimony of the New Testament witnesses ... is testimony to His resurrection as His self-attestation in respect of the universality, inclusiveness and continuity of His particular being and action, of its outreaching, embracing and comprehensive character" (IV/3, 281–82). Barth's understanding of the resurrection asserted the universal and the inclusive connection of Jesus Christ with all peoples, as attested in the New Testament and in Christian theology. He described the "particular event of His resurrection [as] thus the primal and basic form of His glory, of the outgoing and shining of His light, of the primal and basic form of His expression, of His Word as His self-expression, and therefore of His outgoing and penetration and entry into the World around and ourselves, of His prophetic work" (IV/3, 281 rev.). Here Barth connected the resurrection of Jesus Christ to the most elemental form of divine glory, the most basic expression of Christ's Word, and the reconciling and self-revealing movement of Christ's ongoing prophetic work. Not only was the resurrection the defining moment of the New Testament—both the reason the New Testament was written and the event to which the entire New Testament points—but it was the resurrection that defined "the universality of the particular existence of Jesus Christ" (IV/3, 281). For Barth, as for Bediako, the ongoing spiritual existence of Jesus Christ who is alive in this world goes hand in hand with an affirmation of Christ's universality. Through the *ongoing activity* of Christ as prophet, God makes Godself known. The revelation inherent in the New Testament witness to the resurrection demonstrates, further, the "inclusiveness" of the impact of the resurrection on all humanity (IV/3, 281). No one is left out, no one bypassed. As Jesus Christ finds "a form among us and in us," the resurrected Christ transforms what it means to be human (IV/3, 281).

This transformation took place as "the primal and basic form" of Jesus Christ entered human existence through Christ's prophetic office (IV/3, 281).[55] This office encapsulated "the outgoing and shining of His light" (IV/3, 281) that penetrates human, earthly existence. Barth was careful to hold together the incarnation and resurrection at this point in his argument. He asks, "What is specifically contributed in the resurrection of Jesus Christ as the commencement of His new coming as the One who came before, and therefore in the revelation of His reconciling being and action in its primal and basic form as the entry into His prophetic office?" (IV/3, 296). One reason for the question was Barth's insistence that Jesus's coming is one continuous event in many forms—that Jesus lives in diverse ways. Twice on the same page he cites Hebrews 13:8 —"Jesus Christ is the same yesterday and today and forever"—to emphasize his point: Jesus lives; his light can never be extinguished (IV/3, 291). Indeed, the living witness of Jesus Christ preceded the earthly existence of human beings and will outlast human earthly existence. (There is a striking similarity here to Bediako's claim that Christ was active in Africa before humans walked the continent.) The life, death, resurrection, and ascension of Jesus Christ are one continuous event; taken together, they are the event of reconciliation. Recall here Barth's claim, "The atonement is history" (IV/1, 157), in the opening line of IV/1, §59. Barth's doctrine of reconciliation is based on the actual events of Christ's life.

Barth offered an expanded explication on the unity of Christ's reconciling and revelatory action in §69: "The New Testament knows of only one coming again of Jesus Christ, of only one new coming of the One who came before, of only one manifestation of His effective presence in the world corresponding to His own unity as the One who came before. But in the time of the community and its mission after the Easter revelation it also takes place in the form of the impartation of the Holy Spirit" (IV/3, 293). Barth's insistence on the "one" coming and the unity of revelation echoed his Trinitarian understanding of one God in three modes of being and prevents falling into polytheism. Yet the "different forms" to which Barth referred are not Father, Son, and Holy Spirit but instead connect back to the true words and parables of the kingdom from IV/3, §69.2. There is one revelation of the triune God in different creaturely forms. No matter *how* revelation occurs, the content of that revelation is always God in Jesus Christ.

The impact of resurrection, for Barth, then, is the actualization of what has been accomplished already in Christ's life and death as well as the public revelation of these accomplishments. The high priestly and kingly work of justification and sanctification has already taken place. In the resurrection, "the alteration of the situation between God and man accomplished by Him was actualized by taking place immediately and completely in noetic form also as the prophecy of Jesus Christ by being brought out of concealment and revealed and made known to the world" (IV/3, 296–97). The work of Christ as prophet in the resurrection unveiled and declared the already accomplished work of Christ as high priest and king. At the same time, Barth refused to allow the priestly, kingly, and prophetic work of Christ to be separated from one another. Together they are the threefold office of Christ, not three distinct offices. They are interconnected and, though distinct, are merely human linguistic and conceptual conventions for describing and attempting to understand the one work of Christ.

Differing Ontologies

For Bediako, the death and resurrection of Jesus Christ answer the question of *how* the universality of Jesus Christ can be understood to penetrate African culture. In agreement with 1 Corinthians, Bediako wrote that "the death of Jesus ... reveals death itself to be a *theological* problem which calls for a *theological* response."[56] Therefore, any theological consideration of ancestors must begin with a theological consideration of death itself and Christ's death in particular. The Ghanaian philosopher Kwame Gyeke described one African cosmology as follows: "The Akan universe is a spiritual universe, one in which supernatural beings play significant roles in the thought and action of the people. What is primarily real is spiritual."[57] The central feature of Jesus's death, then, is less a sacrifice than it is a triumphant and victorious return to the spirit world through Christ's resurrection and ascension. As the supreme, universal ancestor, Jesus Christ is both mediator (priest) and ruler of the spiritual realm (chief). Since Jesus's death and resurrection have spiritual ramifications, his death affects the ancestors and the spiritual realm in which they are understood to preside. Bediako further develops this point about the interconnectedness of culture and revelation when he claims that the primal imagination is part of an African Christian's "ontological past."[58]

In contrast, Barth argues that human ontology is solely to be understood in relation to God's self-revelation in Jesus Christ. Barth claims, "Man is not a person, but he *becomes one* on the basis that he is loved by God and can love God in return" (II/1, 284; emphasis added). In Barth's view, since "'God is' means 'God loves,'" the being of God as the One who loves constitutes humans as beings who receive love and give love (II/1, 283–84). Barth's understanding of human ontology lies in human correspondence to God's loving command and differs from Bediako's view. Barth stated, "Thus to know, to will, and to act like God as the One who loves in Himself and in His relationship to His creation means (in confirmation of His I-ness) to be a person. God is a person in this way, and He alone is a person in this way. He is the real person and not merely the ideal" (II/1, 28). Bediako made a claim about the scope of divine revelation penetrating African religion and culture; Barth, especially after II/2, developed a full-blown theological anthropology. Particularly for Barth, Jesus Christ defines what it means to be human. Jesus Christ is the Elect One; all humanity is thereby elect in Christ.[59] Bediako would insist on the ontologically shaping role of the primal imagination *in addition to* Christ's defining role in shaping human identity.

For Barth, if someone came to a later awareness of one's election or one's identity as rooted in the being of God, this later awareness did not create a period of "ontological past." This human awareness is simply coming to know what had always been the case. To express it colloquially: just because the news arrives late does not change the news (that an event previously occurred); when the event occurs is not based on when one receives the news. Barth described the situation as follows: "And in this name we may now discern the divine decision as an event in human history and therefore as the substance of all the preceding history of Israel and the hope of all the succeeding history of the Church" (II/1, 53). New information (the *name* Jesus Christ, for both Barth and Bediako) changes how we *understand* the past and hope for the future. Barth's view, in sum, was that humans have *always*, from all eternity, been defined by Jesus Christ and *only* defined by Jesus Christ. Barth would therefore challenge the idea that there is as an ontological past.

Bediako might respond to Barth by claiming that it is actually knowledge, and the existential human condition, that he finds most interesting. Individuals and cultures have been shaped by what they know (or think they know) and what they believe. These forces are powerful and formative. Bediako seeks to leave some of those cultural forces in the past while preserving and assimilating them, to allow for a present and a future shaped by Jesus Christ. The overriding question for him was, how is belief in the ancestors (as an embodiment of the past) continuous with belief in Jesus Christ? And the answer for Bediako was that Jesus himself is one of the ancestors and that Jesus has power over the entire spiritual world, including the realm of the ancestors. Christ is "the only real and true Ancestor and Source of life for all mankind, fulfilling and transcending the benefits believed to be bestowed by lineage ancestors" (JAC, 31). At this point, then, Bediako presented his own "christologized epistemology."[60] Jesus Christ is the key to knowledge about God, humanity, the spirits, and all created things.

Bediako's inclination to start with Christ's divinity and move toward Christ's humanity can be seen as a consequence of his understanding of the Spirit of Jesus Christ. The Spirit of Christ lives in the spiritual realm, giving the omnipotent and omnipresent Spirit more power to affect events on earth than would be possible for one particular Jewish man born in first-century Palestine. In contrast, Barth carefully attempted to hold together the divine and the human within the God-man Jesus Christ by using nonmetaphysical categories,[61] never losing touch with the particular Jewish individual, Jesus of Nazareth. To articulate his ancestor Christology, Bediako turned to the Epistle to the Hebrews. For his part, Barth employed Hebrews in the development of his understanding of the ongoing prophetic activity of Jesus Christ.

Differing Universalisms

Discussing the topic of universalism in a chapter on context may appear to be a category mistake until one considers that Bediako treated African culture as universal revelation to all Africans. Hence Bediako began with universal revelation through African culture that was true, though partial, revelation and then added the name Jesus Christ and the Christian scriptures. This completed, full revelation informs Africans of God in Jesus Christ with whom they were already in relationship. The atoning work of Christ made possible this continuing relationship. In Bediako's work, the concept of reconciliation was rarely treated, and when it was, it often referred to reconciling ethnic groups or philosophical ideas, not the divine-human relationship. In contrast, Barth titled the fourth volume of his *Church Dogmatics* (of which IV/3 is one part-volume) *The Doctrine of Reconciliation*.

Both Bediako and Barth were unapologetically Christocentric, and neither was certain that human beings are eternally saved regardless of their actions on earth. Both would reject the appellation "universalist" while also hoping that all people may be saved. Barth would disagree with the moniker because universalism is a principle that departs from the actual history of Jesus Christ and because he did not see sufficient biblical evidence to *prove* that all humanity is saved in Christ.[62] Instead, Barth saw a clear hope that it was so. Bediako's understanding of evangelical Christianity required him to insist on a personal response to the gospel as an ingredient in personal salvation. Nearly all of his sermons concluded with a call for a response from the listeners.[63] As Kwabena Asamoah-Gyadu remarked in the first Kwame Bediako Memorial Lecture, "He is the only African evangelical theologian and preacher that I have personally witnessed calling for people to physically come forward to offer their lives to Jesus Christ in a Billy Graham–style Altar Call."[64] Yet since Bediako did not think of himself in the categories of Western thinkers like John Calvin, Jacobus Arminius, and John Wesley, and he did not articulate a formal doctrine of atonement, it is difficult to label Bediako's stance on *how* a person is saved. Bediako's understanding of salvation attempted to combine the cosmology of ATRs with an evangelical emphasis on a personal response to the gospel of Jesus Christ.

Bediako believed that the Christian faith has been universally revealed by God to all, including Africans, at first through African traditional religions and then later through Christian churches by Africans and Europeans alike. He also nowhere advocated a version of "universal reconciliation" that Barth promoted. This omission comes, in no small part, from the general lack in Bediako's work of discussions of personal sin. In his most sustained treatment of sin, Bediako claimed that in African traditions, "the essence of sin is in its being ... an antisocial act. This makes sin basically injury to the interests of another person and damage to the collective life of the group. ... [Yet] sin is more than antisocial act; the sinner sins ultimately against a personal God with a will and purpose in human history" (JAC, 26). Without an emphasis on sin (particularly on sins by individuals), Bediako did not seek the same "universal reconciliation" that Barth offered. Bediako's understanding of sin was consistent with other African Christians who view salvation as a "holistic experience ... [of] total well-being"[65] that "embrac[ed] both the physical and the spiritual"[66] and addressed "physical and immediate dangers that threaten individual or community survival, good health and general prosperity or safety." "Salvation," he wrote, "is not just an abstraction, it is concrete."[67] Consistent with an African cosmology, Bediako's understanding of the Christian faith sought access to God without needing to overcome separation from God. Yet, for Bediako, the universal revelation called for an individual, personal response. Without this individual response, salvation was not possible. In contrast to both Barth's belief in the universal reconciliation of all humanity and his hope that all *are already* saved in Jesus Christ, and also to the traditional African understanding that God has fully revealed who God is in and through traditional African religions in such a way that demonstrates God's universal presence among, with, and *within* African peoples and African cultures, Bediako asserted universal revelation but not universal reconciliation or salvation. (Barth presented universal revelation through universal reconciliation.)

To better understand Bediako's appropriation of universal revelation in ATRs, a comparison with Kofi Asare Opoku, a fellow Ghanaian (and Akan), is helpful. Opoku interpreted traditional African religions as presenting an understanding of universal revelation within what he described as "the wisdom of openness to truth. ... Truth does not lie within the grasp of one culture or religious tradition."[68] Further, Opoku's African cosmology resulted in no need for an ultimate salvation, as humanity has never been ontologically separated from God. Though their conceptions of who God is and of the meaning and place of Jesus Christ differ, both Barth (at least it is Barth's hope) and Opoku end up with God (or Nyame, as Opoku would refer to the divine) and all of humanity together. Bediako, on the other hand, holds to a position that a personal conversion experience (much like his own and the apostle Paul's) is needed for each individual who would spend eternity with God.

Still, given these different perspectives on revelation and reconciliation, the possibilities for fruitful dialogue with other religious traditions can be seen. Opoku understood the traditional Akan religious beliefs to be an "open tradition" that is willing to accept all that is true. Thus he can accept Christianity, up to the point that Christians make exclusive claims to truth or salvation. Opoku believed that truth about God is revealed in Christianity—and in Islam—and is willing to stretch to consider that Christ is actively revealing God through other religions, as they can represent "parables of the kingdom" and ways that God is revealing who God is to the world. Yet Barth did not believe that the truth in non-Christian religions is complete or fully reveals who God is, since God can only be fully known in Jesus Christ. However, because of Christ's ongoing prophetic activity, Barth sought to remain attentive to wherever God may be revealed.

In spite of being the recipients of an incomplete revelation of God, adherents of non-Christian religions still are reconciled to God in Christ, for Barth, even if they are not living in correspondence with God's command. While Barth may have intended this as gracious and comforting to his non-Christian dialogue partners, they may resist his assertion that God would make possible their reconciliation without their express consent.

Bediako agrees with Barth that the revelation that occurs within non-Christian religions is incomplete and insists that adherents of non-Christian religions must come to a saving knowledge of God in Jesus Christ in order to receive salvation. None of the terms "pluralist," "inclusivist," and "exclusivist" are sufficient to capture the complexities of Barth's position or the creativity of Bediako's views.[69] It is interesting to note here that Barth, the European, seems closer to Opoku, the practioner of ATRs, than is Bediako, the African. Bediako's early exposure to American evangelicalism likely shaped but did not define his understanding of salvation.

Faithful Contextualization

In Bediako's earliest published writings, he articulated the challenges of African Christians seeking to shape an African Christian identity. His very first publication questioned the exportability of Western theology: "If much of the theological effort in the non-western world merely reproduces replays of the original western versions, we must ask ourselves whether the Christianity that was planted was such as would allow emerging Christian thinkers to answer their own questions."[70] Already, Bediako was asserting the need for Africans to think for themselves and not to allow the dominant Western thought patterns to go uncriticized. His third publication contains a virtual précis of his entire career. He was convinced that God is always "addressing himself to the questionings and longing of [non-Western] minds and hearts in the concrete realities of their environments."[71] Here we see the active God of Bediako's faith, a God who directly addresses the concerns of non-Western peoples in their specific context. This was an important determination that holds together various claims. Against a critic of contextualizing Christian theology, Bediako responded with characteristic boldness: "The answer to 'false contextualization' is not no contextualization, but faithful contextualization."[72] The proclamation of God in revelation comes to humanity in cultural embodiment—an embodiment that is necessarily unavoidable, yet while revealing its "cultural blinkers" also obscure. Faithful contextualization, for Bediako, involved receiving God's revelation in and through African religions and culture as well as through the biblical scriptures.

For Bediako, the gospel must be contextualized but not to the point where its distinctiveness is lost to the host culture, or context. He was vehemently against the idea of a "pure Gospel devoid of cultural embodiment," which, he said, "is simply imaginary."[73] Or, at least, no human being can encounter such a "pure gospel" without any "cultural blinkers." So, on the one hand, purity is not the goal, or even a possibility, for the church's understanding of the gospel. On the other hand, the gospel must not be so fused to its host culture that the blinkers obscure the distinctiveness of the gospel. Although he never expressed it directly, Bediako was convinced that Western Christianity was not faithful to the gospel but was actually a projection of Western culture.

Bediako's work suggests an equation for the production of theology: Gospel + Culture = Theology. Yet in this equation neither "gospel" nor "culture" is an independent variable; instead, they exist in dialectical tension. "Gospel" cannot be apprehended apart from "culture" and "culture" cannot be understood apart from "gospel." Throughout his work, two themes are pervasive: identity and integration (for Bediako a better term than "indigenization"). These themes first appear in the title of his unpublished dissertation, *Identity and Integration: An Enquiry into the Nature and Problems of Theological Indigenization in Selected Early Hellenistic and Modern African Christian Writers,* and never disappeared from his concerns.[74] "The argument of the thesis," Bediako wrote, "attempts to validate the claim that theology is called to deal always with culturally-rooted questions" (*TI*, xv). At a fundamental level, Bediako was interested in questions of how God speaks and through whom. He was wholly convinced that God did not speak exclusively to and through white Europeans. He also knew that this claim of white privilege in matters of revelation had impeded the development of a distinctive African Christian identity.

Revelation, Religion, and Culture

Historically, Bediako's interest in African Christian identity arose in response to how the Europeans conducted their missionary efforts. He wrote, "The ethnocentrism of a large part of the missionary enterprise not only prevented sufficient understanding of African religious tradition, but also led to a *theological* misapprehension of the nature of the Christian Gospel itself" (*TI*, xvii; original emphasis). Viewing the gospel of Jesus Christ from an exclusively white, European, colonialist perspective prevented any honest engagement with African traditional religions and perpetuated an understanding of the gospel as being on the side of the powerful. As African theologians began to discover their voices in the 1960s, their theology was "as much a response to missionary underestimation of the value of African pre-Christian religious tradition, as it [was] an *African* theological response to the specific and more enduring issues of how the Christian gospel relates to African culture." (*TI*, xvii; original emphasis). In sum, African Christian theology began as an alternative to missionary theology. As such, early African theology lacked a sense of internal coherence, since its agenda had been set by outsiders and its content was a response to European emphases. "Thus," Bediako concluded, "modern African Theology emerges as a theology of African Christian identity" (*TI*, xvii). Bediako pursued questions of identity such as, Who are we as African Christians? What does it mean to be African and Christian? Is an African Christian somehow different from a European Christian? And, if so, different in what ways? Different beliefs? Practices? Theological emphases?

Not only did the unreflective and unintentional ethnocentrism of European colonial missionaries forcibly separate Africans from their own history and traditions. A broader problem resulted: the theological myopia of the missionaries conveyed "a *theological* misapprehension" of the gospel (*TI*, xvii; original emphasis). Given this historical legacy, African Christians could not and cannot merely appropriate the "gospel" of colonial missionaries—a gospel that, because of its cultural wrappings, was never wholly good news for Africans. Bediako's project, then, was to "discover fresh insights into the eternal purposes of God towards His creation. These could well be such as Western Christianity has culturally been unable, hitherto, to see."[75] By receiving the gospel of Jesus Christ afresh with African ears, and bypassing Western intermediaries, Bediako aimed to articulate a distinct African Christian identity.

Bediako's later work intensified this line of thought: He came to understand his entire intellectual project as indigenous, in that it originated in and was written for Africa. As a self-consciously autochthonous thinker, he sought to articulate and explain the African roots of his personal identity and that of African Christianity as a whole. In doing so, he argued that the insights of African Christianity were revelatory for the understanding of the Christian faith worldwide. Indeed, for Bediako, the process of translating the gospel of Jesus Christ into African languages and African concepts provided a fuller understanding of the gospel. Bediako understood that "the very process of the cross-cultural transmission of the Gospel can also be revelatory" (*CiA*, 214), such that the experiments in Christian thought within the "laboratory" of Africa reveal who God is (*CiA*, 252).[76] Most strikingly, he claimed that God's revelation might have an impact on all Christians and understandings of the essence of Christianity. These experiences of African Christians, and African Christian theology, more broadly, encouraged the remaking of Christian theology itself.

This need for the remaking of Christian theology was precisely what Stokely Carmichael and James Cone were describing. One's contemporary situation radically affects what one believes about God and the world. To paraphrase Carmichael, everyone's theology comes from what one sees when one gets up in the morning.[77] And Cone's critique was that Barth's context was too different from that of blacks in the southern United States.

The next chapter focuses on one aspect of context as it explores the relationship between the gospel of Jesus Christ and human cultures. As Bediako put it, "In short, the challenge is that of relevance without syncretism" (*CiA*, 85).

FIVE

Cultural Reflection

The Location of Revelation

Culture is the location of revelation. The point of engagement between divine action and human action occurs within the spaces of human cultures. Previous chapters have established that revelation, and therefore contemporary theological reflection, is to be not only Christological but also contextual, for there is no such thing as "a pure gospel." Just as God's Son assumed human flesh in the incarnation, so also the good news must take on cultural forms. The following analyses of Bediako and Barth demonstrate that understanding and articulating the role of the cultural in theological reflection is challenging and complex. The chapter begins with Barth's love of "high culture" in the music of Wolfgang Amadeus Mozart, then examines Barth's and Bediako's explicit definitions of culture, before engaging Bediako on "folk culture."[1]

Barth and Mozart

On May 11, 1953, 120 theology students gathered in a lecture room in Basel for that day's lecture in systematic theology by Professor Barth. To their surprise, instead of hearing the latest draft installment of *Church Dogmatics*, they heard a trio of two flutes and a viola performing Mozart. The musicians had performed the piece by Barth's all-time favorite composer a day earlier in celebration of his sixty-seventh birthday.[2] Barth valued instrumental music as a tool for theological instruction,[3] and he wrote about surprising his students with Mozart, "Even in this place there was an unusual splendor of light."[4]

Barth's love of Mozart is well documented. He owned vinyl records of every piece of Mozart's work that had been recorded, fell asleep listening to Mozart, was awakened to Mozart's music, and even died in his sleep while Mozart was playing.[5] For Barth, Bach was like John the Baptist, preparing the way for Mozart. In an article commemorating Mozart's birth, Barth displayed his affinities: "If I ever get to heaven, I shall ask first after Mozart, and only then after Augustine and Thomas, Luther and Calvin and Schleiermacher."[6] In his study in Basel, Barth hung pictures of Calvin and Mozart next to each other and at the same height.[7]

One of the highlights of Barth's career was the opportunity to offer a public tribute to Mozart at the Music Hall in Basel on January 29, 1956, the two hundredth anniversary of Mozart's birth, which he called "Mozart's Freedom."[8] Near the end of his speech, Barth came very close to naming Mozart's music as a parable of the kingdom. These are his words: "How can I as an evangelical Christian and theologian proclaim Mozart? After all he was so Catholic, even a Freemason, and for the rest no more than a musician, albeit a complete one. He who has ears has certainly heard."[9] Barth continued with a nod to his critics and those who might be wary of hearing the voice of God in Mozart's music: "May I ask all those others who may be shaking their heads in astonishment and anxiety to be content for the moment with the general reminder that the New Testament speaks not only of the kingdom of heaven but also of *parables* of the kingdom of heaven?"[10] Barth was hinting that God in Jesus Christ divinely proclaims and reveals an analogy of who God is through Mozart's compositions (IV/3, 73).[11] That is, the distinction between the kingdom of heaven itself and parables of the kingdom differentiates between the sign and the thing signified.[12] The parables point to the kingdom but are not the kingdom itself.

For Barth, Mozart's music was the epitome of the good that Western culture could offer, whereas religion was a hindrance to the gospel of Jesus

Christ, as I noted in the previous chapter. In this way, Barth differentiated between his understandings of religion and culture. As early as 1936, Barth had offered a theological definition of culture: "Culture is the task set through the Word of God for achieving the destined condition of man in unity of soul and body."[13] He offered a more succinct definition on the next page: "Culture means humanity."[14] Most commonly, when scholars are discussing Barth on culture—which is relatively rare within the scope of Barth studies—appeals are made to Barth's discussions of culture in IV/3, §69.2, and his Mozart essays. However, I agree with Jessica DeCou, against Paul Metzger and Robert J. Palma, when she claimed, "Barth *had* a theology of culture (defined here as a practicable method for understanding, analyzing and engaging with cultural forms theologically), even if he did not explicitly *articulate* it. . . . Though Barth expressed a profound interest in culture and wrote often on politics and the arts, he did not spell out the particular methods and theories underpinning these analyses in relation to his larger theological program."[15] For Barth, culture was assumed: assumed to be Western culture and assumed to be expressed in the arts.

Bediako, as well, did not have a clearly articulated theology of culture. When Bediako provided the "Culture" entry in the *New Dictionary of Theology*,[16] he began with a disclaimer: "Culture is a term that is not easily definable."[17] Yet the challenge did not deter him. Bediako continued by restating a wider consensus—that culture is the ways of thinking and behavior shared by a group of persons that gives them identity—before pushing his main point, "that all persons participate in one culture or another. There is no individual who has no culture." Indeed, "culture . . . give[s] . . . identity."[18] Bediako's own wrestling with identity as an African and a Christian (and with the concerns of fellow Africans) led him to better understand and articulate the discontinuities of African culture; that is, culture must emerge from within a group of persons and not be imposed externally. In this way, culture and identity were inseparable. Bediako routinely insisted that no person or group of people could exist outside of culture. Thus not only people but also their thoughts, convictions, and theologies are rooted in culture. Culture, then, is "all-embracing" and "inescapable."[19] Further, culture is not fixed; instead, "like human life itself, culture is dynamic, adaptable and open to transformation both within itself, and in response to new and external factors."[20] While culture is the collection of human thinking and behavior that a group of people

Compares culture & gospel

shares and that gives them identity, in practice, individual cultures are *fluid and ever changing* in response to internal and external developments. African cultures, then, are the combination of their histories and present circumstances.

In contrast to the fluidity of culture, the gospel is *fixed* on the person of Jesus Christ. Bediako defined "the Gospel, in the true sense of the word, [as] who Christ is, and what he means, in his person, his life on earth, his work, his death, his resurrection and its aftermath, and how all that concerning him relates to all human beings, in all our cultural traditions, histories, and environments."[21] Even though the "gospel was before the New Testament,"[22] Bediako saw it as having historical roots in the person of Jesus Christ. In part this conviction amounted to the rationale for why the "gospel and culture cannot be separated,"[23] for Christ cannot be separated from his earthly body. Bediako based his conviction on John 1:14. Since "'the Word became flesh' [is] not some abstract, general humanity,"[24] the gospel (God's Son coming to earth as a human being) is concretized in a specific way. This connection of gospel with culture is then rooted and given in the incarnation. Bediako wrote, "If the Gospel, therefore, is the person of Jesus Christ of Nazareth, his ministry, his death, his resurrection and its aftermath, as given us in the Scriptures, then it shows the Gospel can no longer be viewed as independent of culture."[25] In the same way that human beings cannot be separated from culture, neither, for Bediako, can the gospel be separated from its human embodiment in Jesus Christ or human cultures. Bediako's understanding here differed from Barth's. While Barth insisted on the uniqueness of the gospel as always identifiable amid culture, Bediako began with the interconnectedness of culture and religion in African cosmology to assert that gospel and culture cannot be separated.

While the mingling of gospel and culture did not worry Bediako,[26] he was concerned that Christian theology could be captured or usurped by culture. In fact, this was precisely the claim he made about most Western theology and some African theologies, such as *Afrikania*.[27] Bediako was wary of any theology claiming to be above, outside of, or apart from culture. But there was also a mutually enlightening relationship between gospel and culture. In the interaction between the two, the gospel teaches about culture and culture teaches about the gospel. Such interaction is an inevitable part of human existence and as such should be welcomed and probed for meaning, without trying to escape or avoid it. Even more than understanding the inevitability of the relationship between gospel and culture, however, Bediako saw potential learning through the interaction. The key question was how to distinguish "bad" interaction between the gospel and culture (such as in colonialism) from "good" interaction. For Bediako, the first step was an awareness of the cultural blinders that everyone brings to the process of biblical interpretation and theological reflection. The second step was for a theology to be examined for cases where culture obscures the gospel.

Culture, then, is not a neutral quantity. Culture is very powerful in shaping the identities of individuals and in pointing them toward or away from Jesus Christ. Bediako believed that "there is within every tradition of culture, history, identity and continuity, elements which lead to Jesus and affirm him as Lord; but equally, there are within every tradition, elements that lead away from Jesus and deny him."[28] Historically, he saw a tremendous amount of Western attention devoted to combating syncretism in churches and theologies of the developing world but "an insufficient alertness to similar phenomena threatening the churches of the West."[29] Bediako's view of Western theology was that it is syncretistic with Western culture and distorts the gospel. Therefore, translating this distorted, Western gospel is not sufficient for churches in the Global South. They must go further. They must seek alternative sources to shape an African Christian identity. And Bediako believed these sources already reside in the heritage of African religions.

As African theologians started to emerge, in their quest to understand their identity as African Christians they found themselves seeking out "their own religious heritage; which is, indeed, a proper task of theology. . . . [T]his new theological approach had no counterpart in the more recent Western theological thought forged within the context of Christendom."[30] In the context of Christendom, religious identity was inherited from one's surrounding culture without intentional effort. Yet in the post-colonial African context, "identity itself thus became a theological category, so that the development of theological concern and the formulation of theological questions were linked as the inevitable by-product of a process of Christian self-definition" (*CiA*, 256). The search for an authentic African Christian identity was a truly theological endeavor as Christians sought traces of religious memory in the past to achieve a better understanding of themselves in the present. This was a shift from unselfconscious inhabitation of context to a purposeful pursuit of identity through the appropriation of African spirituality and religiosity within Christianity.

Bediako repeatedly stressed that African Christians had a past and that they need to know it, "for theological consciousness presupposes religious tradition, and tradition requires memory, and memory is integral to identity: without memory we have no past, and if we have no past, we lose our identity."[31] For Bediako, people without a history have no identity. And this poses a significant problem: Bediako understood part of the colonial project as interjecting a substitute past into the African past. Colonialism "threatened to deny African Christians their own past and sought instead to give them a past which could not in any real sense become fully theirs" (*TI*, 237).[32] Yet each culture can and should experience the gospel of Jesus Christ directly based on its own experiences. Just as Aimé Césaire and other authors of négritude reconnected the black peoples brought to Martinique and the Antilles to their African past, so Bediako sought to connect African Christians to their dual heritage as Africans and as Christians.[33]

Culture: Primal Imagination as the Substructure of African Christianity

The significance of the spiritual realm in African cosmologies cannot be overestimated, especially for Western readers. Remembering Gyeke's claim that in the Akan universe "what is primarily real is spiritual,"[34] many Africans believe that what is *primarily* real is not what is seen but what is unseen. The spiritual, the spirit world, is the primary reality of human existence; the tangible, visible world is secondary and subservient.

Bediako insisted on the integrity of "the primal imagination" in his understanding of Christianity (*CiA*, 92).[35] The primal imagination he understood as an outlook of "a spiritual universe which was both simple and complex, and yet ... able to [be] embraced as a totality" (*CiA*, 92). Further, the maintenance of the primal imagination must derive from ATRs; it cannot be imposed from without. Bediako wrote, "A starting point for appreciating the primal imagination must be in primal religions themselves" (*CiA*, 93). Bediako saw the primal imagination as the core of what is distinctive about African Christianity.

The Christian gospel requires sharing and preserving this view of the primal imagination within African life, not condemning it as many Europeans had. Bediako wrote, "Far from obliterating the African primal view of things, in its essentially unified and 'spiritual' nature and replacing it with a two-tier modern Western view comprising sacred and secular dimensions, the Christian faith has in fact reinforced the African view" (*CiA*, 176). Bediako was thus seeking to "restore the ancient unity of theology and spirituality" (*CiA*, 105). When he "engages the tradition," he considers the Old and New Testaments *and* African philosophy, culture, and traditions. In contrast, Barth's understanding of "engaging the tradition" meant the last two thousand years of Christian thought (which he considers different from Western philosophy and culture) as well as the Old and New Testaments.

In that Bediako constantly sought to bring together the ancient Christian tradition (including the gospel) with the present context (i.e., African culture), he was self-consciously following in the line of the Ghanaian philosopher J. B. Danquah, an author who understood how to link the past with the present so as to lead to the future.[36] The work of translation into and out of African languages and thought forms further highlighted the intersection of the gospel and culture. The intended goal was a diminishing of the influences of the Enlightenment and an increased influence of precolonial African religions and culture, particularly of primal religions in the interaction.

Bediako believed that primal religion is "the Christian substructure[,] ... the foundation of Christian faith."[37] In his telling of the history, Christianity "builds on" primal religion; "the Enlightenment project obscured this understanding."[38] Only recently have African theologians identified the "primal substructure" that had been covered by a European, Enlightenment understanding of the Christian faith. In his work, he sought "a theological interpretation of this Christian substructure."[39] Bediako was adamant that this substructure is primal, not pagan.

While Bediako's understanding of "the Enlightenment project" may be a bit of a caricature, there was enough truth in it to demonstrate the stark contrast between the understanding of the world in primal religions and an Enlightenment understanding. The foundation of African Christianity must be African primal religion, not Enlightenment philosophy.

Bediako explicitly referred to this primal religious foundation as *the substructure of African Christianity*.[40] If, following Clement of Alexandria, the Christian faith was going to absorb the pre-Christian religion that it encounters, then Bediako was also aware that the prior religion will not merely have an impact on, but be integral to, the Christianity that emerged afterward. The early church was deeply influenced by Greco-Roman religion, and Christianity in the modern West was deeply influenced by the Enlightenment. Bediako's argument was that African Christianity was valuably and strongly influenced by African culture and primal religion. (Of course, there remains a more fundamental substructure to Christianity: Israelite cultic religion and Second Temple Judaism. However, the place of Judaism in Bediako's understanding of the Christian faith is much less clear.)

Bediako's argument concerning primal religions as the substructure of Christianity built on an understanding of the primal imagination that was nearly absent from his discussions of Hellenistic religion in *Theology and Identity*. At the same time, this appeal to the primal imagination complicated Bediako's understanding of history. In *Theology and Identity*, Bediako's thought was presented in terms of a chronological past. Yet, for the later Bediako, although the primal religions of Africa belong to the African religious past, "this is not so much a chronological past as an 'ontological' past."[41] By "ontological," Bediako meant that the very being of an African—Christian or non-Christian—has been indelibly formed by the primal imagination of African spirituality and religion, including beliefs about ancestors. Thus, while many Africans now understand themselves as Christians (or Muslims), they remain indelibly formed in their being and identities as Africans by the primal religions of Africa. In this way, though a smaller percentage of Africans actively practice African traditional religions than before colonization (the "chronological past"), the legacy of the primal imagination continues. The impact of the primal religions remains in the being of Africans. Even when Africans convert to Christianity, they do not—in fact, cannot—simply leave the primal religions behind them. Primal religions have shaped who they are and who they will be. Thus, "for the African theologian . . . the traditional religions, even if they constitute his past, are of the nature of an 'ontological' past, which means that together with the profession of the Christian faith, it gives account of the same entity—namely the history of the religious consciousness of the African Christian" (*CiA*, 258). The identity of an African Christian is shaped by the past through the influences of pre-Christendom Christian theology and precolonial African primal religions. And this twin heritage of African Christianity described the presence of an indigenous Christianity in modern African culture.

Perhaps the clearest example of Bediako's perspective can be found in his hope for his own Ghanaian Presbyterians. He writes of how every Christmas Day the Presbyterians in Akropong sing a hymn celebrating Jesus's birthday: "They sing this hymn without any awareness that Christmas itself was originally a Christian substitute for a pre-Christian New Year religious festival in pagan Northern Europe. My earnest prayer and hope is that they will one day sing it at the traditional New Year festival of *Odwira* to welcome and worship the one who achieved once and for all purification for their sins, their greater Ancestor, Nana Iesu Kristo" (*CiA*, 86).[42] Bediako's intent here was to expose and embrace the pre-Christian foundations of many Western Christian traditions, to imagine, positively, how African pre-Christian customs can be embraced in African Christianity.

The impact of the primal imagination, furthermore, kept African Christianity grounded in everyday realities and not abstracted to the realm of speculative ideas. By rediscovering the primal elements within the Christian faith, one gains a greater appreciation of the Christian gospel as not simply a "system of ideas[,] . . . [but] a system of power and of living religiously as being in touch with the source and channels of power in the universe" (*CiA*, 106). Bediako's viewpoint, based in African cosmologies, refused to separate belief from action, theology from concrete realities. In the end, "Christianity in Africa is a truly African experience."[43] What defines African Christianity are the experiences of Africans as shaped by the primal imagination in indigenous African cultures that are continuous with Christianity through ATRs because of the infinite translatability of the gospel.

Continuity: Religion within Culture

Bediako's positive assessment of ATRs and African culture countered the prevailing assumptions of European colonial missions, in particular, the 1910 Edinburgh conference that declared Africans without a religious heritage and their rituals pagan. Instead of viewing ATRs and African culture as problems for African Christianity, Bediako viewed them as full of possibilities. He wrote, "Rather than constituting a prison that inhibits our human development, and therefore a prison from which we are to break free in order to experience salvation in a so-called 'Christian culture' brought in from outside, our African cultural heritage is in fact the very place where Christ desires to find us in order to transform us into his image."[44] African culture, in short, is the site of the engagement between the gospel and Africans. I build on Bediako's understanding of the indigeneity of the Christian faith to Africa (see ch. 3) by exploring the primal imagination and how both contribute to Bediako's understanding of culture.

The first step in identifying and articulating the African religious aspect of the twin heritage of African Christianity was to undo the assumptions of many Western colonial missionaries about traditional African religions. Bediako first conducted this ground clearing in *Theology and Identity*. The first assumption to undo was that of a religious vacuum, that Africans were a religious tabula rasa. Following the Cameroonian theologian Mulago gwa Cikala Musharhamina, Bediako embraced the role of a Christian theologian retrieving African religious identity. He took "theological responsibility for one's cultural community" (*TI*, 353) by retaining and translating its resources in light of the gospel. Indeed, all of Bediako's work, starting in *Theology and Identity*, has attempted to valorize, or at least give a positive account of, the traditions and rituals of African traditional religions. He has demonstrated that Africans have a religious past that makes constructive contributions to African Christian thought that had been elided by Western, colonial presuppositions.

As Bediako understands it, Africans worshipped God even before they knew the name of God as Jesus Christ. However, instead of treating traditional religions as "paganism," Bediako highlighted Africa's pre-Christian religious history that he claimed had prepared Africans for Christianity. In the most basic terms, African Christian thought combines the Christian faith with African primal religious traditions. For Bediako, "primal" is not a euphemism for primitive; it is a positive term in its own right, meaning "universal, basic elements of human understanding of the transcendent and of the world, essential and valid religious insights that may be built upon or may be suppressed but that cannot be superseded."[45] Further, the uniqueness of African Christian thought lies in its appropriation of this primal imagination. Bediako turns to the primal to articulate an authentic African Christian identity. He does so in part by claiming that the names given to deities in African mother tongues can and should be applied to God in Jesus Christ. One God has been active in Africa.

The appropriate name(s) used to refer to God is a key topic in the discussion about the indigenous nature of Christianity in Africa. The basic contrast that Bediako draws is between what happened in Europe and what happened in Africa when the Christian religion was first introduced. Before Christianity was introduced in northern and western Europe, the European primal imagination fostered numerous deities, often associated with aspects of the natural world: earth, fire, water, fertility, and so on. Meanwhile, "Hellenistic Christians had identified the God of the Bible with the 'God' of Plato and the concept of the highest good in the Greek philosophical tradition—a 'God' without a name, generally described in negative categories and usually spoken of in abstract terms."[46] The proclamation of this "God" over and against the gods of the Western primal imagination—often by forced conquest and conversion— eradicated these primal gods.

The process of evangelization in Africa was radically different. In Africa, wrote Bediako, "the bearers of the Christian faith encountered a well-rooted belief in one great God, Creator and Moral ruler of the universe and one not too distinguishable from the God of the Old and the New Testament traditions."[47] The response of the European missionaries was to identify this One with the God of the Bible, to claim continuity with the African religious tradition, not discontinuity. In contrast to the conquerors of Europe, many missionaries to Africa sought out the name for God in an African culture and identified that name with God in Jesus Christ. While this may certainly be viewed as a totalizing move by an occupying power, it has allowed for continuity between African primal religions and Christianity that has encouraged the primal religions to continue. In a footnote in *Christianity in Africa*, he observed, "It is extraordinary, for instance, how the African names for God in African indigenous languages have made an easy transition into Christian vocabulary to designate the God of the Bible—a feature which was lacking in the earlier missionary history of Europe" (*CiA*, 99). As a result, "the God of the Bible turned out to be the God whose name has been hallowed in vernacular usage for generations. This did not happen in Europe" (*CiA*, 55).[48] Put more boldly, Bediako wrote that "in Africa the God whose name had been hallowed in indigenous languages in the pre-Christian tradition was found to be the God of the Bible, in a way neither Zeus, nor Jupiter, nor Odin could be. Onyankopon, Olorun, Ngai, Nkulunkulu are the names of the God and Father of Jesus Christ; Zeus, Jupiter, and Odin are not."[49] Ironically, then, the decision of European missionaries to use African names for the divine being, God, highlights the continuity between ATRs and Christianity.

Yet this claim of continuity also implies that the Akan people can no longer maintain a partial or incomplete understanding of Nyame, the Twi name for God. For Bediako, Nyame has been revealed to be the God and Father of Jesus Christ. This revelation of the fullness of who God is supersedes the prior understanding of the human person in African thought. Indeed, the coming of God in Jesus Christ changes what it means to be a human being; or at least, the revelation of God in Jesus Christ reveals who all humanity—including Africans—have been, are, and will be, whether they knew it or not. Put differently, while the traditions and the imagination of traditional African religions remain in the twenty-first century, the understanding of human beings in their relationship to the divine has been radically altered. The ancestors do not mediate the relationship between Nyame and humanity; instead, mediation occurs through the Supreme Ancestor, Jesus Christ, the Son of God. Furthermore, the direction of the relationship has been reversed. Instead of the living seeking help from the ancestors to communicate with Nyame and the spirit world, in Jesus Christ, Nyame has sent his Son to lead people into full relationship with God through the Holy Spirit.

A more critical claim ventured here is that European Christianity is relatively impoverished. Although "Europe shares with Africa an identical pre-Christian heritage in the primal religious traditions of the world" (*CiA*, 260),[50] Bediako argues, the Christianization of Europe happened through forces that "proceeded on a basis of substitution to such an extent that the primal traditions were virtually completely wiped out."[51] Scant traces of European primal religions remain in Western culture today. The wholesale substitution of the Christian religion in place of European primal religions, "together with the fact that there was no sustained interest in the use of indigenous European languages and their pre-Christian world-views for Christian purposes,"[52] has damaged the Western religious memory beyond recovery. Yet, as Bediako points out, "the old beliefs had

not entirely lost their hold upon people's minds,"[53] as "Christians continued to name the days of the week after pre-Christian deities, and
pre-Christian elements and notions made their way into the celebration
of Christian festivals."[54] These semantic connections, such as Sun-day,
point to a primal European past that has largely been lost.

In a sense, then, it appeared to Bediako that many European missionaries to Africa simply proceeded to "do" missions as missions had been
"done" to their ancestors—by wiping out the local traditions and wholly
substituting a Western understanding of the Christian God. Yet with
some unexpected benefits: European colonization was not (primarily)
military conquest but instead a process of "civilization" with an economic
upside. The European colonizers, moreover, did not eliminate all traces of
African primal religions. Bediako saw this situation as a tremendous opportunity for African Christian thought. He wrote, "It may be that in Africa the opportunity lost in Europe for a serious and creative theological
encounter between the Christian and primal traditions, can be regained."[55]
Thus the requisite task of African Christian theologians has been to articulate the internal dialogue between their Christian faith and the spiritualities
of their African primal heritage. These expressions have the essence of their
"Christian intellectual activity on the frontier with the non-Christian
world."[56] African Christian thought, from its origins, has been well placed
to imagine Christianity anew as an encounter between the gospel and culture. From Bediako's vantage point, "African theological writing came to
focus on giving a more positive interpretation of the African religious past
than the missionary assessment had done, and so demonstrated the continuity of the religious past with the Christian present" (*CiA*, 76). The Christian faith is continuous with the religious past of Africans.

Barth and Culture

The themes of revelation, religion, and culture that arise from a comprehensive analysis of Bediako's corpus also intersect in Karl Barth's late
Christology in *Church Dogmatics* IV/3. Barth wrote during and after the
"shattering events" (IV/3, 30) of the twentieth century: two world wars,
the Nazi Holocaust, atomic warfare, the Cold War between rival political
and economic systems, and independence movements in colonized na-

tions. Barth's late Christology, in IV/3, §69, "The Glory of the Mediator," is suitable for in-depth examination here specifically because of its overlap with Bediako's theological emphases. Barth's account of the ongoing prophetic activity of Jesus Christ provides a useful comparison to Bediako's understanding of the "translatability of the gospel of Jesus Christ." The ongoing, prophetic activity of Jesus Christ reveals (and thereby communicates) who God is in a similar manner for Barth.

Barth envisioned "a deep shadow" (IV/3, 19) as having fallen on the church in the years following the Reformation.[57] Preceding and continuing through this deep shadow, Barth perceives the shining of the "Light of Life," the God-man Jesus Christ. Barth's use of the imagery of light, life, and darkness echoes the prologue to the Gospel of John: "In him was life, and the life was the light of all people. The light shines in the darkness, and the darkness did not overcome it" (John 1:4–5; IV/3, 9, 167). In IV/3 Barth described the *diastasis*, or rupture, that he observed between the Christian community on earth and its beginnings in the life, death, resurrection, and ascension of the God-man Jesus Christ as a response to "the question of the responsible explication and application of the Word of God attested in Scripture" (IV/3, 32) that failed to assert "the sovereignty of the word of Scripture over all man's self-understanding" (IV/3, 32). In the modern period, Christians had turned the faith into a religion that was based on abstract principles and not on the person of Jesus Christ. Barth seeks to overcome this rupture by maintaining a consistent focus on the actions of Jesus Christ, understood as history.

The life, death, resurrection, and ascension of Jesus Christ illuminate who God is (as God's self-revelation) and proclaim God's reconciliation for all. Thus Barth often repeated the phrase, "Reconciliation is also revelation" (IV/3, 38).[58] With these words, Barth succinctly articulated his actualistic understanding of revelation as coextensive with, and in some way identified with, God's redemptive activity. Humans know who God is in and through God's action in the world in Jesus Christ. And this proclamation of Jesus's life is "eloquent and radiant" communication (IV/3, 79)[59] to those who have ears to hear and eyes to see that God is for humanity in the past, present, and future.[60] The life of Jesus Christ is a life of grace and offers a life of grace to all humanity. This grace "would not be grace if it were to remain mute and obscure . . . or were not eloquent and radiant. As such, it is eloquent and radiant. As such, it is prophecy" (IV/3, 81).[61]

Below I examine Barth's exposition of the ongoing prophetic activity of Jesus Christ, specifically in parables of the kingdom.

Parables of the Kingdom

The starting point for Barth's reflections on revelation and culture is the incarnation of the Son of God in the human flesh of a Jewish Nazarene, Jesus Christ. In this consideration of revelation and culture, I analyze *Church Dogmatics* IV/3, §69.2, "The Light of Life," by asking the question, what does it mean that revelation takes place in nonreligious parables? Barth's understanding of how revelation occurs, that is, God's self-revelation in Jesus Christ, is particular. Revelation is always mediated in specific cultural forms, most notably in the person of Jesus of Nazareth. Barth went to great lengths, particularly in *Church Dogmatics* IV/1, to stress Jesus's Jewishness. For Barth, this emphasis underlined both that Jesus is human and, more specifically, that Jesus possessed a specific ethnic identity, like all humans, that located him within God's chosen people of Israel, not some sort of generic human essence. The revelation of God that took place in Jesus Christ occurred within and through the Jewish culture of first-century Palestine. The incarnation encompassed a particular culture and history.

By extension, one might say that all ongoing revelation through the prophetic activity of Jesus Christ must also take cultural forms. In *Church Dogmatics* IV/3, §69.2, Barth discussed "true words" and "parables of the kingdom" as two forms of revelation God uses today. Certainly, revelation is *always* in Christ, by Christ, and from Christ. But revelation is not restricted to the Bible and the Christian community. Barth defined true words as follows: "true words, i.e., words which, whatever their subjective presuppositions, stand objectively in a supremely direct relationship with the one true Word, which are not exhausted by what they are in themselves, which may even speak against themselves, but which are laid upon their lips by the one true Word, by Jesus Christ, who is their Sovereign too" (IV/3, 125). While it may appear that Barth views true words as an overcoming of culture, I read Barth as valuing cultural forms, including language, preserving their authenticity while filling them with additional meaning as "true words."

In the end, Barth saw a "positive relationship" between "the light of life [and] the lights" (IV/3, 165). Jesus Christ was, is, and will be the light of life (IV/3, 135). All lesser lights are not deemed "revelation" because "no faith is needed to grasp them" (IV/3, 143), implying that the human reception of revelation is a matter of faith. Meanwhile, the "world as such can produce no parables of the kingdom of heaven" (IV/3, 143). Only God can ordain creaturely media to (temporarily) serve as vehicles for divine self-revelation. Therefore, creaturely truths are only partial truths (IV/3, 159), the lesser lights cannot replace the *one* light of God's self-revelation (IV/3, 153), and the little lights are integrated into the one great light (IV/3, 156).

Barth used the concept "parables of the kingdom," sometimes translated as "parables of the kingdom of heaven," to explain the relationship of the Light (Jesus Christ) to the lights in the best-known section of *Church Dogmatics* IV/3, §69 (114–35). In contrast to the lack of scholarly attention to the bulk of §69 and to Barth's treatment of Christ as prophet, Barth's "parables of the kingdom" have received careful scholarly treatment, most significantly as "Secular Parables of the Truth" by George Hunsinger in his epilogue to *How to Read Karl Barth*.[62]

Hunsinger's exposition seeks to correct a misperception that Barth's "exclusivist Christology is incompatible with recognizing truth (i.e. theological truth) in non-Christian sources and writers."[63] In doing so, he helpfully demonstrates how these "secondary forms of the one Word of God" outside of the scriptures or the church drive the community back to the scriptures.[64] Pace Hunsinger, I do not believe that the qualifier "secular" helpfully captures the significance of Barth's claims about the parables of the kingdom of heaven in §69.2. In fact, in Barth's *Dogmatics*, there is only one mention of a *secular* parable (IV/3, 115). Hunsinger imports the sacred/secular dualism without sufficient textual support from Barth's work. His reading seems to suggest that Barth distinguishes between the "secular" and the "holy." While the significance of Barth's "parables of the kingdom" is certainly that God's revelation occurs *outside* the Bible or the church, calling everything outside the church "secular" is obstructive and possibly even pejorative. The parables of the kingdom that Barth described in §69.2 are not "secular" per se; it is rather that they occur "in the secular sphere" (IV/3, 117). Barth's word translated here as "secular" means all that is profane, that is common or ordinary. "Secular" here describes *where* the parables occur (outside the Christian community), *not* the character of the parables themselves. The imagery Barth employed, then, seeks to encourage Christians to "eavesdrop in the world at large" (IV/3, 117) to hear true words that are not directly addressed to the Christian community yet may be beneficial to them to hear.

Appealing to the parable in John 10, Barth suggests that one "hears the voice of the Good Shepherd" in parables of the kingdom (IV/3, 117).[65] Barth's central claim had to do with God's sovereignty in revelation. God's self-revelation through the prophetic activity of Jesus Christ can happen anywhere, not simply within the walls of the church or only through previously sanctioned mediums or oracles. Barth was diminishing the force of the distinction between the church and the world, the so-called sacred and secular—not intensifying the distinction as Hunsinger risks doing. Specifically, Barth is simultaneously trying to disrupt those Christians who have become comfortable and complacent within European Protestant culture while opening up the possibility of the work to achieve political justice for peace, for the poor, and so on, being done by socialists and other left-leaning activists as the work of God's kingdom.[66] The parables of the kingdom, then, are not secular in and of themselves but instead underline that parables can still happen today. This is a claim about the ongoing nature of Christ's prophetic activity.

All interpreters would agree that in the New Testament Jesus used parables to explain God's character and intentions in the world. Barth used the phrase "parables of the kingdom" only twice in his *Dogmatics* outside of §69. The first is in IV/2, §64, to refer to the parables Jesus told in the synoptic gospels about practices of the kingdom of heaven (IV/2, 174). The second use is in IV/2, §67, where Barth referred to "the synoptic parables of the kingdom" (657). The other ten uses of "parables of the kingdom (of heaven)" in the *Church Dogmatics* all appear in §69.2.[67] There are three uses outside of that work that shed additional light on Barth's use and understanding of the term: in Barth's teaching on the Heidelberg Catechism (1948), in his previously mentioned tribute to Mozart (1956), and in *The Christian Life* (1962).[68]

In response to Question 28 in the Heidelberg Catechism, "What advantage comes from acknowledging God's creation and providence?," Barth described patience based in "the fact that God will act in his good time, which does not despair when it sees no parables of the kingdom of heaven."[69] Barth was already deploying, a decade before the composition of *Church Dogmatics* §69.2, the category "parables of the kingdom of heaven." Barth may have borrowed the language itself from C. H. Dodd's book *The Parables of the Kingdom*,[70] which Barth alluded to in a letter to the French Jesuit theologian Jean Daniélou in October 1948.[71] This usage in his commentary on the catechism pointed to how parables of the kingdom of heaven can provide hope to a community of faith where God is at work in spite of the present adversity they are facing.

In the posthumously published *The Christian Life*, which contains drafts of what would have been the first half of *Church Dogmatics* IV/4, in §77.2, "Zeal for the Honour of God: The Known and Unknown God," which John Webster describes as "an especially important commentary on *CD* IV/3,"[72] Barth asked, "When we meet outspoken children of the world, and read expressly secular literature, do we not sometimes at least, quite unexpectedly and to our shame, get the impression that God the Creator does not contradict the contradiction of his creature for nothing?" (*TCL*, 121–22). While being careful to avoid any tinge of natural theology, Barth could not help but "not[e] that Jesus obviously in his addresses . . . found very worldly (profane) processes and relations apt and worthy for use as parables of the kingdom of heaven" (*TCL*, 121–22). This commentary on IV/3 that Barth provided in §77.2 highlighted the main point of §69.2: the revealing of veiled knowledge of God in so-called worldly forms outside the church or the Bible. The source and content of this revelation is the Word of God, Jesus Christ. Barth named these "processes and relations . . . parables of the kingdom of heaven" (*TCL*, 122). Barth's late claim, in *Church Dogmatics* IV/3 and *The Christian Life*, was that God used contemporary images (i.e., updated and contextualized from the Sower and the Seed or other parables in the Bible) to reveal who God is.

Always for Barth Jesus Christ is the source of revelation; otherwise, words, or a parable, are not "true words," not God's self-revelation. Barth was quite clear that listening for the distinct sound of the Word of God in the secular sphere is *not* "natural theology" (*TCL*, 121–22; IV/3, 117). As opposed to a "natural theology" that allegedly enables a degree of knowledge about who God is to Christians and non-Christians alike, the audience of Barth's parables of the kingdom is those who already have faith in Christ. Similar to the parables of Jesus in the New Testament,[73] the message, the truth, of the parables of the kingdom is for those with "ears to hear" (Mark 4:9, 23).[74] At the same time, these parables of the kingdom truly offer "attestations of the self-impartation [of God]," not "only abstract impartations" (IV/3, 117). The truth that is imparted is real, not abstract, and personal, not formal. Certainly, these "attestations" must "be materially tested by and compared with this witness . . . present in Scripture" (IV/3, 117). In these parables of the kingdom, unlike natural theology, "we do not leave the sure ground of Christology" (IV/3, 117). Barth appealed to Christ's sovereignty in his resurrection whose witness is "not restricted" to the Bible and the church (IV/3, 118). The unrestricted nature of the freedom of God in Jesus Christ to reveal God is the central meaning of Barth's parables of the kingdom. He states his argument succinctly: "Our thesis is simply that the capacity of Jesus Christ to create these human witnesses is not restricted to His working on and in prophets and apostles and what is thus made possible and actual in His community. His capacity transcends the limits of this sphere" (IV/3, 118). The significance of Christ's unrestricted revelation is that it can (and does) make other women and men into "His witnesses, speaking words which can be seriously called true" (IV/3, 118). The revelation of God in Jesus Christ is not merely informative, but transformative. The words, indeed the very lives, of ordinary human beings are transformed by the living Word of God to be God's witnesses in the "wider sphere" (IV/3, 118).

"Secular" and "Periphery"

At this point in his argument concerning the parables of the kingdom, Barth paused to ask, "But what is this wider sphere? To whom or what do we refer when we speak of the secular world in contrast with that of the Bible and the Church?" (IV/3, 118). In answering his question, Barth seeks to minimize, if not eliminate, the sacred/secular dichotomy, or rather to prevent it from having any kind of traction. He distinguished between a closer and a more distant periphery, a secularism that is in "a pure and absolute form" as compared to another secularism that is "mixed and relative" (IV/3, 118). He preferred the imagery of a sphere with a center and a more distant periphery. This unified, inseparable view of the world allows for *degrees* of secularization rather than a strict binary with a distinct secular sphere and a distinct Christian or church sphere. For Barth, "Jesus Christ can raise up extraordinary witnesses to speak true words" from both spheres.

Instead of neatly demarcated boundaries, the world is in the church and the church is in the world. While there is "a pure and absolute form"

(IV/3, 118) of secularism, there is also "a world of mixed and relative secularism" (IV/3, 121). What this meant for Barth was that *"there is no secular sphere"* (IV/3, 119; emphasis added) that has been abandoned by God. To make such a claim would both limit the power and scope of the resurrection and inhibit one from recognizing the voice of God in the world. For Barth, humans must "be prepared at any time for true words even from what seem to be the darkest places. Even from the mouth of Balaam the well-known voice of the Good Shepherd may sound, and it is not to be ignored in spite of its sinister origin" (IV/3, 119). Regardless of the appearance or form of the witness or what appears to be "the darkest places," God in Jesus Christ can and does speak true words of revelation. God does not abandon a so-called secular sphere unto itself but instead remains actively present to all humanity.

The revelation of God in Jesus Christ pervades the entire worldly sphere. Barth developed his imagery of the sphere with Jesus Christ as the center of the circle that constitutes a periphery in order to assert the in-breaking of God's kingdom into human existence. God's prophetic self-revelation in "true words . . . pierce the secularism of the worldly life surrounding it in closer or more distant proximity" (IV/3, 122). This passage reaffirmed Barth's point that revelation that occurs through human words comes from and has its origin in the one, solitary Word of God. He wrote, "All human words can be true only as [the Word's] genuine witnesses and attestations" (IV/3, 122). Further, this indirect revelation is partial and incomplete. Nonetheless, this revelation has the power to "pierce the secularism of worldly life" (IV/3, 122) both in its "pure" and "mixed" forms. The witness of revelation defines worldly life as secularism, categorizes it as pure or mixed, and constitutes the sphere of divine-human relating by providing its center.

Barth articulated and explained the relationship between the Word and true words, the center and the periphery, by using an illustration of the one Word of God, Jesus Christ, as both the center of the circle and the whole of its periphery. All human words are "only genuine witnesses and attestations" (IV/3, 122) as the one Word of God—either in the center or at the periphery. Barth did not allow the witness of Jesus Christ to be confined to the center, lest he underplay the "out-shining" power of the resurrection. While the centrality of revelation constitutes the circle and alone occupies the center, the "truth of the one Word of God" is also found in the whole of the periphery.

Though the periphery represents the secular, even there the revelation of God in Jesus Christ is present. Barth continued, "[True words are] genuine witnesses and attestations of the one true Word, real parables of the kingdom of heaven, if . . . the centre and therefore the whole of the periphery, i.e., Jesus Christ Himself, declares Himself in them" (IV/3, 122–23). While the parables of the kingdom are found on the periphery, not in the center, they contain and convey the same Word of God as constitutes the center because they are products of Christ's self-revelation. These parables communicate true words and are "true segments of the periphery" and their role is to "point to the whole" (IV/3, 123).

The significance, again, is that "Jesus Christ Himself, declares Himself" in the whole—the center *and* the periphery. Since Jesus Christ himself is present in the periphery as well as the center, then the true words, the parables of the kingdom, "do not express partial truths, for the one truth of Jesus Christ is indivisible. Yet they express the one and total truth from a particular angle, and to that extent only implicitly and not explicitly in its unity and totality" (IV/3, 123). Barth reaffirmed that Jesus Christ is *the* Light of Life; there is only *one* truth, not multiple truths. He wrote, "They manifest the one light of the one truth with what is from one standpoint a particular refraction which as such is still a faithful reflection of it as the one light" (IV/3, 123). Yet, even though revelation through true words and parables of the kingdom is incomplete (meaning that it does not present the whole picture), the truth that the periphery conveys is not partial, for—to express it tautologically—the truth is entirely true. Barth demonstrated that revelation is *ongoing* through the prophetic activity of Christ.

Hunsinger helpfully articulated the relationship between the center and the periphery: "whereas the truth of the periphery imparts itself to the center by participating in and manifesting the totality which the center has established, the truth of the center imparts itself to the periphery by filling it and endowing it, at each and every point, with the fullness of uncreated light."[75] The Light of Christ fills and penetrates the entire worldly sphere, both the center and the periphery. Thus, for Barth, "we must be prepared to hear, even in secular occurrence, not as alien sounds but as segments of that periphery concretely orientated from its centre and towards its totality, as signs and attestations of the lordship of the one prophecy of Jesus Christ, true words which we must receive as such even though they come from this source" (IV/3, 124). The Christian community can in fact *expect* revelation in true words to come from secular parables and not simply from the Bible, the church, or preaching. Why? Because of its encounter with Christ's extravagant light.

At same time, Hunsinger identified the potential difficulties of navigating this discernment process. He wrote, "This point about the contextual ambiguity of secular parables—their immediate context being merely apparent, their true context being veiled though real—suggests the extent to which Barth tends to think in terms of differing contextual wholes that are at once inwardly integral and mutually incompatible."[76] These differing contexts serve as containers for revelation in Jesus Christ. In his analysis, Hunsinger retracted his designation of the words and parables of the kingdom as "secular": "The real contextual whole in which these words participate is only apparently secular, in reality it is actually Christocentric."[77] The parables of the kingdom are not secular because they exist under Christ's sovereign rule and as a result of Christ's ongoing prophetic activity. Barth's view of the world is not split into two distinct realms. There is not a worldly, secular realm and a godly, Christian realm. Nor are there a City of God and a City of Man. Nor even a visible and invisible church. Instead, Barth offered a Christocentric view of the world in which Christ is present in and within the entire created order. Because of Christ, the church is in the world and the world is in the church.

At points, Barth presented the prophetic activity of Christ as the response to the decline of the Christian church. At this point, recall that Barth did not consider Calvin's "re-discovery" of the prophetic office an accident (meaning chance or coincidence; IV/3, 18, 38) but as a product of his era. The European reformations themselves pointed to a need for the outward-facing Christian community to remember the prophetic office of Christ. This need only intensified in the ensuing 450 years as the pace of secularization quickened and intensified. Barth was deliberately talking about the secular, in §69, as he explicated his Christological understanding of the ongoing prophetic activity of Jesus Christ. The prophetic and the secular are interconnected. The outreaching of prophetic activity permeates the secular realm. But more than that, Christ's ongoing prophetic activity is not bound to a "Christian/Church" realm or to a "secular" realm; Christ is active everywhere. In fact, the Christian community must pay attention to Christ's prophetic activity in the secular realm to learn from Christ there. In this way, seemingly secular political acts can serve as "true words" to and for Christians and Christian communities. The "secular" in §69 served as a reminder of the political in Barth's writing. The prophetic office of the God-man insisted not that Christendom be reinstated but that lives be lived in correspondence to the life and teachings of Jesus Christ in response to God's grace with a vocation of fulfilling Christ's commission of service *for* others. In §72, Barth applied his understanding of the ongoing prophetic activity of Christ ecclesiologically as the sending of the Christian community in service *for* the world.

While Barth does not even hint at the possibility of primal religious forms being used by God as parables of the kingdom of heaven, in chapter 6 I take up the question of whether African traditional religions could be considered parables of God's self-revelation in Jesus Christ as an expression of Christ's ongoing prophetic activity. Barth's deeply Christocentric account of revelation in the event of reconciliation and the ongoing prophetic activity of Jesus Christ within and outside the walls of the church allow a reassessment of Barth's understanding of the category of religion and can reopen the question of revelation and culture.

As North America becomes more ethnically and religiously diverse, pluralism will only increase and expressions of the Christian faith will take on cultural forms. This process of translation will transform what it means to be "Christian" from one culture to another. Thus, as individuals seek to understand and establish their own Christian identity, these identities are constantly in flux as their culture changes and their understanding of the Christian faith changes.

SIX

Constructive Reflection

Imaginative and Prophetic

In 1990, at the Odwira Thanksgiving nondenominational service to mark the end of the weeklong Odwira festival in Akropong-Akuapem, Bediako preached a sermon titled "Christ, Our Odwira" based on two texts from Hebrews, 1:1–5 and 10:1–10. Bediako named the connection between Hebrews and Odwira in the very first line of his sermon: "It may seem to some persons that culture and tradition have nothing to do whatsoever with Christ. And yet, our Scripture reading from Hebrews shows us that our present great festival of Odwira is itself mentioned in the Bible."[1]

He obviously did not intend this provocative claim literally. The claim is based on the use of the Twi verb, *dwiraa,* in the vernacular translation of Hebrews 1:3, translated into English variously as "purgation," "forgiveness," or "purification"—as in "When he had made purification for sins" (*CiA,* 70–72). This verb is also the root of the name of the festival, Odwira. The local Akan chief Oseadeeyo Addo Dankwa III defined Odwira as "the period of purification." He said, "As human beings, we have, over the past years, committed a lot of mistakes, and as we enter this period of purification, we should ponder over our past mistakes and resolve to improve upon our behavior."[2] Significant here is the admission of wrongdoing and the possibility of future correction as connected to a time to pause, reflect, and steel oneself for future challenges during this period of purification. Through a Christian lens, one sees here elements of confession but not forgiveness; there is future resolve but without the sanctifying power of the Holy Spirit.

A local Bible study group Bediako led in Akropong brought him to connect Odwira to Hebrews. The group had been studying the Epistle to the Hebrews in Twi when "it seemed to have occurred to our group members that *Odwira* had something to do with Jesus, and that the atoning work of Jesus could be related to the traditional *Odwira* rituals and its anticipated benefits" (*CiA*, 71). For Bediako, this was a significant realization, one that now informs his interpretation of Jesus as Ancestor. He wrote, "The vernacular scriptures became the means of gaining a further insight into the traditional culture, whilst the meaning of the Scriptures was also illuminated in a new way, in relation to a vital aspect of the traditional culture" (*CiA*, 71).

This example demonstrates the interplay for Bediako between the Bible and elements of African culture. While reading Hebrews in Twi, the connection of Jesus's work, bringing about "purification for sins" (1:3), to the purification sought in the Odwira festival was readily apparent linguistically. Through the use of the mother tongue, a connection between Christ and culture was drawn. No longer could Christ's purification and Odwira be considered separately; now, by reading "ɔde n'ankasa ne ho dwiraa yɛn bɔne no" (Hebrews 1:3), the connection between Christ's purification and the Odwira festival was unavoidable.[3]

Not only did the Twi translation allow for a connection to be made between the Bible and Akan culture; this connection also had theological import for Bediako. Because the linguistic connection existed (i.e., both Christ and Akan culture present a way to offer purification) Bediako made the theological claim that this connection demonstrated God's providential provision. He used the Bible study group's conclusion to express his theological methodology and underlying conviction: "Christ had a stake in the spiritual universe of traditional religion" (*CiA*, 72). Bediako's conclusion connected his reading of Hebrews to the means of God's revelation through a traditional festival. Bediako used Hebrews to connect Jesus Christ not only to the ancestors but also to the traditional Akan festival of purification, reconciliation, and renewal that marks the end of one year and the start of the next (*CiA*, 71). He claimed the Epistle to the Hebrews for all Africans, referring to it as "OUR Epistle!" (JAC, 27). Any consideration of practicing the Christian faith in a religiously pluralistic society or of introducing the Christian faith to a previously isolated society quickly raises a number of questions, including the following: How can the gospel of Jesus Christ and a given culture interact? Does translating the gospel into cultural forms always result in syncretism? Historically, accusations of syncretism flourish in times of pluralism or whenever the prevailing religious consensus is threatened. From the early centuries of the Christian church to colonial Africa to Nazi Germany to modern-day Europe or twenty-first century America, we find allegations of syncretism against some group that is combining gospel and culture in ways we deem inappropriate.[4] In Calvin's Geneva, for instance, those who wanted to place images inside the sanctuary were labeled syncretists.[5]

If a "pure gospel" is an impossibility and God's self-revelation occurs through cultural media (human flesh, the texts of the Bible, the acts of individuals or communities, etc.), then revelation and culture, or gospel and culture, will always be intertwined. Often the nature of the interconnectedness between the gospel and human cultures is fraught with conflict. Charges of syncretism are levied when one believes that a particular theological formulation has too much culture and not enough gospel. Others may cry, "Irrelevant!," when they sense that a theological formulation is too disconnected from the people it is seeking to address.

One way of thinking about the relationship of the gospel and culture is as a continuum with the gospel on one side and culture on the other. Since the pure gospel pole is uninhabitable and the pure culture pole is undesirable for Christians, contemporary theological reflection takes place between the poles, one hopes closer to the gospel side so as to avoid the dreaded syncretism. After all, syncretism was the epithet applied to many early versions of African Christianity that made colonial Europeans nervous. Could you have Christians who played drums or danced in worship, who visited "traditional" healers, or who did not wear neckties? Many Africans learned about neckties at the same time and from the same people who taught them about Jesus Christ. Today many African men are tired of wearing neckties (and other Western and colonial trappings), but they want to hold on to Jesus Christ. So they are trying to figure out what it was they learned about Jesus Christ that was so wrapped up in Western culture that it should be thrown out with the necktie and what about Jesus is authentic revelation that should be kept and repackaged in African cultural categories.

Typically, the label of syncretism has been applied by those in power to discredit a differing or a challenging view. "Syncretism" thus often has a negative connotation. Barth barely referred to syncretism at all, and when he did it was clearly something to avoid or overcome.[6] Bediako quipped that the goal of theological reflection was "relevance without syncretism." More recently, some postcolonial theologians and others on the underside of power have sought intentionally to embrace the label of syncretism. While each case would need to be evaluated on its own, the actions of these authors raise an important question: to some degree, are all Christians syncretists? If all theology is engaged and articulated in cultural categories and a pure gospel is not possible, then all of us are mixing theology and culture and all of us are syncretists. The charge then becomes that you are more syncretistic than I am. In response to centuries of Westerners labeling African Christianity as syncretistic, Bediako replied that he believed that Western Christianity was more syncretistic than African Christianity and that Western syncretism was *worse* because Westerners did not know where their cultural convictions stopped and their theological convictions began.[*]

The flat continuum of gospel and culture, with syncretism somewhere in the middle, fails to account for real-life complexities and also treats the gospel and culture as polar opposites instead of culture as a means to convey the gospel. Our understanding of syncretism needs to be revised and rethought. For those who find cultural expressions of the gospel threatening, what if syncretism was not hurled as an insult but instead was considered as an opportunity to expand one's understanding of the gospel,[7] or even of expanding the gospel itself?

This chapter engages syncretisms near and far to assess the lenses employed to evaluate theological reflection and also to reflect critically on one's own cultural blinders. The chapter has three sections. In the first, I present Bediako's theology of ancestors as a case study of the interrelationship of revelation, religion, and culture in theological reflection. In the second section, I employ insights from Bediako and Barth to engage more deeply contemporary questions of syncretism. In the third section, I examine Bediako's and Barth's approaches to theological reflection in relation to each one's exegesis of John 1 and Hebrews 1. The overarching point I want to make is that contemporary theological reflection must be constructive. Regurgitating former theological positions in response to new questions is irrelevant. As I demonstrate the methods of Bediako and Barth below, I apply their shared emphases, Christological, contextual, and cultural, in their constructive moves. For Barth, revelation occurs *by means of* cultural media. For Bediako, revelation occurs *in and through* culture. To begin, let us examine Bediako's theology of ancestors as an example of revelation occurring in and through culture. As we will see, these are not theoretical questions but have deep repercussions in daily life.

A Theology of Ancestors: The Interrelationship of Revelation, Religion, and Culture

The most honored aspect of many African cultures, including the Akan in Ghana, is the place and role of the ancestors. Important rulers and members of a clan who have died are honored for their lives by being designated as ancestors (*CiA*, 80).[8] These ancestors are referred to as "the living dead" and form the basis of African traditional religions. According to Anthony Ephirim-Donkor, "African religion, that is, ancestor worship[,] . . . [is] the continued notion that the ancestors are intimately involved in the affairs of their posterity and therefore the need by the living to worship them in order to receive favor, blessing, and protection from the ancestors and deities."[9] Through seeking intervention in everyday affairs and the offering of food and drink in ritual libation ceremonies,[10] Africans are understood to continually "*live* with their dead."[11] These honored dead are believed to speak from beyond the grave and to influence events on earth.

For Bediako, the initial focus in African Christian thought on identity, alongside quests to situate African Christianity historically and to pursue the indigenous nature of the Christian faith in Africa through the use of mother tongue scriptures and vernacular concepts, inevitably led to the development of a theology of ancestors.[12] And more than a theology of ancestors, Bediako articulated an ancestor Christology. He wrote, "Jesus Christ is the only real and true Ancestor and Source of life for all mankind, fulfilling and transcending the benefits believed to be bestowed by lineage ancestors" (JAC, 31). Bediako was not unique in articulating an ancestor Christology.

Though different theologians used different Christological titles, Bediako saw all of them as seeking to connect African culture with the gospel of Jesus Christ. Bediako wrote, "African Christological titles like 'Eldest Brother' (H. Sawyerr), 'Ancestor,' 'Great Ancestor' (J. S. Pobee, C. Nyamiti, K. Bediako), are neither 'from below,' nor strictly 'from above;' rather they are indicative of the way the primal imagination grasps the reality of Christ in terms in which all life is essentially conceived—as spiritual" (*CiA*, 176). By asserting the "continuity of God in African experience" (*CiA*, 225), African theologians needed to interpret "the past in a way which shows that the present experience and knowledge of the grace of God in the Gospel of Jesus Christ have been truly anticipated and prefigured in the quests and the responses to the Transcendent in former times" (*CiA*, 224–25). These interpretations constitute "a theology of ancestors." Once an African identity in Jesus Christ was established, then investigating the cultural continuity backward, from the present to the past, occurred. The question for many Africans was more personal and pointed than the hypothetical questions that many Western Christians may ask aloud: What about the people who were born before Jesus lived? Or what about those who never heard of Jesus? Are they saved? While Westerners can develop theological responses to account for the salvation of Abraham, Moses, David, Ruth, and the "unreached" peoples of Papua, for Africans in the twentieth century, relatives, perhaps even grandparents, may have died before hearing European missionaries explain the gospel of Jesus Christ. What about them? And what about the famed African kings from centuries past who continue to be remembered and revered? Are they saved? Can they be saved?

Beyond these personal and individual questions, broader cultural questions loom large. The deep interconnection of the living and the dead among the Akan people (and many other African peoples) demonstrates a great deal about their understanding of human community and their culture. In particular, the Ghanaian attitude to death and funeral observances reveals much about cultural ideas of personal and group security and well-being.[13] Bediako described the relationship: "In traditional Akan understanding, the dead and the prominent dead especially—go to join the ancestors bearing messages from the living."[14] Those members of the clan who have died and who are honored for their lives by being designated as ancestors continue to live on from the other side of the grave. These "ancestors, from the realm of their continuing existence, [are held to] play a decisive role in the affairs of the society."[15] The connection between generations was understood to pass from an ancestor to his descendants. Danquah described this connection as a "spark": "For the Akan the central fact of life is not death but life, the means whereby the blood of an ancestor, the spark of the race, is generated for a descendent, bearer and vehicle of the spark."[16] The spirit of life itself is passed from generation to generation through the lineage ancestors. Though death is inevitable and the ancestors are venerated, life itself remains the focus, not fearing or embracing death.

Bediako's strong desire to integrate what he understood as the twin heritage of African Christian identity—African culture and the gospel of Jesus Christ—motivated him to address his Christian convictions to the core African religious belief in the ancestors. For him, the question was, how is belief in the ancestors continuous with belief in Jesus Christ? Bediako answered this question in two parts. In so doing, the interrelationship of the three themes that pervade his work—revelation, religion, and culture—was on full display.

First, Bediako asserted that Jesus was revealed as an ancestor of Africans and that Jesus had power over the entire spiritual world that was ordinarily attributed to lineage ancestors. Second, Bediako described how Christianity desacralized Akan cultural and political convictions. Starting from the conviction that Jesus Christ is the "*Universal* Saviour" (JAC, 230; original emphasis), Bediako wrote that there has been a "continuity of God from the pre-Christian African past into the Christian present . . . [such that African traditional religions were] . . . a vital preparation for the Gospel" (JAC, 21). This belief in Christ's universality led Bediako to claim that "Christianity is, among all religions, the most culturally translatable, hence the most truly universal, being able to be at home in every cultural context without injury to its essential character" (JAC, 32). The analysis in this chapter draws on the prior exposition of Bediako's insights about translatability, continuity, indigeneity, and the primal imagination while deepening and complicating Bediako's understandings of revelation, religion, and culture.

The African understanding of ancestors lies within, not outside, Christian theology. In Bediako's view, "all Christians in every place and time, not only need to have a past, but indeed do have a past, a pre-Christian past that connects with the present. All Christians have need of ancestors, pre-Christian ancestors!"[17] Specifically, the ancestors are the most direct link to the African heritage of African Christianity. The stories in the Bible told Africans of their spiritual ancestors, their predecessors in faith. The Old Testament in particular "validates . . . a theology of ancestors" (*CiA*, 226). At the heart of African traditional religions, the ancestors "represent a more enduring problem theologically than divinities" (*CiA*, 98). The theological issue was about mediation between God and humanity, not the existence of other gods. As noted earlier, Bediako applied his understanding of the Trinity to account for the presence of multiple "divinities" in ATRs—which he understood as a monotheistic religious system. Yet how then was the role of the ancestors to be understood? The answer to this question intersected the understanding of humanity, of divinity, and of Jesus Christ as fully divine and fully human.

Bediako approvingly quoted his fellow Ghanaian theologian Christian Baëta when he claimed that Africans "*live* with their dead."[18] Bediako also described the role and significance of ancestors to African culture, including the ruler, or chief, of the tribe. He noted that since the traditional belief attributes the well-being of society to maintaining good relations with the ancestors, the tribal rulers fulfilled the important function of serving as intermediaries between the living and the dead for the help and protection of society. Yet, truly, "in the traditional world view, royal ancestors are not 'dead,' they have simply joined their grandsires in the realm of the spirit-fathers, from where they continue to show interest and to participate in the affairs of the society through the channels of spiritual intervention by the appropriate rituals."[19] Frequently, when someone is ill or if the crops are not producing, the first explanation is that the ancestors are unhappy; the first recourse, then, is to find a way to appease them. Thus the understanding of the place and role of the ancestors in Ghanaian society cuts to the heart of cultural assumptions and the articulation of an African Christian identity.

According to Bediako, after Danquah's 1944 book, *The Akan Doctrine of God*, "no African Christian theology that took seriously its African context, could ignore ancestors . . . [since he] had virtually set the agenda for all subsequent intellectual discourse on the matter."[20] A key concern for Bediako in his understanding of African Christian identity was to prevent and counteract the experience of many African Christians of "'living at two levels,' half African and half European, but never belonging properly to either" (JAC, 23). Since many African Christians were unable to see how to integrate or reconcile their African cultural heritage with their Christian beliefs, they simply held them both simultaneously, thereby living a bifurcated existence.

Bediako laid the blame for this disjointed understanding of African Christian identity on the churches and their theology, not on individual Africans. He wrote, "Up to now, our churches have tended to . . . present the Gospel as though it was concerned with an entirely different compartment of life, unrelated to traditional religious piety" (JAC, 23). Sermons did not indicate how Jesus "saves them from the terrors and fears that [African Christians] experience in their traditional worldview" (JAC, 23). This disconnect between the African cultural and religious worldview and Christian theology and practice was precisely the problem Bediako sought to address in his theology of ancestors. His hope was that all Africans may "meet God in the Lord Jesus Christ speaking immediately to us in our particular circumstances, in a way that assures us that we can be authentic Africans and true Christians" (JAC, 23).

Questions have been posed to Bediako about his ancestor Christology in light of his claim that the ancestors do not have power. First, Robert Owusu Agyarko criticized Bediako by saying that if the ancestors do not have power, then why would Bediako want Jesus as the all-powerful incarnate son of God to be a (powerless) ancestor?[21] Second, if the ancestors are powerless, because they are *dead*—for even if they are understood as the *living dead* they are still *dead*—then why would Bediako want the resurrected and ascended Jesus Christ, who is *alive*, sitting at the right hand of the Father, to be a dead, powerless ancestor? These critics suggested leaving the ancestors alone (i.e., ignoring them), since they are merely part of the myth of ATRs, and preserving Jesus's uniqueness. There is no need to force Jesus to be an African ancestor, they say.

Yet Bediako cannot simply leave the ancestors alone. In my view, there are two reasons for his ancestor Christology, both of which derive from his understanding of culture. First, if African traditional religions are *praeparatio evangelica*, there must be seeds of Christianity within ATRs. By working backward, Bediako demonstrated the seeds of Christianity by identifying the "fruit": Jesus as Ancestor. Second, if the gospel of Jesus

Christ can be translated into any culture, then the gospel must have something to say about the cult of the ancestors. Ephirim-Donkor made the point that ancestor veneration is at the heart of ATRs.[22] As such, Bediako wanted to demonstrate the relevance of Jesus Christ to the most central belief of ATRs.

Jesus Christ is the only human being who has died who can still have an impact on earthly life. Dead persons honored as ancestors do not and indeed cannot have an impact on human events; only Christ has authority and power. Bediako is simply not willing to give mediatory power to any human being—living or dead—except Jesus Christ. He is not willing to grant lineage ancestors the power of influential spirits as in ATRs or even the role of saints in the Roman Catholic tradition.[23] Bediako challenged the African understanding of ancestral power: "If authority does not reside with the merely human, then why should it be located in the realm of the essentially *human* spirits of the ancestors? So, in the perspective of Christian ideas, ancestors too become desacralized. Authority truly belongs only to God" (*CiA*, 244). In the death, resurrection, and ascension of Jesus Christ, God has been shown to be a more powerful spirit, the Great Spirit, than the human spirits of the ancestors. Due to the close connection in African life between ancestral function and politics, particularly tribal politics, Bediako acknowledged that "the whole realm of politics is sacralised[;] ... the traditional world-view makes no sharp dichotomy between 'secular' and 'sacred' realms of existence" (*CiA*, 241). This unified understanding of the holy and the profane in African cosmologies differentiates them from Western understandings. Authority, specifically, belongs to and derives from the transcendent, spiritual realm. The spirits interceded to shape the earthly realities. "Jesus' way of dealing with political power," Bediako wrote, "represents the perfect desacralisation of all worldly power."[24] The work of Christ asserted his spiritual authority and exposes the ancestors' lack of spiritual authority.

In this way, Bediako can write that "Christianity desacralises, [yet] it does not de-spiritualise" (*CiA*, 246). Every challenge to political authority is an attack on the ancestors.[25] Bediako saw that one "of the values of an Ancestor-Christology is precisely that it helps to clarify the place and significance of 'natural' ancestors. ... Just as there exists a clear distinction between God and divinities, so also there exists a qualitative distinction between Christ as Ancestor and natural ancestors" (*CiA*, 217–18). The distinctive clarification that Bediako achieved—that Christ is a unique ancestor and that natural ancestors were merely the common memories of deceased human beings—placed him in conflict with other African understandings of ancestors, both non-Christian and Christian. Though articulating an ancestor Christology was not unique to Bediako, his formulation remains vulnerable to the critique of African Christianity of failing to regard African traditional religions on their own terms that is offered by two prominent non-Christian African philosophers, Ali Mazrui and Okot p'Bitek. Other Christian theologians, including the South African Tinyiko Sam Maluleke, contested Bediako's understanding of the ancestors. In "African Traditional Religions in Christian Mission and Christian Scholarship: Re-Opening a Debate That Never Started," Maluleke considers Bediako's approach to the ancestors overly triumphalistic, and he accused Bediako of merely viewing ATRs as preparation for Christianity.[26] Maluleke even applied p'Bitek's epithet, "intellectual smuggler," to Bediako.[27] "We must do better," Maluleke wrote. "The possibility is not only for Jesus to become the Supreme Ancestor, but he could simply join the ranks of other ancestors who are at the service of the Supreme Being in Africa."[28] Maluleke seeks to retain the place of lineage ancestors while exalting Jesus to join them.

While Maluleke criticized Bediako for replacing the cult of ancestors with Jesus Christ, for our purposes, the significance of Maluleke's critique is that he wholly agrees with Bediako that the dead have an impact on the living in African culture, though Bediako modifies the claim to indicate that the impact of the dead is through story or myth, not real power. Neither theologian sides with the initial Western viewpoint that the ancestors are demonic, as many early missionaries did. Both offer a positive assessment of African primal religions, even as Maluleke criticizes Bediako's view that ATRs are legitimate religious traditions *only* as preparation for Christianity. Both affirmed the place and value of ATRs in making significant cultural and religious contributions to the lives of Africans. Bediako's view articulates a third way of understanding African ancestors. For him, the ancestors are neither demonic and irrelevant (as in the Western view) nor deities and essential (as in many ATRs); rather the ancestors are to be honored and revered (but not worshipped) in the religious, cultural, and social lives of Africans.

Bediako appealed to scripture to explore theological and cultural insights that desacralize the ancestors and offer revelation of God in Jesus Christ. A concrete illustration is his method of reading Colossians

1:15–17: "He is the image of the invisible God, the firstborn of all creation; for in him all things in heaven and on earth were created, things visible and invisible, whether thrones or dominions or rulers or powers— all things have been created through him and for him. He himself is before all things, and in him all things hold together." For Bediako, in reading and studying this passage in the vernacular Twi version, "the potency of the New Testament world of spiritual powers does not seem to be remote at all."[29] Specifically, he is interested in the translation of the Greek word θρόνοι, translated into English as "thrones" and into Twi as "nhengua." For the Akan, the Twi-speaking people of Ghana, "'nhengua' are the sacred, ritually preserved thrones of departed royals. As royal ancestors, such departed rulers, [are] presumed [to be] still connected with the community and continuing to be concerned with the affairs of the community."[30] Most significant is Bediako's conclusion: "By using the term, *nhengua*, therefore, the Scriptures clearly declare that Jesus Christ reigns supreme over that world also, as living Ancestor there in his own right. . . . Jesus Christ has something to do with what happens in the throne room of the royal palace."[31] Bediako attributed divine authority to the choice of the word *nhengua* in Colossians and takes that usage to assert the authority of Jesus Christ as superior to Akan rulers and ancestors past, present, and future. Bediako reflected on the insight he received from the mother tongue scriptures, that "'nhengua' were created through Christ and were created for Christ, was a revolution and a new revelation!"[32] Bediako's understanding of Christ's providential role in history includes the translation of the Bible from Greek to Twi, the use of *nhengua* in Akan culture, and the mediating role of the ancestors in Akan religious life. Language— as an artifact of culture—leads Bediako to a new theological understanding, a "new revelation" of who God is. The use of the mother tongue scripture demonstrated the possibility of culture offering a new revelation of who God is: Jesus Christ is a living ancestor of all Africans.

Based on his underlying belief that the gospel of Jesus Christ is infinitely translatable, Bediako used his understanding of pre-Christendom Christianity and precolonial African traditional religion to shape a history for the Christian faith that is indigenous to Africa. This indigenous Christian faith can be expressed through mother tongue scriptures and vernacular concepts, including, significantly, a theology of ancestors. Methodologically, Bediako insists that "the cross-cultural transmission did not *bring* Christ into the local African situation. If that were to be the case, then, in African terms, Christ would be a disposable divinity, actually able to be taken, carried and brought . . . and presumably also, disposed of if not needed" (*CiA*, 226; original emphasis). For Bediako, the deeper insight was that Christ was already present in Africa—that Christ brought missionaries to Africa. The missionaries did not, indeed could not, bring Christ to Africa. The history of the spread of the Christian faith was about "divine initiative in the local situation," not the heroic efforts of European missionaries (*CiA*, 226).

The examination of Bediako's theology of ancestors demonstrates the close interrelationship of revelation, religion, and culture in his thought. For him, God's revelation in Jesus Christ is primary and occurs through the mediums of the Christian scriptures and African traditional religions and cultures. Thanks to his understanding of revelation through the translatability of the gospel, Bediako understood Christ as an ancestor and sought to alter traditional understandings of the ancestral cult by placing Christ at the center of African religious life.

Syncretisms Near and Far: Toward an Understanding of Revelation in the Twenty-First Century

For Bediako, African Christianity does not present a rupture but continuity with its primal religious past.[33] Even when Africans convert to Christianity, they do not, and in fact cannot, simply leave the primal imagination behind them. Instead, the impact of the primal religious imagination remains with them "in their being." Primal religions have shaped who Africans *are* and who Africans *will be*.[34] The identity of an African Christian is shaped by the past through the influences of pre-Christendom Christian theology and precolonial African primal religions. This twin heritage of African Christianity describes the presence of an indigenous Christianity in modern African culture.[35] As such, Bediako considered the traditional religions of Africa evangelical preparation for Christianity.

The presence of Christianity in Africa is the result of a movement of God from within African culture, not a foreign imposition from without. Such claims as these—that African Christian identity is singular and indigenous and requires reclaiming from European influences—set

Bediako in stark opposition to a leading theorist of postcolonial identity, Homi Bhabha.

On the boundaries of spaces, cultures, borders, or historical ages, Bhabha theorized that *hybridity* occurred when a past and a present come together and make something new.[36] Bhabha's theory treats African Christians as a hybrid of two distinct entities, the African and the Christian. The African is the past, the prior identity that encounters the possibility of a Christian identity and results in a hybrid African-Christian future identity. Bhabha's approach therefore assumes difference where Bediako posits similarity and continuity. For both the African past and the Christian past are part of the history and identity of Africans, says Bediako. Neither one is foreign; there is not a hybrid but a unified whole. In fact, Bediako understands the entire postcolonial trope as detrimental to African Christian theology: "In positioning oneself as postcolonial, one is handicapped to understand one's indigenous heritage."[37] By identifying oneself primarily with an "after," such as after colonialism, one risks separating oneself from more basic or elemental truths about one's being, one's identity. Bediako did not want to lose the insights of the primal imagination from the precolonial period through a too hasty jump to the post-colonial.

Bediako resisted postcoloniality, then, because he understood it as still defined by Western categories in its opposition to colonialism. He rejects the postcolonial paradigm, because he advocates an indigenous African Christian identity that is not entirely shaped, much less solely defined, by Western, European, or colonial history and ideas. Africans can encounter Jesus Christ without Western intermediaries by extricating African Christianity from the influence of Western Christianity, so that "African Christian theological scholarship will be making African Christianity less provincial but instead more truly universal!"[38] As Christianity reconnects with its primal roots and relies on the scriptures of the Old and New Testaments, a more universal and missional Christianity is revealed than the Western model of captivity to Western culture. And the implication of this possibility is nothing less than the remaking of Christian theology itself. In fact, he muses hopefully, "the present shift in the centre of gravity may have secured for Christianity a future that would otherwise be precarious in the secularized cultural environment of the modern West."[39] For Bediako, Africa may have saved Christianity itself.

His interest in articulating an indigenous understanding of Christianity where Christian identity comes from the gospel and not from cultural categories—whether colonial or post-colonial—is not limited to Africa. Bediako referred to this process as the remaking of Christian theology. He appealed to the imagery of the Peruvian theologian Gustavo Gutiérrez: African theologians need to guide people to "drink from their own wells"—prepared by God in Jesus Christ—while themselves drinking from these same wells.[40] In this way, the future of African Christian theology can move forward without losing its roots in its primal imagination. Such an identity may free African theology from any captivity to colonial or postcolonial categories toward the remaking of Christian theology for the world. In one of his earliest publications, Bediako mused, "Why worry about syncretism in Africa, but not also in the West?"[41] Bediako sought to assist Western Christians in identifying the cultural blind spots in their faith understandings.

Barth, of course, was very careful to make sure that nothing and no one impinges on the sole mediatorship of Jesus Christ. He wrote, "That He is the one Word of God means further that His truth and prophecy cannot be combined with any other, nor can He be enclosed with other words in a system superior to both Him and them" (IV/3, 101). Barth was delimiting two hypothetical possibilities that are theologically unacceptable. First, no combination or synthesis of the Word of God, Jesus Christ, and *any* other word, idea, religion, culture, and so on, is allowed. There should be no Jesus *plus* culture or religion. If this addition is attempted, then the sole witness and mediatorship of Jesus Christ is violated and the resulting combination is not Christian. Second, any attempt to place a system of thought above the Word of God, to subsume or confine Jesus Christ or rein in his ongoing prophetic activity, distorts "His truth and prophecy" and is theologically unacceptable.

In the midst of drawing these boundaries, Barth was quick to affirm God's sovereignty and the unstoppable, uncontrollable, and, for us, unpredictable ongoing prophetic activity of Jesus Christ. That the Word of God "cannot be combined with any other" truth or prophecy does not restrict the Word from revealing who God is through true words or other media. Barth continues, "As the one Word of God, He can bring Himself into the closest conjunction with such words. He can make use of certain [people], making them His witnesses and confessing their witness in such a way that to hear them is to hear Him (Luke 10:16)" (IV/3, 101). Though humans are not theologically justified in using the Word of God for their purposes, the Word of God can use human words and even humans themselves as witnesses for the Word of God. In fact, God has done this before and will do it again, for previously God "entered into a union of this kind with the biblical prophets and apostles" (IV/3, 101).

A connection can be identified between Barth's understanding of the ongoing prophetic activity of Jesus Christ and Bediako's understanding of traditional African religions as evangelical preparation for Christianity. Expressing Bediako's view in Barth's language: Jesus Christ, the Word of God, has chosen to bring himself "into the closest conjunction" with the traditions and expositors of African traditional religions. Christ makes them "His witnesses[,] . . . confessing their witness in such a way that to hear them is to hear Him" (IV/3, 101). Barth certainly never considered this application of his understanding of Christ as Prophet. And both Barth and Bediako would be quick to point out that any such revelation that would occur through ATRs would be partial and incomplete. Kofi Opoku would disagree with both theologians. As he expressed it (in relation to Bediako, but it would also apply to Barth): "Kwame was wrong about this [*praeparatio evangelica*]. In traditional religions, Kwame saw the seeds of Christianity. I see the seeds and the fruit."[42] However, Bediako and Barth share an understanding of the universality of revelation that allows for (and, in Bediako's case at least, mandates) revelation through traditional religions in Africa, and presumably elsewhere as well.

For Barth, the Word of God, Jesus Christ, cannot be prevented from speaking through anyone and anything. After his claim earlier in *Church Dogmatics*—that God could speak through a dead dog or a flute concerto—Barth clarified that no one can prevent God from entering into unions with the words of people "outside the sphere of the Bible and the Church . . . as a form of [God's] free revelation of grace" (IV/3, 101). All revelation is in, by, and about Jesus Christ. Yet revelation can come *through* a variety of media. The revelation of God in Jesus Christ, whether through true words, parables of the kingdom, or traditional religions, can, at least in principle, be understood by Barth as gifts from God to humanity, expressions of God's grace.

God is active in revelation, while humanity is receptive; God in Christ speaks through the Holy Spirit, while humans listen. However, Barth sees an inversion of the proper mode of revelation when Christians or non-Christians create syntheses between Jesus Christ as the one Word of God and any other words. These syntheses imply a control over Jesus Christ, to which none of us has any right, and which can be only the work of religious arrogance (IV/3, 101). Barth's Christocentric focus of his trinitarian theology is on full display in his insistence on the unidirectional movement of revelation from God to humanity, never from one human to another—though at times the Word of God may choose to use humans to witness to revelation. Humans, as recipients of God's self-revelation, must always be *testing* human words to see if they are pointing beyond themselves to *the* one Word of God, the Lord, the Prophet, Jesus Christ.

For Barth, the problem with Bediako's claim that humans can come to know God through traditional African religions would be the abiding connection that Bediako posited between Christianity and African traditional religions. Barth's fear would be that if Christ were constantly revealed through traditional religions, then the freedom and distinctiveness of Christ would be lost. So does Bediako's understanding of Christ's revelatory presence within African traditional religions amount to a "suspiciously loud but empty utterance," in Barth's words (IV/3, 102)? For Bediako, God intentionally used and uses traditional religions to prepare Africans for the full revelation of God in Jesus Christ as revealed through the scriptures of the Old and New Testaments. Bediako's understandings of creation, divine providence, and even history were displayed in his belief in the infinite translatability of the gospel.

Barth used the imagery of Jesus as the Light of Life to express the irrepressible nature of God's self-revelation. The Light of Life permeates all places and may use a parable of the kingdom to reveal who God is, but God's presence (and corresponding revelatory intent) does not remain within the creaturely medium indefinitely. The revelation is real and true, though partial (as it was for Bediako). For Barth, the revelation that resulted from the parables and true words is ad hoc. An illustration: in the parable of the Sower (Mark 4:1–20, Matt. 13:1–23, and Luke 8:1–15), there is nothing special about the Sower, the seed, or the soils. This ordinary event *became* a parable of the kingdom through the way that Jesus incorporated it into his teaching. The revelatory meaning in the parable lies not in the medium (the Sower, seed, or soils) but in the (true) words of Jesus Christ that reveal the Word (Logos)—God in Jesus Christ. God is not orchestrating events to create parables of the kingdom. The light of Jesus Christ shines widely on all people, just for the sake of it, without requiring a deeper significance.

For Barth, humanity cannot apprehend a pristine gospel unadulterated by human culture. The church is in the world and the world is in the church. While they can be distinguished, they cannot be separated. Barth is quite clear that in many ways the identity of Western Christians has become too cozy with Western cultural assumptions, including the exceptional view that a peculiar form of Western Christianity is best for the entire world. If one cannot identify the gospel in the life of a Christian or a Christian community, then the distinctiveness of the gospel has been lost.

The works of Bediako and Barth—in spite of their differences in theological emphases and sociocultural locations—point to the *impossibility* of apprehending a "gospel" apart from material culture. Both appealed to the incarnation of the Son of God in the person of Jesus of Nazareth as the key moment of gospel and culture coming together. Thus, though a pure gospel is not apprehensible, neither is the gospel inseparable from, or identical with, culture.

Both Bediako and Barth point to a necessary relationship between God's revelation and human cultural forms as the medium of that revelation. Is any such relationship necessarily syncretistic? If so, then all Christians are inherently syncretists. Yet such an understanding mistakes any synthesis for syncretism and ignores the complexity of the diversity of encounters between the gospel and culture, including hybridity. Simply because a theologian embraces insights from culture does not necessarily imply "theological syncretism" (*CiA*, 67). Instead, Bediako understood that "this engagement between Gospel and culture [is] inescapable. It is not possible any longer to say, 'This is culture and we cannot intermingle it with the Gospel.' What is our identity? We cannot take ourselves out of our cultures and stand in sanitized, disinfected isolation from them. At the same time, this process need not cause anxiety. It need not terrorize us, *because* the engagement between Gospel and culture is what God has been about all along."[43]

Bediako stressed the use of vernacular languages and concepts in order to engage local cultures theologically. Since the human flesh that Jesus Christ, the divine Son, assumed in the incarnation is understood to be common to all humanity—all colors, races, ethnicities, and cultures—

then the presence of Christ and the accompanying conversations about the gospel and culture cannot be foreign to any culture. That is, every culture needs to navigate these questions in their own terms and their own language. Bediako summarized his position: "In short, the challenge is that of relevance without syncretism" (*CiA*, 85).

Barth demonstrated a similar awareness in his early *Göttingen Dogmatics*. He wrote, "Of none of us is it true that we do not mix the gospel with philosophy."[44] Barth deeply understands that one's culture, or worldview as he often called it, always shapes one's readings of the gospel. All human beings are intimately affected by their worldviews and the philosophy they have imbibed. Barth understood that in God's self-revelation God always uses creaturely media. Whether the self-revelation uses scripture, humanity, or other media, the process is one of God's continual veiling and unveiling of Godself. The light of Jesus's life shines and illuminates who God is and what God has done in reconciliation. The shining light of Christ's ongoing prophetic activity brings clarity and attention to the work of God that has already been accomplished in Jesus Christ and whose grace continues to work toward God's purposes in the world.

Bediako believed that one's identity is primarily rooted in Jesus Christ. The gospel of Jesus Christ was then infinitely translatable into any and all human cultures. Barth emphasized the priority of God's self-revelation over culture. Both authors developed Christocentric theologies—including their understandings of revelation, religion, and culture—that interpret the person and work of Christ. Bediako understood Christ's universality through his divinity by articulating an understanding of Christ as Spirit that enables him to be universally revealed to African peoples as an ancestor. Barth understood Christ's universality through his resurrection by articulating how Christ's atoning work achieved universal reconciliation for humanity with God. Both theologians appeal to the Epistle to the Hebrews—Barth offered a dogmatic reading, and Bediako offered a cultural reading—to make distinctly theological claims about Jesus Christ and God's revelation. Both understood the encounter between the gospel and culture to occur in specific locations. At these moments, God's revelation intersects with religion and culture. Bediako described revelation through his concept of translatability that expresses how the gospel was contextualized in cultural forms. Barth used the imagery of light to convey how God's self-revelation flows outward toward all people. Their views on religion demonstrated an unexpected convergence as both theologians offer strong critiques of religion as human projection that seeks to displace God's revelation in Jesus Christ. Their understandings of universal revelation (for Bediako) and universal reconciliation (for Barth) highlighted Bediako's insistence on Christ's revealing presence within African culture and Barth's insistence that reconciliation must always precede revelation. For Barth, reconciliation is revelation, but revelation is not necessarily reconciliation. Revelation is a constituent part—the outward movement—of reconciliation. For Bediako, the revelation of God in Christ through African cultures and religions proclaimed the possibility of eternal life with God.

Syncretistic Exegesis

Both Bediako and Barth spent quite a bit of time and space exploring the prologue to the Gospel of John and the Epistle to the Hebrews as biblical sources for their Christological reflection. As I discuss below, Bediako's Christology is based more in Hebrews with reference to John; Barth's Christology is based more in John and then connected to Hebrews, particularly the exordium. Bediako emphasized Christ's high-priestly role and the connection of Jesus Christ to the ancestors—both Israelite and African. Barth emphasized the person of the Word of God and the incarnation of the Word as the God-man Jesus Christ.

Although both John 1 and Hebrews 1 are known for focusing more on the divine aspects of Christ than the human, Barth did not allow his understanding of the second person of the Trinity to be separated from the concrete human being, Jesus Christ. McCormack described Barth's understanding as follows: "John 1.1, then, does not refer to an eternal Word abstracted from the humanity He would assume in time but to Jesus Christ and, therefore, to a Word whose identity is given through the relation in which He stands to Jesus of Nazareth. Jesus Christ is simply called 'the Word' in v.1 because He is the Revealer, the personal address of God to those who live in darkness."[45]

More than one hundred times in *Church Dogmatics* (including eight times in IV/3, §69), Barth cited John 1:14: "And the Word became flesh and lived among us, and we have seen his glory, the glory as of a father's only son, full of grace and truth."[46] The six-page excursus in §69.3 on the history of the prophecy of Jesus Christ (IV/3, 231–37) demonstrates the importance of the Gospel of John to Barth's entire project in IV/3 and in §69 in particular. Barth wrote:

It is especially relevant that we should consider the verdict of this Gospel in the present context because the terms Word, light, revelation, speech and witness denote the specific angle from which the history of Jesus Christ is seen and recounted in this Gospel. Epigrammatically, *we might almost say that the Gospel of John is the Gospel of the Gospel itself, i.e., of the prophetic work of Jesus Christ.* (IV/3, 231; emphasis added)

Barth cited John 1:14 three times in the space of these six pages, both to emphasize the union of God with human flesh in the person of Jesus and to point to the glory (remembering here the connection Barth drew between glory and light), "full of grace and truth," that is visible in the incarnate Son. As Barth understood it, "the Johannine description points from above downwards to the human being of the eternal Son of God" (IV/2, 156). The origin of the incarnate Son and of revelation itself comes from God above.

So Barth found in the Gospel of John the very rationale for the prophetic office of Jesus Christ,[47] whereas Bediako found in Hebrews the rationale for Christ's sole mediatorship and priesthood as well as his ancestor Christology. Along the way, Barth buttressed his case using the intertwining themes of sonship and priesthood in Hebrews, while Bediako used "the early verses of John's Gospel . . . [to] insist on the primacy of Jesus' universality."[48] In many ways, their particular emphases here, while articulated and defended theologically, can also be viewed in light of their respective contexts. It is not surprising that Barth's theological exposition of the doctrine of reconciliation culminated in a presentation on Jesus as Prophet after spending a lifetime seeking to be a witness to Christ in the political arena. Neither is it surprising that Bediako's work focused on mediation (as priesthood), as much of his argument was intended as an attack on the history of the indirect communication of the gospel to Africans by Europeans and a defense of the direct communication of the gospel through its infinite translatability. As always for both, the proclamation of the gospel occurs in specific cultural settings.

Reading the Epistle to the Hebrews Theologically

Examining their engagement with the Epistle to the Hebrews reveals particular Christological elements in both Bediako's and Barth's theologies. We have seen that Bediako, in contrast to many Western missionaries, believed that a theology in and of Africa is not complete without a theology of the ancestors, a theology of the dead.[49] The late Cameroonian Catholic priest Jean-Marc Éla agreed; he argued that "there is a great need to rediscover within Christianity an African vision of humanity—which is precisely what is at stake in dealing with the cult of the ancestors . . . [since] the deep communion established among the members of a family is not broken by death."[50] Bediako's treatment of the Epistle to the Hebrews provided an exegetical exposition of the ancestors—both African and Christian—as I explore below, following an exposition of Barth's dogmatic reading of Hebrews.

Karl Barth's attention to the Epistle to the Hebrews, while not as extensive as his attention to other biblical works (he never wrote a commentary on Hebrews or even lectured on it), is nonetheless significant—particularly his use of the exordium, the opening four verses.[51] Following McCormack's insights into Barth's practice of "theological exegesis,"[52] I claim that we can discern Barth's understanding from his forty-two citations of Hebrews 1:1–4 in *Church Dogmatics*.[53] McCormack understands Barth's practice of theological exegesis to be a different type of reading from that practiced by many historical-critical scholars of the New Testament. He describes Barth's method as follows: "The task of the theologian is not simply to ask what the author of Hebrews said but to ask what the New Testament (and the Bible as a whole) have to say—a task which requires us to read *across* documents in a synthetic fashion."[54] This approach leaves Barth relatively uninterested in questions of authorial intent or reader-response criticism. His method was a narrative exegesis—treating the parts of a text as part of a larger whole—yet his focus was not on an individual book but on the whole of the biblical witness.

Barth frequently cited and commented on the Epistle to the Hebrews in his *Church Dogmatics*. Confining my analysis to IV/3, §69, Barth employed Hebrews to present Christ as a witness and apostle (IV/3, 12) who as one and the same person proclaimed his work as high priest (IV/3, 13) that destroyed (IV/3, 169) and overcame evil and death (IV/3, 238). In

Hebrews, Barth found justification for identifying Christ as prophet within the structure of the biblical witness whose power upholds all things as the one Word of God (IV/3, 195). Hebrews underlined Barth's claims about the sole revelation of God in Jesus Christ as prophet (Hebrews 1) and the sole reconciliation of Christ as priest (Hebrews 10). And, as mentioned in chapter 4, Barth appeals to Hebrews 13:8 to demonstrate that as Jesus Christ lives, both light and revelation are ongoing.

As I explore in more detail below in the examination of Hebrews and revelation, Barth connected the Christological expressions in the exordium of Hebrews with the prologue to the Gospel of John and discerned a shared focus in these two books on the divine of the God-man over the human. This scriptural connection undergirded Barth's belief in the movement of revelation from God to humanity and human cultures. God's self-revelation originates within Godself and radiates outward, enlightening the world and enkindling human understanding of God through the work of Christ on behalf of humanity. Barth harvested insights from Hebrews—particularly about Christ as prophet and priest—that he applied dogmatically in a coherent and systematic approach to Christology.

Bediako took a different tack by focusing on the cultural relevance of Hebrews to Africans, yet he also made use of Hebrews' descriptions of Jesus's divinity. As demonstrated in the opening of this chapter, Bediako employs a type of cultural exegesis to explore the themes of sacrifice, priestly mediation, and ancestral function in his exposition of Hebrews.[55]

Hebrews and Revelation

We can recognize each theologian's overall understanding of and approach to revelation by examining how he reads the Epistle to the Hebrews. In *Church Dogmatics* IV/3, §69.2, Barth explored Hebrews 1:1–4 by considering the meaning of Jesus Christ as the Light of Life and the reality of ongoing revelation. He uses the opening verses of Hebrews to demonstrate that the author of the Epistle does not anticipate any materially new revelations after the ascension of Jesus Christ. Barth wrote that "the circle of Old Testament expectation and New Testament recollection is for the author of the Epistle a closed one outside of which there cannot be considered, nor is there to be expected, any other speaking on the part of God"

(IV/3, 94). Bediako also noted in Hebrews 1:1 "the use of the past tense—'he spoke' (Twi: ɔkasa kyerɛɛ yɛn), indicating that God's speaking is complete."[56] However, Bediako goes further than Barth:

> The text does not itself make this limitation [of God's past speaking] to Jewish ancestors. It states quite simply: 'God spoke to the fathers.' The Twi here is more accurate: 'kasa kyerɛɛ agyanom.' There is a point to the text using the absolute term, 'the fathers,' rather than the interpreted and specific 'our fathers.' For the text thus leads to the recognition that the universal relevance of the revelation in Christ applies equally to the revelation given in the former times.[57]

Bediako's point was that God has spoken to all peoples "in all contexts . . . in the One who is a Son."[58] Further, since the content of God's speaking is "not a secret," we know that God spoke differently—though consistently and through Jesus Christ—to the Israelites than to Jewish Christians in the first century. A God who could speak differently in one context than in a previous one—in a separate context—can and does continue to speak today: differently in different contexts. The hermeneutical move made by the author of the Hebrews to construct a Christology as a Jewish Christian was precisely the move Bediako made.[59] Bediako intentionally constructed his Christology as an African Christian.

Barth agreed with the author of the Epistle that revelation is complete (though he would add, unfinished and ongoing) in the life, death, resurrection, and ascension of Jesus Christ, but he also claimed that Jesus continues to reveal who God is—not necessarily new aspects or attributes of who God is but the same being of God in new ways to changing cultural contexts. Barth quoted additional scriptural texts to demonstrate that God's work on earth is not finished and that Christ as Prophet continues to reveal who God is in ways that the author of the Epistle never imagined (IV/3, 94). Bediako's reasoning on this point was not as nuanced. He continued to claim that all revelation is in and through Jesus Christ. Christ continues to work through cultural forms, including traditional African religions, but these ongoing revelations are partial and incomplete. Only the revelation of God in Jesus Christ as conveyed in the scriptures of the Old and New Testaments is the full and complete revelation of God in Jesus Christ. As I explain more fully in the final section of this chapter, the main difference between Bediako and Barth regarding the ongoing nature of revelation is that Bediako posited a perpetual relationship between ATRs and revelation while Barth insisted that revelation *extra muros ecclesiae* (outside the walls of the church) was only occasional, or ad hoc. For Barth, Christ's revelatory presence does not remain within cultural media indefinitely.

Regarding the understanding of revelation articulated in the opening verses of the Epistle to the Hebrews, this comparison demonstrates that Bediako's views more closely adhere to the plain sense of the exordium read on its own terms than do Barth's. Barth read Hebrews 1 through the lens of John 1. McCormack described the connections that Barth saw: "The high Christology of the Johannine prologue does indeed find a parallel in the exordium. But it must also be conceded that Barth found in John 1 a key to the gradual unfolding of a Christology which would eventually become a material key for understanding his exegetical work even on Hebrews 1:1–4."[60] Barth's expansive understanding of Christ as prophet allows for, and truly mandates, the real revelation of who God is through Jesus Christ by the Holy Spirit in and through contemporary human cultures in true words and parables of the kingdom, in ways that the author of the Epistle never could have imagined. In an excursus, Barth appealed to Mark 10:17 ff., Mark 2:5 ff., 1 Corinthians 8:6 ff., 1 Timothy 2:5, and Romans 3:29 ff. to distinguish the one God as "the Word spoken in the existence of Jesus Christ from all others as the Word of God" (IV/3, 99). Bediako did not explore Christologically the notion of prophet that Barth offers. Bediako was much more interested in Jesus's mediatory role between God and humanity (as priest). In fact, for Bediako "the gospel"—understood in the sense of the totality of Christ's saving work—does much of the work that Barth attributes to Christ as Prophet. Whereas Bediako elucidated the infinite translatability *of the gospel*, Barth spoke of Jesus's prophecy as the Light of Life and seeks to hold together Christ's threefold office—priest, king, and prophet.

For Barth, the sole revelation of God in Jesus Christ (as expressed in the exordium of the Epistle to the Hebrews) was inextricably connected to the sole reconciliation in Jesus Christ (expressed as sacrifice and offering in Hebrews 10). The uniqueness of Christ's prophecy, witness, and proclamation was thus tied to Hebrews 10:12 and 10:14, which "speaks of the one exclusive θυσία (sacrifice) or προσφορᾷ (offering) which Christ has made for sins, which is followed by His session at the right hand of God, but by which He has perfected forever them that are sanctified through Him" (IV/3, 110). Jesus is the sole mediator of both revelation and reconciliation. Indeed, in Christ, reconciliation *is* revelation! Barth, then, does not allow Christ to be confined to one historical epoch or the pages of a human book (the Bible); Christ the Prophet continues to speak "good words . . . *extra muros ecclesiae*" (IV/3, 110), if and when God so chooses.

"God spoke to our ancestors" (Hebrews 1:1), "God has spoken to us by a Son" (Hebrews 1:2), *and* God continues to speak, as Barth expressed it: "words of genuine prophecy . . . that meet and match with the one Word of God Himself and therefore with that of His one Prophet Jesus Christ" (IV/3, 111 rev.). In spite of the completeness of the self-revelation of God in Jesus Christ through the witness of the Bible, through the "universal prophecy of Jesus Christ" (IV/3, 129), God can choose to reveal who God is in distinct and novel ways through contemporary forms. While affirming God's self-revelation outside of the Bible or the church, Barth is also preserving a kind of occasionalism. The chosen medium—whether a religion, a sunset, or a farmer sowing seeds—does not *possess* God's self-revelation. Instead, the medium is a conduit for the light of Christ's prophetic activity that shines on Christ's reconciling life. Revelation itself is an *act* of God. Revelation does not exist in a vacuum apart from Christ's ongoing prophetic activity.

While Bediako would affirm God's ongoing activity, his understanding of revelation is more static and less dynamic than Barth's. In many ways, Bediako's project was an ongoing process of trying to understand and appropriate in light of African culture the God who has been revealed in Jesus Christ. He was continually seeking to strip away Western interpretations of the scriptures of the Old and New Testaments to get a better grasp of the revelation of God that has already occurred—without looking for additional sources of revelation in contemporary cultural forms—while also binding the gospel to ATRs. In this way, Bediako was seeking to separate Jesus Christ and the gospel from Christianity as a Western religion and was consistent with the evangelical heritage of his early theological education—a heritage that generally regarded Barth's ideas on revelation with considerable skepticism.

Bediako saw tremendous possibilities in reading the Epistle to the Hebrews today: "It seems to be that the new African theology will have to attempt what the writer of the Epistle to the Hebrews did: that is, to make room, within an inherited body of tradition, for new ideas, for new realities which, though seemingly entering from the outside, come in to fulfill aspirations within the tradition, and then to alter quite significantly the basis of self-understanding within that tradition" (*CiA*, 84). Bediako viewed Hebrews as a way of reading the presence of Jesus Christ in African culture from the inside out. His starting point was within African culture and sought to understand and appropriate revelation from within culture. Bediako described his method in one of his earliest publications: "My own approach is to read the Scriptures with Akan traditional piety well in view. In this way, we can arrive at a Christology that deals with the perceived reality of the ancestors. I also make the biblical assumption that Jesus Christ is not a stranger to our heritage."[61] On the other hand, Barth began with an understanding of God's self-revelation that cannot be separated from the unique person of Jesus Christ. For him, revelation began outside culture and penetrated culture through Christ's ongoing prophetic activity. These differences in their understandings and appropriations of revelation are closely related to their Christocentric theological positions. The revelation of God is ongoing in and through the forms of material culture.

SEVEN

Collaborative Reflection

Learning, not Helping

The Christian churches must meet the challenges of globalization by
appropriating their own normative potential more radically.
                    —Jürgen Habermas, "A Conversation about God and the World"

The truth of the matter is that, after five centuries of "teaching" the world,
the global North seems to have lost the capacity to learn from the experiences
of the world. In other words, it looks as if colonialism has disabled the global
North from learning in noncolonial terms, that is, in terms that allow for the
existence of histories other than the universal history of the West.
                    —Boaventura de Sousa Santos, *Epistemologies of the South*

On April 20, 1968, Monsignor Ivan Illich addressed the Conference on
InterAmerican Student Projects (CIASP) in Cuernavaca, Mexico, by criticizing the abuse of privilege by North Americans seeking to help those
south of the border. His speech, "To Hell with Good Intentions," concluded with these words:

I am here to suggest that you voluntarily renounce exercising the power which being an American gives you. I am here to entreat you to freely, consciously and humbly give up the legal right you have to impose your benevolence on Mexico. I am here to challenge you to recognize your inability, your powerlessness and your incapacity to do the "good" which you intended to do.

I am here to entreat you to use your money, your status and your education to travel in Latin America. Come to look, come to climb our mountains, to enjoy our flowers. Come to study. But do not come to help.[1]

Illich's half-century-old remarks remain poignant today, not only in regard to Christian service and mission but for the contemporary practices of Christian theological reflection as well. During the colonial period and beyond, Western theologians have sought to "help" indigenous peoples in Africa, Asia, and Latin America with their spiritual and religious lives. This colonial approach embodied three main assumptions: (1) that Westerners knew something about God that indigenous peoples did not; (2) that Westerners believed that what they thought they knew would be "helpful" to indigenous peoples; and (3) that Westerners had nothing to learn from formerly colonized peoples who were considered primitive. This book addresses the third assumption through a careful engagement with Kwame Bediako's thought. By juxtaposing Bediako with Karl Barth, the preceding chapters have demonstrated the usefulness—and I daresay necessity—of reading Western and non-Western theologians *side by side* in the twenty-first century. Further, no one can decide what would be "helpful" for another's sociocultural context. Each person has to do that for himself or herself. This concluding chapter offers some general suggestions for the practice of theological reflection in the twenty-first century while also consolidating the findings of the previous chapters.

The Power of Listening

For anyone seeking to offer sustained theological reflection today—whether formally or informally—the most important point in this book is, *listen to voices from outside your context.* All of us must especially seek out voices from the underside of power, those seeking liberation, and those whose voices may have been (or still are) silenced by majority cultures.

For Westerners, this means listening to—and taking seriously—four types of theological voices. And hearing those voices on their own terms.

1. Voices from the Global South (like Bediako's)
2. Indigenous writers in our own countries (including Native Americans or those from Canadian First Nations)
3. Writers from currently or historically oppressed groups (African Americans, immigrants, those who are called undocumented, impoverished persons)
4. Female authors, since in many cultures women have been less respected as thinkers and authors.

This list recalls the words of Jesus in the Sermon on the Mount: "Blessed be the meek. . . . Blessed be the poor . . . for they will inherit the earth . . . for theirs is the kingdom of heaven" (Matt. 5). The works of Bediako and Barth demonstrate that the revelation of God comes in many and diverse forms. The challenge is that these contributions are not something to "try on" but to learn from. All of us must listen in the places in which God is already active, to which God has already pointed, and in which God is already speaking.

For those in the Global South, the skill of listening remains an important task. Yet how the task is carried out differs.

1. Listen to the voices of the women among you.
2. Seek out voices from other parts of the world; for example, a theologian in Ghana could seek the perspective of a Dalit theologian in India.
3. Read Western theologians and biblical commentators with a grain of salt. Certainly Westerners will be reading you that way. Glean what you can. Do not expect to accept Western assumptions that shape method and interpretive conclusions.
4. Practice the art of theological reflection in community with others, particularly with those from different sociocultural contexts.

None of these suggestions is meant to imply that those with the most privilege (i.e., those in Western culture, especially white males) are somehow incapable of insight or of being used by God. Yet there is much benefit if the privileged learn to be quiet, listen, and let others speak. In addition, all contributions from any author must be interrogated for assumptions of privilege that may have unwittingly corrupted his or her interpretations. Certainly this critique applies to the present book as well. My unending gratitude is to those from other contexts than my own (particularly Africa) who by pointing out to me my assumptions and privileged perspectives have made this a better (though by no means perfect!) book.

Setting aside my personal experiences and context, the next section harvests the insights of the preceding chapters by asking, What can be learned about contemporary theological reflection amid globalization and secularization through this juxtaposition of Kwame Bediako and Karl Barth for Westerners and Africans? Even in the phrasing of the question, I am aware of the implicit reinforcing of a problematic Western/non-Western dichotomy. While I deeply regret the colonial assumptions that this dichotomy promulgates, the need for contemporary theological reflection to be contextual requires acknowledgment of the vast differences in philosophical and cultural assumptions as well as in power and privilege that remain today as part of the colonial legacy. Truly, the learnings outlined in this book will be of the most use when individuals apply the insights gained from juxtaposing Bediako and Barth specifically in local contexts. With this disclaimer in mind, in what follows I describe what I have learned from reading Bediako and Barth together that many Westerners and Africans may likewise find useful in their own cultural and theological contexts.

Most basically, what might Africans gain by reading Bediako and Barth together? Barth offers an understanding of God's close and active presence in the world (through the incarnation) that many Africans desire. Barth, rightly understood, offers a robust understanding of the Holy Spirit and the spirit world.[2] After all, while Bediako did not speak of exorcisms, Barth recounts the exorcism of Gottheim Dibelius in §69 and titles §69.3 "Jesus Is Victor" after the demon's confession prior to departing from her.

Barth offers an account of the role of culture in revelation that allows for African Christian theologians to avoid the false dichotomy of either fully embracing or fully rejecting ATRs. Barth's parables of the kingdom and "true words" describe how some aspects of ATRs can often communicate or reveal who God is while not positing the abiding presence of

God in Jesus Christ in any particular festival or custom within ATRs. Thus, by reading Barth and Bediako together, African Christian theologians can offer a positive account of ATRs without blindly or wholly embracing all that ATRs teach. In this way, the theologies of Africa can be both *African* and *Christian*.

In a similar vein, what might Westerners gain by reading Barth and Bediako together? To begin with, in Bediako, Westerners can gain an appreciation for the primal imagination, a connection to God, one another, and the earth that is good. Second, the juxtaposition of these two authors allows us the opportunity to be self-critical about Western combinations of the gospel and culture that take the form of religion more than revelation. Third, Westerners are able to discover kinship with brothers and sisters in Africa by exploring the breadth of Christian theology—not simply the (historical) length. All told, this study provides tools for discerning and appreciating God's self-revelation in cultural forms that appreciate culture by

a. defining culture broadly by looking at the underlying factors that shape culture, not simply the cultural artifacts;
b. acknowledging the ad hoc self-revelation of God through cultural media; and
c. acknowledging God's sovereignty in revelation and human frailty, brokenness, and fallibility in accessing or receiving revelation.

The live issue remaining is the discernment of God's self-revelation amid myriad cultural forms. When one observes a potential parable of the kingdom or a true word, the first step is to turn to scripture and test the meaning of what one hears or sees against the scriptures of the Old and New Testaments. All the while, one must hold lightly the possibility of God's self-revelation. Do not look for the event to be repeated, but do look for other ad hoc situations that proclaim a similar word, meaning, or insight.

The Contemporary Context

The end of Christendom is an opportunity, not a threat. The unyoking of the Christian faith from institutions of power and prestige allows for, even necessitates, a rethinking of the Christian faith for the twenty-first century. This process of rethinking and rearticulating Christian theology—and of holding all theological convictions loosely—is necessitated by changing contexts. The times they are a'changin'. And theology must change too. This is an insight that African Christian theologians, especially Kwame Bediako, have understood deeply and that some Western theologians have struggled to grasp. Some Westerners have claimed that the methods may change, but the message never does.[3] This belief asserts that there is a pure gospel that offers a plain-sense reading of the biblical text that results in static theological claims and doctrines.

As this engagement with Bediako and Barth has demonstrated, all theology is contextual. Or, at the very least, attempts to treat theology without context or to apply theology formed in one context to another are ineffective, or worse, harmful. In the recent past, the most obvious example of the attempt to export theology was the failed colonial project. As Fanon noted, the failure of colonialism not only left the formerly colonized peoples with corrupted understandings of identity, power, and the Christian faith but also corrupted the colonizers' understandings of identity, power, and the Christian faith. The end of colonialism formally marked the demise of the global reach of Western, Christian powers while also exposing the errors and blatant sense of superiority in Western theological understanding that supported and encouraged the colonial project. The twenty-first century calls for moving through and beyond the colonial, theological categories of saved/damned, Christian/heathen, white/black, and even Western/African. For Westerners, Africa is no longer a destination for missionaries, nor are we to mine it for its theological resources. Instead, the powerful and the privileged in the West must learn with and among our African sisters and brothers as well as others in the Global South. The future of constructive theology lies not in North America, Europe, or among white peoples. Instead, the future of constructive Christian theology lies in collaborations across cultural, ethnic, economic, and gender lines.

In the near term, I believe that there is a place for marginalized groups to think theologically among themselves. But for the rich, the powerful, the privileged, there is no theological future within that safe, comfortable bubble. There are some resources in the history of Western theology (as I hope has been demonstrated by the engagement with Barth's late

Christology in this book), but they must be viewed with a hermeneutic of suspicion. The context of the production of these theologies (power, privilege, safety) has unavoidably shaped the questions asked and the answers given. As Western society has become increasingly secularized and globalized, the context of theological reflection has changed. The questions asked and the answers given must change as well. The task of this book has been to demonstrate that these changes cannot take place without engaging thinkers and ideas from other sociocultural contexts with differing values and worldviews. My hope is that other comparative studies follow after mine and continue to juxtapose Western and non-Western Christian theologies. My deeper and longer-term hope is that the stark distinction between Western and non-Western theologies will disappear. I hope that deeply contextual theologies flourish around the globe and that thoughtful engagements arise across boundaries. These engagements will allow for both cross-fertilization of new ideas and self-critical reassessment of one's own theological method and assumptions.

My fear with this proposal is that it places an unequal (and *unfair*) burden on Christians and theologians of the Global South and others who are disenfranchised throughout the world (including within powerful nations, such as the United States). In effect, my proposal says, "We Westerners need your help because of what we did to you. Now that we exploited you for our own power and wealth, help us fix our theological and identity crises." This trope is a form of continued exploitation of people of color for the sake of white theology and white privilege. Such a move must be named and avoided.

The book demonstrates the power and possibilities of reading African theologians as bona fide theologians alongside the so-called theological giants of the Western academy. While Bediako's corpus is not as comprehensive as Barth's, nor was that Bediako's goal, his significant insights on the gospel of Jesus Christ as indigenous to Africa, the primal imagination as the substructure of African Christianity, and the possibilities of revelation through culture deserve further and deeper analysis. These insights, in particular, push Barth's understanding of the interrelationship of revelation, religion, and culture in helpful ways.

Together, Bediako and Barth challenge aspects of classical theism and offer alternative proposals. They both stress God's ongoing activity in the world. They both stress that God's self-revelation is ongoing and that

God uses creaturely media to reveal who God is to the world. Some may find these media and their uses surprising—whether they be indigenous religious festivals, communism, or contemporary music, art, or film. The point here is that God can and does use creaturely forms for self-revelation and that human beings can and should be looking for the true words that God is communicating through them. Of course, as is the case with all theological claims, the identification and interpretation of these words must be tested against scripture and are provisional.

My hope is that Westerners can recognize their cultural blinders more clearly, can name them, acknowledge them, and begin to remove them. While all of God's self-revelation will be mediated through cultural forms and all theology is contextual, the ability to name, understand, and assess the cultural influences on one's own Christian theological reflection can help ameliorate the deleterious effects of coming to understand and explain the gospel of Jesus Christ from positions of power, authority, wealth, and comfort. Further, Western Christians must pause to hear Bediako's claim about the paucity of their primal imagination. Many Westerners would agree that they are not connected to the earth or to their ancestors or to the spirit world. Indeed, many Christians would claim that such connections are pagan—which is exactly Bediako's point. Is there, can there be, any possibility of Westerners recovering their primal imaginations? Honestly, I do not know, yet there seem, at the least, to be opportunities to expand Western understanding and appreciation for the primal by listening to Christians from the Global South and from marginalized communities within Western nations. A greater appreciation for the frequency of divine activity in everyday life would then help facilitate the identification of parables of the kingdom and true words that God uses to reveal Godself to humanity.

Religious Pluralism

Since virtually all Christians around the world live in societies with persons of other religious faiths or of none,[4] a Christian theology of religious pluralism is a necessity for twenty-first-century Christians. Bediako saw that Africa had much to contribute to the development of a theology of religious pluralism while "the modern West has less to offer than may be readily recognized, unless it be the lessons from the disaster that was Christendom."[5] For Africans, "pluralism is primarily a lived experience"[6] among Muslims, Christians, and practitioners of traditional religions. Thus Bediako contended that "Christian theology has not had the option, generally speaking, of establishing its categories in isolation, as though in a Christendom in which all possible religious alternatives are presumed to be non-existent, or in a secularized environment in which specifically religious claims are held to be no longer decisive."[7] African Christians have always had to consider the claims of primal religions and Islam while understanding and articulating their faith. In particular, since all Africans have been indelibly formed by the primal imagination, the primal cannot be ignored in interreligious dialogue.[8] Bediako distinguished between the context of religious pluralism and the theological agenda of a Christian identity. He wrote, for "modern African theologians, religious pluralism is their *experience*; Christian identity is the *issue*" (*CiA*, 257; original emphasis). Bediako understood early Hellenistic and African Christian theologians to have had an identical "experience" and "issue" (*CiA*, 257).[9] Pluralism is assumed; shaping a Christian identity is the theological task in response to this context.

Many Western theologians, whose social contexts are no longer homogeneously Christian but are increasingly pluralistic, have tried to maintain a prior understanding of Christian identity (and its relationship to culture) in spite of changing circumstances. The "new" religious pluralism in the West has been "normal" in Africa for centuries. African theologians have suggested other ways of pursuing contemporary theological reflection.

As a result of the context of religious pluralism, Bediako viewed Africa as "the privileged Christian laboratory for the world. . . . [T]he 'normal' African (as other non-Western) experience of religious pluralism as the framework for Christian affirmation, means that 'Christian uniqueness' or distinctiveness need not be lost in the midst of pluralism."[10] Bediako asserted the uniqueness of the Christian faith as one option among many, not as an authority ruling over others. Bediako understood the Christian faith in Africa to have preserved its uniqueness and grown exponentially while not seeking religious hegemony. For Bediako, "a Christian theology of religious pluralism becomes an exercise in spirituality, in which one affirms a commitment to the ultimacy of Christ, whilst accepting the integrity of other faiths and those who profess them."[11] He understood a theology of religious pluralism to entail dual, simultaneous affirmations: the uniqueness of Jesus Christ and the integrity of other faiths. These affirmations were to be maintained "in Christ-like humility and vulnerability."[12]

African theologians who were trained in the West were "forced by the very demands of Africa's religious pluralism, to move into areas of theological activity for which no Western syllabus prepared them" (*CiA*, 258), according to Bediako.[13] Their theological activities attested to what Bediako has claimed on a number of occasions—that Africa is a Christian theological "laboratory for the world" (*CiA*, 252).[14] More generally, Bediako claimed that the recent history and present realities of Christianity in Africa allowed for "experiments" that are instructive for the wider world and for the future of Christianity. Bediako's central contention was that the setting of Christianity in Africa has always been religiously pluralistic: "Long before pluralism—religious as well as cultural—became a subject of serious discussion in the Western world, many of the Christian communities of Africa had been living, witnessing and learning to survive and grow in the context of religious pluralism" (*TI*, 433). From the beginning "in modern Africa, the Christian churches have had to learn to evangelize, grow and affirm that Jesus Christ is Lord in the midst of other religious options, notably the pervasive spiritualities of both the indigenous primal religions and Islam."[15] The Kenyan theologian John Mbiti acknowledges that this process of shaping a new identity for African Christianity can be messy as theologians from the Global South "must be free to hatch their own heresies and theological errors, for often it is only in response to heresies and errors that sound theological orthodoxy is generated."[16] The work of African theologians in shaping a distinctive Christian identity in religiously pluralistic societies can be a guide to Western theologians facing a similar task. To do so, however, Bediako claims that Western theology must be fundamentally remade. Contemporary theological reflection must adopt the posture of learners, not of helpers.

These differences manifest themselves in interesting ways as Bediako and Barth engage questions of religious pluralism—a context that Bediako lived amid and with which he was very familiar and one that Barth treated more theoretically.

My hope is that Africans can see that there are theological lessons to be gained from Western theologians. Yet, as a Western theologian myself, I hesitate to prescribe what lessons Africans might learn from Barth. Instead, by expositing Barth in juxtaposition to Bediako, I hope to have demonstrated and laid bare aspects of Barth's thought that I think *might* be helpful in a contemporary African situation. Any assessment or implementation of those potential resources is for the reader to decide, not me. In spite of the lack of engagement with the primal imagination and the corrupting influence of colonialism and neocolonialism, I contend that there are aspects of Western theology that demonstrate faithful interpretations of scripture. Some of these nuggets are well worth claiming and employing in the task of articulating Christian theological responses to contemporary African situations going forward.

Good theological reflection cannot be done in a vacuum—particularly when that vacuum was achieved by intentionally, systemically excluding rival or discordant voices. For those with privilege, listening to theologians from the majority world and those on the underside of power is essential. Listening is the first step toward radically altering theological convictions that have appropriated divine authority toward abusive or prejudicial ends. Over the past five hundred years, the social consequences of Western Christian theological beliefs have been decidedly mixed. Alongside all the good works done in the name of the gospel are stacked the horrors of the transatlantic slave trade, the Holocaust, the Rwandan genocide, and other atrocities supported and endorsed by Christian theologians and the church. For non-Western theologians, particularly postcolonial theologians who know the temptation of replacing Western cultural hegemony with another, "better" system, a goal can be to make use of Western theological insights without rejecting the entire Western project.

If such deep listening and learning can occur, such that the Western agenda can be interrogated and laid aside and the anti-Western rhetoric of some postcolonial theology can be suspended, there exists the possibility of true dialogue within world Christianity. Indeed, the goal would be dialogue, not a monolithic, global theology. Such dialogue would allow for the exchange of ideas in order to better interpret biblical texts and encourage the development of local, indigenous theologies that are not isolated but in conversation with other contextual theologies around the world. One of the results of globalization is that peoples in distant geographic locations may be facing similar theological challenges, including varieties of secularization. Globalization also brings the opportunities for Christians in distant lands to share their responses to these contemporary challenges. In this way, Barth can be read as a theologian within world Christianity. Most certainly, not as first among equals, but as *a* voice, indeed as a witness pointing to Jesus Christ, from a particular sociocultural moment in human history—a voice who *may* be considered because a given theologian finds Barth's insights helpful for her project, not a voice who *must* be considered because others have venerated Barth in the past. And for Bediako, there is a similar opportunity to be read alongside other theologians of the past who have shaped the course of Christian theology.

The most significant adjustment would be one of orientation. In a pluralistic culture, the church will need to focus itself outward, to be sent out, as Jesus commanded his followers in Luke 10, to be, in the words of Dietrich Bonhoeffer, a "church for others" in a "world come of age."[17] Through presence, service, and humility, the Christian churches can begin to truly communicate with those outside their bounds.

Some may feel that this call for collaboration makes the task of contemporary theological reflection impossible. A single theologian cannot possibly be conversant with the ever-increasing variety of theological perspectives, some might object. In response, I would submit that anyone asking these questions is already missing the point. There is an assumption underlying these questions that there is *one* right way to do contemporary theological reflection or *one* set of *right* conclusions. Instead, the claim of this book is that there are some principles that should be kept in mind for contemporary theological reflection but that these principles are not a checklist. I think of these five elements more like the Chalcedonian Definition than the Nicene Creed. The creed offers a list of beliefs to assent to: belief in one God, one Lord Jesus Christ, begotten, not made, being of one substance with the Father, and so on. The achievement in 325 CE was unanimity of belief. The resulting choice for theologians was conformity or heresy. Today, we all must choose what to believe. Returning to the root meaning of heresy in Greek, *heresis*, meaning "to choose," we are *all* heretics.[18] Contemporary theological reflection requires guidance as those choices are made, not instructions. In contrast to Nicaea, the Chalcedonian Definition offers boundaries within which belief can flourish. The definition is known for its four adverbs when it confesses "one and the same Christ, Son, Lord, only begotten, recognized in two natures, without confusion, without change, without division, without separation." While certain Christological understandings are ruled out of bounds, at the same time space has been created for a range of theological interpretations.

My hope is that these five elements culled from the theological legacies of Bediako and Barth—the Christological, contextual, cultural, constructive, and collaborative—form a similar space for contemporary theological reflection. Admittedly, this space is larger than the one intended at Chalcedon. Strong disagreements over method and doctrine are likely within this space. The boundaries themselves are porous, not fixed. The porous boundaries allow for listening and collaboration among those currently within the bounds of contemporary theological reflection and those outside. This call for contemporary theological reflection to be collaborative is not only possible but necessary if contemporary theological reflection is to remain vibrant and outward looking.

NOTES

1. See Lactantius, "On the Deaths of the Persecutors," 44.5, in *Fathers of the Third and Fourth Centuries*, vol. 7, *The Ante-Nicene Fathers* (Buffalo, NY: Christian Literature Company, 1886; Peabody, MA: Hendrickson, 1999), 301–22; Eusebius, "Life of Constantine," in *Eusebius: Church History, Life of Constantine the Great, and Oration in Praise of Constantine*, vol. 1, *The Nicene and Post-Nicene Fathers*, 2nd ser. (New York: Christian Literature Company, 1890; Peabody, MA: Hendrickson Publishers, 1999), 405–610.

2. See, e.g., Andrew Porter, *Religion versus Empire? British Protestant Missionaries and Overseas Expansion, 1700–1914* (Manchester: Manchester University Press, 2004), esp. 91–115.

3. Andrew F. Walls, "Kwame Bediako and Christian Scholarship in Africa," *International Bulletin of Missionary Research* 32.4 (October 2008): 192.

ONE. A Crisis of (Shifting) Authority

1. When in secondary school in Cape Coast at the Mfantsipim School, Bediako's classmates referred to him as "Joe Noir"—the quintessential black man ("Call to Glory," funeral program for Kwame Bediako, July 2008, 3).

2. The first use of *négritude* in print appeared in 1939 in Aimé Césaire's *Notebook of a Return to My Native Land = Cahier d'un retour au pays natal*, trans. Mireille Rosello and Annie Pritchard (Newcastle upon Tyne: Bloodaxe Books, 1995). Négritude derives from the French *nègre*. The term is a neologism, made up by Césaire as part of "a family of words based on what he considered to be

the most insulting way to refer to a black. . . . It signified a response to the centuries-old problem of the alienated position of the blacks in history, and implicitly called upon blacks to reject assimilation and cultivate consciousness of their own racial qualities and heritage. For Césaire, identity in suffering, not genetic material, determined the bond among black people of different origins" (Translator's footnote in Aimé Césaire, *Notebook of a Return to the Native Land*, trans. and ed. Clayton Eshleman and Annette Smith [Middletown, CT: Wesleyan University Press, 2001], 60).

3. Kwame Bediako and Gillian Mary Bediako, "'Ebenezer, This is how far the Lord has helped us': Reflections on the Institutional Itinerary of the Akrofi-Christaller Memorial Centre for Mission Research and Applied Theology (1974–2005)" (Unpublished handbook, Akropong-Akuapem: ACI, 2005), 4.

4. Hans Visser and Gillian M. Bediako, Introduction to *Jesus and the Gospel in Africa* (Oxford: Regnum, 2000), xi–xii.

5. Kwame Bediako, "Worship as Vital Participation: Some Personal Reflections on Ministry in the African Church," *Journal of African Christian Thought* [hereafter *JACT*] 8.2 (2005): 4.

6. Kwame Bediako, "Andrew F. Walls as Mentor," in *Understanding World Christianity: The Vision and Work of Andrew F. Walls*, ed. William R. Burrows, Mark R. Gornik, and Janice A. McLean (Maryknoll, NY: Orbis, 2011), 8.

7. The source of this phrase is Geoffrey Parrinder's claim, "Africans have been called incurably religious," in *Religion in Africa* (Harmondsworth: Penguin Books, 1969), 235. Parrinder's viewpoint has been strenuously contested. See Jan Platvoet and Henk van Rinsum, "Is Africa Incurably Religious? Confessing and Contesting an Invention," *Exchange* 32.2 (2003): 123–53; Kehinde Olabimtan, "'Is Africa Incurably Religious?' II: A Response to Jan Platvoet and Henk van Rinsum," *Exchange* 32.4 (2003): 322–39. When he wrote his response, Olabimtan was on the staff of the Akrofi-Christaller Centre, where Bediako was the founder and director.

8. Bediako and Bediako, "'Ebenezer,'" 4.

9. For more on Bediako, see two books that were released too recently to be engaged here: Bernhard Dinkelaker, *How Is Jesus Christ Lord? Reading Kwame Bediako from a Postcolonial and Intercontextual Perspective* (Bern: Peter Lang, 2017); Sara Fretheim, *Kwame Bediako and African Christian Scholarship: Emerging Religious Discourse in Twentieth-Century Ghana* (Eugene, OR: Pickwick Publications, 2018).

10. Karl Barth, "Evangelical Theology in the 19th Century," in *Humanity of God* (Louisville, KY: Westminster John Knox Press, 1960), 14. Translated from Karl Barth, "Evangelische Theologie im 19. Jahrhundert," *Theologische Studien*, Heft 49 (Evangelischer Verlag, Zollikon-Zurich, 1957), 6.

11. For an excellent and detailed description of *Kulturprotestantismus*, see Gangolf Hübinger, *Kulturprotestantismus und Politik: Zum Verhältnis von Liberalismus und Protestantismus im Wilhelminischen Deutschland* (Tübingen: J. C. B. Mohr, 1994).

12. Martin Rumscheidt, Foreword to *Fragments Grave and Gay*, by Karl Barth (London: Fontana, 1971), 1. When informed of the pope's comment, Barth quipped, "This proves the infallibility of the Pope." See "Witness to an Ancient Truth," *Time* 79.16 (April 20, 1962): 61–69.

13. The polemics that Bediako and Barth present against nineteenth-century Protestantism may not measure up to reality. For more balanced accounts of liberal Protestantism, see Claude Welch, *Protestant Thought in the Nineteenth Century*, 2 vols. (New Haven, CT: Yale University Press, 1972); Bernard M. G. Reardon, *Liberal Protestantism* (Stanford, CA: Stanford University Press, 1968); Gary J. Dorrien, *Kantian Reason and Hegelian Spirit: The Idealistic Logic of Modern Theology* (Oxford: Wiley-Blackwell, 2012), esp. "Idealism as White Supremacist Ordering," 542 ff.

14. John Lardas Modern, *Secularism in Antebellum America* (Chicago: University of Chicago Press, 2011), 3.

15. "America's Changing Religious Landscape," Pew Research Center, May 12, 2015, www.pewforum.org/2015/05/12/americas-changing-religious-landscape/.

16. After advancing the secularization theory in his book *The Sacred Canopy: Elements of a Sociological Theory of Religion* (New York: Anchor Books, 1990), Peter Berger later retracted his thesis that humanity was abandoning religion in favor of secularity. José Casanova initially followed Berger's lead in his *Public Religions in the Modern World* (Chicago: University of Chicago Press, 1994) but revised those claims a decade later and has helpfully pointed toward aspects of globalization missing from discussions of secularization. Charles Taylor's massive tome, *A Secular Age* (Cambridge, MA: Belknap Press of Harvard University Press, 2007), sought to demonstrate the conditions for belief in the early twentieth century. Two additional significant voices in conversations about secularization are Sara Mahmood (*Religious Difference in a Secular Age: A Minority Report* [Princeton, NJ: Princeton University Press, 2016]) and Talal Asad (*Formations of the Secular* [Stanford, CA: Stanford University Press, 2003]).

17. Louise Bennett, *Selected Poems* (Kingston, Jamaica: Sangster's Book Stores, 1982), 107.

18. See Robert P. Jones, *The End of White Christian America* (New York: Simon & Schuster, 2016).

19. See Sandra L. Colby and Jennifer M. Ortman, "Projections of the Size and Composition of the U.S. Population: 2014 to 2060," Current Population Reports, P25-1143, U.S. Census Bureau, Washington, DC, 2014; "America's Changing Religious Landscape."

20. Robert Stam and Ella Shohat, "Whence and Whither Postcolonial Theory?," *New Literary History* 43 (2012): 379.

21. Ibid.

22. Marcel Gauchet, *The Disenchantment of the World: A Political History of Religion*, trans. Oscar Burge (Princeton, NJ: Princeton University Press, 1997), 4; original emphasis.

23. Berger, *The Sacred Canopy*, 113.

24. Berger traces the rise of secularization from its roots in Israelite religion through formation of the Christian church and the Protestant Reformation (which he calls "a historically decisive prelude to secularization") to reach his conclusion about the current condition of Christianity in the West. See Berger, *The Sacred Canopy*, 123. Casanova makes a similar claim in his *Public Religions in the Modern World*, 11–39.

25. James Davison Hunter, *American Evangelicalism: Conservative Religion and the Quandary of Modernity* (New Brunswick, NJ: Rutgers University Press, 1983), 16.

26. For more on attempts to preserve the political status quo in political discourse in the United States, see Jones, *The End of White Christian America*.

27. Berger, *The Sacred Canopy*, 145, 138; original emphasis.

28. Ibid., 160.

29. James Davison Hunter, "The Culture War and the Sacred/Secular Divide: The Problem of Pluralism and Weak Hegemony," *Social Research* 76.4 (Winter 2009): 1309.

30. Ibid., 1318.

31. Berger, *The Sacred Canopy*, 27.

32. Taylor, *A Secular Age*, 3.

33. Ibid.

34. Ibid., 20.

35. Ibid., 13.

36. Karl Barth, *Das Evangelium in der Gegenwart* (Munich: Chr. Kaiser Verlag, 1935), 33–34. Quoted by Eberhard Busch in *The Great Passion: An Introduction to Karl Barth's Theology* (Grand Rapids, MI: Eerdmans, 2004), 170; Barth's emphasis.

37. The very yoking of religious power and influence to official, state power began the confusion between the "secular" and the "religious" that later led to the need to disambiguate the two. In this way, Casanova's first definition of secularization as the "differentiation and emancipation of the secular spheres from religious institutions and norms [that] remains a general modern structural trend" is essentially a premodern (and pre-Christendom) trend as well (*Public Religions in the Modern World*, 212). Clearer demarcation in institutions and norms is a welcome development for contemporary theological reflection.

38. Casanova, *Public Religions in the Modern World*, 25–35.

39. The decline of religious beliefs and practices has certainly occurred in Western Europe but *not* in the developing world. In the United States, while there has been a decline in formal participation in religious institutions, there also has been a dramatic rise in those who identify with the phrase "spiritual, but not religious." The United States continues to confound secularization theorists as a modernized nation that has remained deeply religious.

40. Taylor, *A Secular Age*, 12.

41. Following Berger's insight, since we all must choose whether or not to believe and also what to believe, we are all twenty-first-century heretics. See Peter L. Berger, *The Heretical Imperative: Contemporary Possibilities of Religious Affirmation* (Garden City, NY: Anchor Press, 1979).

42. Taylor, *A Secular Age*, 304.

43. Philip Rieff, *Triumph of the Therapeutic: Uses of Faith after Freud* (Chicago: University of Chicago Press, 1987), 5.

44. Ibid.

45. Philip Rieff, "Reflections on Psychological Man in America," in Philip Rieff, *The Feeling Intellect: Selected Writings*, ed. Jonathan Imber (Chicago: University of Chicago Press, 1990), 7.

46. Robert Bellah et al., *Habits of the Heart: Individualism and Commitment in American Life* (Berkeley, CA: University of California Press, [1985] 2007), 221.

47. Rieff, *Triumph of the Therapeutic*, 25.

48. Ibid.

49. Ibid., 56.

50. Ibid., 245.

51. Ibid., 22.

52. Rieff writes, "In the religious period, the symptom was called sin, and the neurotic, a sinner, self-convicted. The task of the clergy was to make the sinner hopefully aware of his sin; the task of the analyst is to make the neurotic therapeutically aware of his neurosis." Philip Rieff, "The American Transference: From Calvin to Freud," in *The Feeling Intellect*, 13.

53. Ibid.

54. Rieff, *Triumph of the Therapeutic*, 242.

55. Rieff, "The Evangelist Strategy," in *The Feeling Intellect*, 126.

56. For a theological analysis of one such case, see Tim Hartman, "Lost in Translation: Postcolonial Reflections on 'The Panare Killed Jesus Christ,'" *Cross Currents* 63.3 (September 2013): 328–49.

57. Rieff, *Triumph of the Therapeutic*, 16.

58. James Davison Hunter, *Evangelicalism: The Coming Generation* (Chicago: University of Chicago Press, 1987), 211.

59. Berger, *The Sacred Canopy*, 153.

60. For an important exception to this claim, see Joerg Rieger, *Globalization and Theology* (Nashville, TN: Abingdon, 2010).

61. Thomas Friedman, *The World Is Flat: A Brief History of the Twenty-First Century*, updated and expanded ed. (New York: Farrar, Straus and Giroux, 2007), 8.

62. Roland Robertson, *Globalization: Social Theory and Global Culture* (London: Sage, 1992), 7.

63. Paul Jay, *Global Matters* (Ithaca, NY: Cornell University Press, 2010), 50.

64. Ibid., 38.

65. Robertson, *Globalization*, 25–31.

66. Jay, *Global Matters*, 39.

67. Amartya Sen, "How to Judge Globalism," *American Prospect* 13.1 (Winter 2002): A4.

68. James Ferguson describes Africa as "an inconvenient case" for globalization theorists, since it does not fit the story line for either proponents or opponents of globalization. Instead, "the recent history of Africa does pose a profound challenge to ideas of global economic and political convergence." Just as the vast continent of Africa defies the generalizing theories of globalization, the same is true theologically. Even when the numerical shift of the center of gravity of world Christianity is identified, the theological contributions are left unexplored. See James Ferguson, *Global Shadows: Africa in the Neoliberal World Order* (Durham, NC: Duke University Press, 2006), 26, 28.

69. "Global Christianity—A Report on the Size and Distribution of the World's Christian Population," Pew Research Center, December 19, 2011, www .pewforum.org/2011/12/19/global-christianity-exec/.

70. David Barrett, "AD 2000: 350 Million Christians in Africa," *International Review of Mission* 59.233 (January 1970): 49–50.

71. Andrew F. Walls, "The Gospel as Prisoner and Liberator of Culture," in *The Missionary Movement in Christian History: Studies in the Transmission of Faith* (Maryknoll, NY: Orbis Books, 1996), 6. Walls first wrote about this change of the center of gravity in Christianity in 1971 in an article published as "Towards Understanding Africa's Place in Christian History," in *Religion in a Pluralistic Society*, ed. J. S. Pobee (Leiden: Brill, 1976), 180–89. See Kwame Bediako, "The Willowbank Consultation, January 1978—A Personal Reflection," *Themelios* 5.2 (January 1980): 26 n. 6.

72. Walls, "The Gospel as Prisoner and Liberator of Culture," 9.

73. Ibid., 10.

74. Kwame Bediako, "'In the Bible . . . Africa walks on familiar ground': Why the World Needs Africa," *AICMAR Bulletin* 6 (2007): 38.

75. Philip Jenkins, *The Next Christendom: The Rise of Global Christianity* (New York: Oxford University Press, 2002).

76. Ibid., 220.

77. Philip Jenkins, *The New Faces of Christianity: Believing the Bible in the Global South* (New York: Oxford University Press, 2006).

78. Barrett, "AD 2000," 50.

79. Kwame Bediako, "'Why has the summer ended and we are not saved?': Encountering the Real Challenge of Christian Engagement in Primal Contexts," *JACT* 11.2 (2008): 5.

80. E.g., Kwame Bediako, "Islam and the Kingdom of God," *JACT* 7.2 (2004): 3–7; Kwame Bediako, "Africa and Christianity on the Threshold of the Third Millennium: The Religious Dimension," *African Affairs* 99 (2000): 316.

81. Of no minor significance here is that Bediako published these words six years before Jenkins's *The Next Christendom*.

82. Bediako insisted on the integrity of "the primal imagination" in his understanding of Christianity (*CiA*, 92). He borrowed the term from C. G. Baëta's *Christianity in Tropical Africa* (Oxford: Oxford University Press, 1968). For Bediako, primal imagination was understood as an outlook of "a spiritual universe which was both simple and complex, and yet ... able to [be] embraced as a totality" (*CiA*, 92). Further, the maintenance of the primal imagination must derive from African traditional religions (ATRs); it cannot be imposed from without. "A starting point for appreciating the primal imagination," wrote Bediako, "must be in primal religions themselves" (*CiA*, 93). Bediako sees the primal imagination as the core of what is distinctive about African Christianity. The term "primal" had no pejorative meaning whatsoever for him.

83. Bediako, "'Why has the summer ended and we are not saved?,'" 5–6.

84. Barth, "Evangelical Theology in the 19th Century," 14.

85. José Casanova, "The Secular, Secularizations, Secularisms," in *Rethinking Secularism*, ed. Craig Calhoun, Mark Juergensmeyer, and Jonathan van Antwerpen (New York: Oxford University Press, 2011), 72.

86. See Casanova, *Public Religions in the Modern World*, 10; and his reassessment of his earlier argument in José Casanova, "Public Religions Revisited," in *Religion: Beyond a Concept*, ed. Hent de Vries (New York: Fordham University Press, 2008), 102.

87. Casanova, "Public Religions Revisited," 104.

88. Sara Mahmood, "Can Secularism Be Other-Wise?," in *Varieties of Secularism in a Secular Age*, ed. Michael Warner, Jonathan Van Antwerpen, and Craig Calhoun (Cambridge, MA: Harvard University Press, 2010), 288.

89. More recently, globalization and religion have begun to be considered together. See Peter Beyer and Lori Beaman, eds., *Religion, Globalization, and Culture* (Leiden: Brill, 2007); Jennifer Reid, ed., *Religion, Postcolonialism, and Globalization: A Sourcebook* (New York: Bloomsbury Academic, 2015).

90. Beyer and Beaman, *Religion, Globalization, and Culture*, 1.

91. George Van Pelt Campbell, "Religion and Phases of Globalization," in Beyer and Beaman, *Religion, Globalization, and Culture*, 282.

92. Roland Robertson, "Global Millennialism: A Postmortem on Secularization," in Beyer and Beaman, *Religion, Globalization, and Culture*, 9.

93. For more on this type of negotiation in one region, see Afe Adogame, "Sub-Saharan Africa," in Beyer and Beaman, *Religion, Globalization, and Culture*, 527–48.

94. José Casanova, "Rethinking Secularization: A Global Comparative Perspective," *Hedgehog Review* 8.1–2 (Spring–Summer 2006): 17.

95. Ibid., 19.

96. John Mbiti, "Theological Impotence and the Universality of the Church," in *Mission Trends No. 3: Third World Theologies*, ed. Gerald Anderson and Thomas Stransky (Grand Rapids, MI: Eerdmans, 1976), 17.

97. Hunter, "The Culture War and the Sacred/Secular Divide," 1311.

98. The social technology theorist Clay Shirky, "Monkeys with Internet Access: Sharing, Human Nature, and Digital Data," paper presented at SXSW (South by Southwest), Austin, TX, March 14, 2010, available at www.shirky.com/weblog/2010/04/the-collapse-of-complex-business-models/, accessed September 1, 2018; and in Clay Shirky, *Cognitive Surplus: Creativity and Generosity in a Connected Age* (New York: Penguin Press, 2010).

99. James Davison Hunter, *To Change the World: The Irony, Tragedy, and Possibility of Christianity in the Late Modern World* (New York: Oxford University Press, 2010), 201–2.

100. Rieff, "The Evangelist Strategy," 124.

101. Hunter, *To Change the World*, 202–3.

102. Roger Finke, "Innovative Returns to Tradition: Using Core Teachings as the Foundation for Innovative Accommodation," *Journal for the Scientific Study of Religion* 43.1 (March 2004): 31.

103. For more on this understanding of translation and the Christian faith, see the work of Lamin Sanneh, esp. *Translating the Message: The Missionary Impact on Culture* (Maryknoll, NY: Orbis, [1989] 2009).

104. Kwame Bediako, "New Paradigms on Ecumenical Co-operation: An African Perspective," *International Review of Mission* (July 1992): 376.

105. Kwame Bediako, "Conclusion: The Emergence of World Christianity and the Remaking of Theology," in *Understanding World Christianity: The Vision and Work of Andrew F. Walls*, edited by William R. Burrows, Mark R. Gornik, and Janice A. McLean (Maryknoll, NY: Orbis, 2011), 248.

106. The presence of a vibrant and growing African Christianity gave Bediako the confidence to claim in his last major lecture in July 2007 that "in the present situation, it becomes less helpful to speak of a 'global Christianity' whereby,

presuming a contest for 'global' hegemony, the new centres of Christian vitality are represented as 'the next Christendom'—a relocation of power from Western churches, and therefore a global threat to the West (pace Jenkins's *Next Christendom*)." Kwame Bediako, "Conclusion: The Emergence of World Christianity and the Remaking of Theology," 248.

107. Bediako, "The Willowbank Consultation," 32.

108. Kwame Bediako, "Reading Signs of the Kingdom," Stone Lecture No. 1, Princeton Theological Seminary, Princeton, NJ, October 20, 2003.

109. Ibid.

110. Kwame Bediako, "A New Era in Christian History—African Christianity as Representative Christianity: Some Implications for Theological Education and Scholarship," *JACT* 9.1 (2006): 4.

111. Émile Durkheim's *The Elementary Forms of Religious Life* was first published in 1912. For more on the history of the connection between Christianity and colonization in Africa, see David Chidester, *Savage Systems: Colonialism and Comparative Religion in Southern Africa* (Charlottesville: University Press of Virginia, 1996).

112. Karl Barth, "Christianity or Religion?," in *Fragments Grave and Gay* (London: Fontana, 1971), 30–31.

113. Karl Barth, "No Boring Theology! A Letter from Karl Barth," *South East Asian Journal of Theology* 11 (Autumn 1969): 4–5.

114. See Mark Gornik, *Word Made Global: Stories of African Christianity in New York City* (Grand Rapids, MI: Eerdmans, 2011); Jacob K. Olupona and Regina Gemignani, *African Immigrant Religions in America* (New York: New York University Press, 2007); Soong-Chan Rah, *The Next Evangelicalism: Freeing the Church from Western Cultural Captivity* (Grand Rapids, MI: InterVarsity Press, 2009).

115. I follow William Stacy Johnson here in understanding Barth as "postmodern." See William Stacy Johnson, *The Mystery of God: Karl Barth and the Postmodern Foundations of Theology* (Louisville, KY: Westminster John Knox, 1997), esp. 184–91. Interestingly, this book is one of the few on Barth in the library of the Akrofi-Christaller Institute. See also Robert Jenson's comment, "Indeed, if there is such a thing as 'postmodernism,' Barth is its only major theological representative so far, for his work is an attempt not only to transcend the Enlightenment but to transcend nineteenth century Protestantism's way of doing the same." Robert Jenson, "Karl Barth," in *Modern Theologians: An Introduction to Christian Theology in the Twentieth Century*, 2nd ed., ed. David F. Ford (Oxford: Blackwell, 1997), 22. Similarly, Graham Ward sees Barth's thinking as pointing "the way towards a postmodern theology of the Word." See his *Barth, Derrida and the Language of Theology* (Cambridge: Cambridge University Press, 1995). For a contrasting view, see Bruce McCormack, "Revelation and History in Transfoundationalist

Perspective: Karl Barth's Theological Epistemology in Conversation with a Schleiermachian Tradition," in *Orthodox and Modern: Studies in the Theology of Karl Barth* (Grand Rapids, MI: Baker Academic, 2008), 21–40.

116. For this imagery, see Bill Ashcroft, Gareth Griffiths, and Helen Tiffin, *The Empire Writes Back: Theory and Practice in Post-Colonial Literature* (London: Routledge, 1989).

TWO. Transcultural Theology through Juxtaposition

1. Andreas Riis, autobiographical account, September 16, 1827. Cited in Brigit Hepprich, *Pitfalls of Trained Incapacity: The Unintended Effects of Integral Missionary Training in the Basel Mission on Its Early Work in Ghana (1828–1840)* (Eugene, OR: Pickwick Publications, 2016), 238.

2. C. G. Blumhardt was the first inspector of the seminary, serving from 1816 to 1838. See Noel Smith, *The Presbyterian Church of Ghana, 1835–1960: A Younger Church in a Changing Society* (Accra: Ghana Universities Press, 1966), 35.

3. Smith, *The Presbyterian Church of Ghana*, 21.

4. Jon Miller, *Missionary Zeal and Institutional Control: Organizational Contradictions in the Basel Mission on the Gold Coast, 1828–1917* (Grand Rapids, MI: Eerdmans, 2003), 14.

5. Yaw Danso, *The Basel Mission in Anum 1863–1918* (Osu, Ghana: Heritage Publications, 2013), 8.

6. Miller, *Missionary Zeal and Institutional Control*, 15.

7. Andreas Riis, letter of December 2, 1832; cited in Seth Quartey, *Missionary Practices on the Gold Coast, 1832–1895: Discourse, Gaze and Gender in the Basel Mission in Pre-Colonial West Africa* (Youngstown, NY: Cambria Press, 2007), 47.

8. Hans W. Debrunner, *A History of Christianity in Ghana* (Accra, Ghana: Waterville Publishing House, 1967), 86, 99.

9. G. G. Gunn, *A Hundred Years 1848–1948: The Story of the Presbyterian Training College Akropong* (Akropong, Akwapim, Gold Coast: Presbyterian Training College, 1948), 16. See also the version in Debrunner, *A History of Christianity in Ghana*, 107, "If you could show us some black men who could read the white man's book, then we would surely follow you," which cites N. T. Clerk, "A Short Centenary Sketch: The Settlement of West Indian Immigrants on the Goldcoast under the Auspices of the Basel Mission 1843–1943," Basel Mission Archives, ref. no. D.076 (1943), 8. Similar versions of the story also appear in Peter Schweitzer, *Survivors on the Gold Coast: The Basel Missionaries in Colonial Ghana* (Accra, Ghana: Smartline, 2000), 50–51; Christ Presbyterian Church, Akropong-Akuapem, Ghana, website, "History," www.akropongcpc.faithweb.com/history.htm, accessed August 8, 2018.

10. Debrunner, *A History of Christianity in Ghana*, 107–8.

11. Christ Presbyterian Church website, "History," www.akropongcpc.faithweb .com/history.htm.

12. More recently, the harm that Riis's personality caused in the Gold Coast has been documented as well. His treatment of many Africans, as well as the Jamaicans he recruited, betrays a sense of cultural and ethnic superiority that should not be lauded. See Miller, *Missionary Zeal and Institutional Control*, 132–33; Quartey, *Missionary Practices on the Gold Coast*, 63 ff.

13. Wilhelm Schalter, *Geschichte der Basler Mission: Mit besonderer Berücksichtigung der ungedruckten Quellen* (Basel: Verlag der Basler Missionsbuchhandlung, 1916), 38–39. See also Miller, *Missionary Zeal and Institutional Control*, 133–34.

14. Ogpu Kalu, *The History of Christianity in West Africa* (London: Longman Group, 1980), 6.

15. William J. Danker, *Profit for the Lord: Economic Activities in Moravian Missions and the Basel Mission Trading Company* (Grand Rapids, MI: Eerdmans, 1971), 95.

16. See Peter B. Clarke, *West Africa and Christianity* (London: Edward Arnold, 1986), 59.

17. Denmark had sold their interests in the Gold Coast to Britain in 1850.

18. For more on the founding and history of the Presbyterian Church of Ghana, see Smith, *The Presbyterian Church of Ghana*.

19. World Council of Churches, www.oikoumene.org/en/member-churches /presbyterian-church-of-ghana, accessed September 1, 2018.

20. See www.acighana.org.

21. See *African Christianity Rising*, directed by James Ault (151 min.), 14:15–16:43.

22. Kwame Bediako, "Education and Human Values in Ghana—A Christian Reflection on our Common Future," *JACT* 18.2 (December 2015): 51. Bediako was quoting Blumhardt from Karl Rennstich, "The Understanding of Mission, Civilisation and Colonialism in the Basel Mission," in *Missionary Ideologies in the Imperialist Era: 1880–1920*, ed. Torben Christensen and William R. Hutchinson (Copenhagen: Aros, 1982), 95. Rennstich, in turn, was quoting Christian Blumhardt, "Die 'Instruction,'" *Evangelisches Missionsmagazin* (*EMM*) (1830): 451–82; specifically 454, 468, 470, 472, 480, 481. See also the posthumously published essay, revised by Gillian Mary Bediako: Kwame Bediako, "An Evaluation of the Achievement of the Christian Ideal in Education in Ghana from the 19th Century to the Early 20th Century," in *Educating a Nation: A Christian Perspective for Our Time*, Andrew McCutcheon Atkinson Memorial Lectures, delivered at the Presbyterian Church of the Resurrection, Accra, Ghana, December 1, 1993, unpublished, 2.

23. Bediako, "An Evaluation of the Achievement of the Christian Ideal in Education in Ghana," Lecture 3, 5–6.

24. Smith, *The Presbyterian Church of Ghana*, 54.

25. J. G. Christaller, *A Grammar of the Asante and Fante Language Called Twi Based on the Akuapem Dialect with Reference to the Other (Akan and Fante) Dialects* (Basel: Printed for the Basel Evangelical Missionary Society, 1875); J. G. Christaller, *A Dictionary of the Asante and Fante Language Called Tshi (chwee, Twi): With a Grammatical Introduction and Appendices on the Geography of the Gold Coast and Other Subjects* (Basel: Printed for the Evangelical Missionary Society, 1881).

26. J. B. Danquah, *The Akan Doctrine of God: A Fragment of Gold Coast Ethics and Religion* [1944] (New York: Routledge, 2006, reprint of 1968 2nd ed.), 185–86.

27. Ibid., 186.

28. Kamau Brathwaite of Barbados describes the experience of colonized peoples in Africa and the diaspora who were given not only a religious system that was foreign to them, but an entire religious and cultural history that was foreign: "People were forced to learn things that had no relevance to themselves. Paradoxically, in the Caribbean (as in many other "cultural disaster" areas), the people educated in this system came to know more, even today, about English kings and queens than they do about our own national heroes, our own slave rebels—the people who helped build and to destroy our society." See Kamau Brathwaite, "History of the Voice," in *Roots: Essays in Caribbean Literature* (Ann Arbor: University of Michigan Press, 1993), 263.

29. Frantz Fanon, *The Wretched of the Earth* (New York: Grove Press, [1961] 2004), 7.

30. Ibid., 6, 15, 43.

31. Kwame Bediako, "[Response to] David Hesselgrave: Dialogue on Contextualization Continuum," *Gospel in Context* 2.3 (1979): 13.

32. J. C. Blumhardt was named after his grandfather, who was also Christian Blumhardt's father.

33. Karl Barth, *Fakultätsalbum der Evangelisch-theologischen Fakultät* (Muenster, 1927); cited in Eberhard Busch, *Karl Barth: His Life from Letters and Autobiographical Texts* (Philadelphia: Fortress, 1976), 84.

34. Karl Barth to Wilhelm Speondlin, January 4, 1915; cited in Busch, *Karl Barth: His Life from Letters*, 81.

35. For a more detailed description of these days, see Busch, *Karl Barth: His Life from Letters*, 83–85.

36. Karl Barth to Wilhelm Speondlin, January 4, 1915, cited in Busch, *Karl Barth: His Life from Letters*, 81, 84.

37. One significant influence is Hermann Kutter's *They Must: Or, God and the Social Democracy. A Frank Word to Christian Men and Women*, American ed. (Chicago: Co-operative Printing Co., 1908). According to McCormack, Kutter "saw in socialism a kind of secular 'parable of the Kingdom'—a demonstration in deeds as well as in words of a vision of a new world which bore clear witness

to that Kingdom which Jesus had proclaimed" (Bruce L. McCormack, *Karl Barth's Critically Realistic Dialectical Theology: Its Genesis and Development 1909–1936* [Oxford: Clarendon Press, 1995], 83). See especially Kutter's quotation (in English) of Friedrich Naumann's *Das Soziale Programm der evangelischen Kirche* (1891), in *They Must*, 65–67.

38. McCormack, *Karl Barth's Critically Realistic Diacritical Theology*, 123.

39. Ibid., 130–31.

40. Ibid., 129.

41. Karl Barth, Afterword to Christoph Blumhardt, *Action in Waiting* (Rifton, NY: Plough Publishing House, 2012), 151.

42. Barth, *Falkultätsalbum der Evangelisch-theologischen Fakultät*, quoted in Busch, *Karl Barth: His Life from Letters*, 84.

43. Karl Barth, "Unscientific Concluding Post-Script," in *Theology of Schleiermacher* (Grand Rapids, MI: Eerdmans, 1982), 263–64.

44. Ibid., 264.

45. McCormack, *Karl Barth's Critically Realistic Diacritical Theology*, 78, 79; original emphasis.

46. Eberhard Jüngel, *Karl Barth: A Theological Legacy*, trans. Garrett E. Paul (Philadelphia: Westminster Press, 1986), 63–65. See also Hans Frei, "The Doctrine of Revelation in the Thought of Karl Barth, 1909 to 1922: The Nature of Barth's Break with Liberalism" (PhD diss., Yale University, 1956).

47. Jüngel, *Karl Barth*, 63.

48. Christian T. Collins Winn, *Jesus Is Victor! The Significance of the Blumhardts for the Theology of Karl Barth* (Eugene, OR: Pickwick Publications, 2009), xix. For his comments on McCormack's omission of the Blumhardts, see 28–31.

49. Timothy Gorringe, *Karl Barth: Against Hegemony* (New York: Oxford University Press, 1999), 34.

50. McCormack, *Karl Barth's Critically Realistic Diacritical Theology*, 125.

51. See also Collins Winn, *Jesus Is Victor!*, 212–13.

52. Collins Winn, *Jesus Is Victor!*, 274.

53. Larry Bouchard, "On Contingency and Culpability: Is the Postmodern Post-Tragic?," in *Evil after Postmodernism: Histories, Narratives, and Ethics*, ed. Jennifer L. Geddes (London: Rutledge, 2001), 25.

54. Ibid.

55. Ibid., 25–26.

56. Of particular note is the final chapter of the Commission IV report. For more on this significant moment in missionary history and the delimiting of Christendom, see Brian Stanley, *The World Missionary Conference, Edinburgh 1910* (Grand Rapids, MI: Eerdmans, 2009), esp. 235–45. See also Bediako's assessment: "The missionary enterprise of the nineteenth century did not see in African

traditional religion and culture a partner for dialogue the way in which it viewed Buddhism and philosophical Hinduism in Asia" (*CiA*, 69).

57. Frantz Fanon, *Black Skin, White Masks* (New York: Grove Press, [1952] 2008), 160.

58. Fanon, *The Wretched of the Earth*, 43.

59. In Hastings's view, "the interplay of the two is what makes his work so exciting." Adrian Hastings, "A New Voice out of Ghana: A Review of Kwame Bediako's *Christianity in Africa*," *Church Times* (January 1996): 15. See also Adrian Hastings, *The Church in Africa: 1450–1950* (Oxford: Clarendon Press, 1994); Adrian Hastings, *A History of African Christianity, 1950–1975* (Cambridge: Cambridge University Press, 1979).

60. Richard Sturch, personal email correspondence, November 7, 2012. Sturch's best-known publication is Richard Sturch, *The Word and the Christ: An Essay in Analytic Christology* (Oxford: Clarendon Press, 1991).

61. Gillian Mary Bediako, personal interview, June 1, 2012, Akrofi-Christaller Institute, Akropong-Akuapem, Ghana.

62. Gillian Mary Bediako, personal email correspondence, June 3, 2013.

63. Robert Aboagye-Mensah, personal email correspondence, June 7, 2012. A fellow Ghanaian, Aboagye-Mensah wrote his PhD dissertation on Barth at the University of Aberdeen while Bediako was there. See Robert Aboagye-Mensah, "Socio-Political Thinking of Karl Barth: Trinitarian and Incarnational Christology as the Ground for His Social Action and Its Implications for Us Today" (PhD dissertation, University of Aberdeen, 1984).

64. The original phrase is, "kohlrabenschwarz, aber mir sehr sympathisch." Quoted in Eberhard Busch, *Karl Barths Lebenslauf: Nach Seinen Briefen und Autobiograph Texten* (Munich: Kaiser, 1975), 410 (English translation in Busch, *Karl Barth*, 396); from a letter from Karl Barth to Christoph Barth, August 25, 1951.

65. Robert Aboagye-Mensah, personal email correspondence, June 7, 2012.

66. Karl Barth, *Der Römerbrief*, 1st ed. (Bern: G. A. Bäschlin, 1919). Subseqent citations are from Karl Barth, *Epistle to the Romans*, 2nd ed., trans. Edwyn C. Hoskyns (London: Oxford University Press, [1933] 1968).

67. For current updates on the Akrofi-Christaller Institute of Theology, Mission, and Culture, see www.acighana.org.

68. Barth, *Church Dogmatics*, IV/1, x.

69. Edward B. Fiske, "Karl Barth Dies in Basel; Protestant Theologian, 82," *New York Times*, December 11, 1968, 1, 42. The original quotation is from Robert McAfee Brown's introduction to Georges Casalis, *Portrait of Karl Barth* (Garden City, NY: Doubleday and Co., 1963), 2.

70. David Neff, "Theologian Kwame Bediako Dies," *Christianity Today Online*, June 13, 2008, www.christianitytoday.com/gleanings/2008/june/theologian-kwame-bediako-dies.html, accessed September 1, 2018.

71. Iwan Russell Jones, "Following the Footprints of God: Kwame Bediako, 1945–2008," www.ship-of-fools.com/features/2008/kwame_bediako.html, accessed September 1, 2018.

72. J. Kwabena Asamoah-Gyadu, "Bediako of Africa: A Late 20th Century Outstanding Theologian and Teacher," *Mission Studies* 26 (2009): 5.

73. Ibid., 9. Recall also Walls's near-hagiographic praise of Bediako in Walls, "Kwame Bediako and Christian Scholarship in Africa," 192.

74. This quotation is McCormack's summary of Friedrich-Wilhelm Marquardt, *Theologie und Sozialismus: Das Beispiel Karl Barths*, 3rd ed. (Munich: Chr. Kaiser, 1972); see McCormack, *Karl Barth's Critically Realistic Diacritical Theology*, 27.

75. Bediako, "'In the Bible . . . Africa walks on familiar ground,'" 36.

76. See Kwame Bediako, "'Whose Religion Is Christianity?': Reflections on Opportunities and Challenges for Christian Theological Scholarship as Public Discourse—The African Dimension," *JACT* 9.2 (2006): 43–48; Kwame Bediako, "Conclusion: The Emergence of World Christianity and the Remaking of Theology," in *Understanding World Christianity: The Vision and Work of Andrew F. Walls*, ed. William R. Burrows, Mark R. Gornik, and Janice A. McLean (Maryknoll, NY: Orbis, 2011), 248; also published in *JACT* 12.2 (2009): 1–12.

77. Kwame Bediako, "Biblical Christologies in the Context of African Traditional Religion," in *Sharing Jesus in the Two-Thirds World*, ed. Vinay Samuel and Chris Sugden (Grand Rapids, MI: Eerdmans, 1984), 121.

78. Kwame Bediako, "Review of *African Theology en Route*," *Journal of Religion in Africa* 11.2 (1980): 159.

79. Ibid., 159.

80. Bediako, "Africa and Christianity on the Threshold of the Third Millennium," 307.

81. Bediako is quoting Andrew Walls's article, "Structural Problems in Mission Studies," in *International Bulletin of Missionary Research* 15.4 (1991): 146.

82. Bediako, "The Emergence of World Christianity and the Remaking of Theology," *JACT* 12.2 (2009): 51.

83. Ibid.

84. Ibid., 54.

85. Ibid.

86. Bediako, "Africa and Christianity on the Threshold of the Third Millennium," 314.

87. Fernando Ortiz, *Cuban Counterpoint: Tobacco and Sugar*, trans. Harriet de Onís (New York: Knopf, 1947), 98.

88. Ibid., 102; original emphasis.

89. Ibid., 103.

90. Ibid.

91. Larry Bouchard, *Tragic Method, Tragic Theology: Evil in Contemporary Drama and Religious Thought* (University Park: Pennsylvania State University Press, 2010), 178.

92. Bouchard, *Tragic Method, Tragic Theology*, 178.

93. Ibid.

94. Bouchard, "On Contingency and Culpability," 38–39.

95. Ibid., 39.

96. For an extended treatment of translatability by Bediako, see "Translatability and the Cultural Incarnations of the Faith," ch. 7 in *CiA*, 109–25.

97. Paul Dafydd Jones, *The Humanity of Christ: Christology in Karl Barth's Church Dogmatics* (New York: T&T Clark, 2008), 252; original emphasis.

Transitional Theological Interlude

1. Barth, "Evangelical Theology in the 19th Century," 14. From Barth, "Evangelische Theologie im 19. Jahrhundert," 6.

2. Bediako and Bediako, "Ebenezer," 4.

THREE. Christological Reflection

1. Letter, Karl Barth to Wilhelm Niemöller, October 17, 1953, cited in Busch, *Karl Barth: His Life from Letters*, 245. See also Arthur Cochrane, *The Church's Confession under Hitler* (Philadelphia: Westminster Press, 1962), 177.

2. For a helpfully more complicated and realistic account of the composition of the confession at Barmen, see Derek Woodard-Lehman, "Democratic Faith: Barth, Barmen, and the Politics of Reformed Confession" in *Thy Kingdom Come: The Contemporary Relevance of the Barmen Declaration*, ed. Frank Dallmayr (Lanham, MD: Rowman and Littlefield, 2019), 74–116.

3. Karl Barth, *Theological Existence Today*, trans. R. Birch Hoyle (Lexington, KY: ATLA, [1933] 1962); and a more recent translation in Mary Holberg, trans. and ed., *A Church Undone: Documents from the German Christian Faith Movement, 1932–1940* (Minneapolis, MN: Fortress Press, 2015). See Busch, *Karl Barth: His Life from Letters*, 226.

4. Barth, "Theological Existence Today!" in Holdberg, *A Church Undone*, 86–87.

5. Karl Barth, in conversation with Tübingen students, March 2, 1964, recorded in Busch, *Karl Barth: His Life from Letters*, 226.

6. Cochrane, *The Church's Confession under Hitler*, 239.

7. Karl Barth, "A Theological Dialogue," *Theology Today* 19.2 (July 1962): 172. The parenthetical note about Berkouwer was added by *Theology Today*.

8. Karl Barth, "Extra Nos—Pro Nobis—In Nobis," in *Hören und Handlen: Festschrift für Ernst Wolf zum 60. Geburtstag*, ed. Helmut Gollwitzer and Hellmut Traub (Munich: Chr. Kaiser Verlag, 1962), 15–27; quoted from George Hunsinger's translation in *The Thomist* 50.4 (October 1986): 511.

9. See Barth's three comments on Christomonism in his *Church Dogmatics*: III/3, preface; IV/3, 713; and IV/4, 23.

10. I use the descriptor African traditional religions (ATRs), not African indigenous religion(s), out of deference to African Christian theologians, such as Kwame Bediako, Bénézet Bujo, and John Mbiti, who sought to articulate indigenous African understandings of the Christian faith based in their belief that God in Jesus Christ has always been present and active on the African continent and with African peoples. From their point of view, both African (traditional) religious beliefs and rituals and African Christianity are indigenous religions of Africa. For representative examples, see Kwame Bediako, *Christianity in Africa: The Renewal of a Non-Western Religion* (Edinburgh: Edinburgh University Press, 1995); Bénézet Bujo, *African Theology in Its Social Context*, trans. John O'Donohue (Maryknoll, NY: Orbis Books, 1992); John S. Mbiti, *New Testament Eschatology in an African Background: A Study of the Encounter between New Testament Theology and African Traditional Concepts* (Oxford: Oxford University Press, 1971).

11. Personal interview, August 5, 2013, Akrofi-Christaller Institute, Akropong-Akuapem, Ghana.

12. Kwame Bediako, "'Missionaries did not bring Christ to Africa—Christ brought them': Why Africa Needs Jesus Christ" *AICMAR Bulletin* 6 (2007).

13. Bediako, "Biblical Christologies in the Context of African Traditional Religion."

14. See Bolaji Idowu, *Towards an Indigenous Church* (London: Oxford University Press, 1965).

15. See John S. Mbiti, *African Religions and Philosophy*, 2nd rev. and enl. ed. (Oxford: Heinemann, 1990).

16. For more on Idowu's position, see Bolaji Idowu, *African Traditional Religion: A Definition* (Maryknoll, NY: Orbis Books, 1973), 205. For more on Bediako's discussion of Idowu, see *TI*, 286–88, and of monotheism in ATRs, see *TI*, 291–93.

17. Kwame Bediako, "Christian Tradition and the African God Revisited: A Process in the Exploration of a Theological Idiom," in *Witnessing to the Living God in Contemporary Africa*, ed. David Gitari and Patrick Benson (Nairobi: Uzima Press, 1986), 77–97; and *TI*, 289.

18. Bediako followed Mbiti's claim that African primal religions are in fact, *praeparatio evangelica* (evangelical preparation for the gospel; *TI*, xvii, 149, 315). See also Kwame Bediako, "'Their past is also our present.' Why All Christians

Have Need of Ancestors: Making a Case for Africa," *AICMAR Bulletin* 6 (2007): 9. Significantly, Mbiti also considered Islam a traditional African religion.

19. Bediako's Christological view of history extended prior to the New Testament itself. He wrote, "Indeed, the gospel was before the New Testament. In that sense, the gospel existed before our traditions, before our cultures." See Kwame Bediako, "Scripture as the Hermeneutics of Culture and Tradition," *JACT* 4.1 (2001): 2. Originally given as lectures, August 9–13, 1999, Akrofi-Christaller Memorial Centre, Akropong-Akuapem, Ghana.

20. Adolf von Harnack, *What Is Christianity?*, trans. Thomas Bailey Saunders (New York: Harper & Brothers, [1900] 1957), 15.

21. Harnack used the kernel and husk imagery on pp. 2, 12, 15, 55, 179, 217, 299.

22. In *Church Dogmatics*, Barth first used *mündig*, meaning maturity or coming-of-age, in I/2 (335); then it was further developed by Dietrich Bonhoeffer (through the influence of Wilhelm Dilthey's work) in his *Letters and Papers from Prison* (Dietrich Bonhoeffer Works, vol. 10 [Minneapolis, MN: Fortress Press, 2010]): letters to Eberhard Bethge on June 8, 1944 (427), July 16, 1944 (478–79), July 18, 1944 (482), and August 3, 1944 (500). For more on the relationship of Bonhoeffer to IV/3, see Charles Marsh, *Reclaiming Dietrich Bonhoeffer: The Promise of His Theology* (New York: Oxford University Press, 1994), 25–33 and 48–50.

23. *Church Dogmatics* IV/3 was published in German in 1959 and in English in 1961, following its debut as student lectures at Basel in the winter term of 1956–57. Geopolitically, the context of the composition of §69 is the Cold War. The first lectures, titled "The Glory of the Mediator," were delivered in late 1956 (the year of Barth's seventieth birthday), just weeks after the Hungarian Revolution and the Soviet occupation. A year before, the Warsaw Pact had been signed and West Germany had joined the North Atlantic Treaty Organization (NATO). A year later, *Sputnik* was launched by the Soviet Union as part of the space race with the United States (Busch, *Karl Barth: His Life from Letters*, 425). Volume IV/3 was completed with the lectures of winter 1958–59 (see Busch, *Karl Barth: His Life from Letters*, 441); it was published in two parts because of its length, 1,107 pages in German, 963 pages in English. Barth wanted to make sure that the reader received "two halves that were 'bearable' [*tragbare*] in the literal sense" (IV/3, preface, xi).

24. For more on Barth's understanding of Christ as prophet, see Georg Pfleiderer, "Das 'prophetische Amt' der Theologie: Zur systematischen Rekonstruktion der Theologie Karl Barths und ihres Entwicklungsgangs," *Zeitschrift für Dialektische Theologie* 17.2 (January 2001): 112–38.

25. For more on the history of the *munus triplex*, see Wolfhart Pannenberg, *Jesus: God and Man*, trans. Lewis L. Wilkins and Duane A. Priebe (London: SCM, 1968), 212–25; Wolfhart Pannenberg, *Systematic Theology*, vol. 2, trans. Geoffrey Bromiley (Grand Rapids, MI: Eerdmans, 1991), 444–49; John Frederick Jansen, *Calvin's Doctrine of the Work of Christ* (London: J. Clark, 1956), 13–38;

Gerald W. McCulloh, *Christ's Person and Life-Work in the Theology of Albrecht Ritschl with Special Attention to* Munus Triplex (Lanham, MD: University Press of America, 1990), esp. ch. 3: "The History of *Munus Triplex* in Christian Thought," 86–144; and David T. Williams, *The Office of Christ and Its Expression in the Church: Prophet, Priest, King* (Lewiston, NY: Edwin Mellen Press, 1997).

26. See John Calvin, *Institutes of the Christian Religion*, trans. Ford Lewis Battles (Philadelphia: Westminster John Knox, 1960), II.xv.1–2. Yet as Geoffrey Wainright helpfully notes, "Calvin was not the first sixteenth-century writer to take up the notion of Christ's threefold office: there are scattered anticipations of his more developed use. Already in his *Commentary on the Second Psalm* (1522), Erasmus speaks of the senseless raging of the prince(s) and peoples of this world against the Lord and his Anointed when in fact Christ has come, full of grace, for the salvation of all nations: 'the prophet of prophets, the priest who has given himself'" (Wainright, *For Our Salvation: Two Approaches to the Work of Christ* [Grand Rapids, MI: Eerdmans, 1997], 103). Pannenberg insightfully identifies that Calvin may have seen Osiander's use of the *munus triplex* in 1530. He writes, "Luther was not the author of the doctrine of the three offices in the Reformation. Luther spoke only of the Kingship and Priesthood of Christ. The figure three [*sic*] seems to go back to Andreas Osiander. In his defense written for the Augsburg *Reichstag* of 1530 he gave the argument, which later became classic, for the necessity of speaking of three offices—or better, of a threefold office—of Christ: 'Since Christ is thus called an Anointed One and only the prophets, kings, and high priests were anointed, one notes well that all three of these offices rightly belong to him: the prophetic office, since he alone is our teacher and master, Matt. 23:8 ff.; the authority of the king, since he reigns forever in the house of Jacob, Luke 1:32 ff., and the priestly office, since he is a priest forever after the order of Melchizedek, Ps. 110:4. Thus it is his office that he is our wisdom, righteousness, sanctification, and redemption, as Paul testifies in 1 Cor., ch. 1.' The threefold character of the offices of Christ achieved general recognition through Calvin, who had used the doctrine after 1536 in the Geneva Confession and in the various versions of the *Institutio Christianae Religionis*. Apparently the subsequent Reformed, as well as Lutheran, orthodoxy took over the doctrine of the three offices from him" (Pannenberg, *Jesus: God and Man*, 213). Pannenberg found Osiander's defense in Wilhelm Gussman, *Quellen und Forschungen zur Geschichte des Augsburgischen Glaubensbekenntnisses*, vol. 1 (Leipzig: B. G. Teubner, 1911), 302. Both Erasmus and Osiander, however, were not inventing but recovering the concept of the threefold office from the early church. Eusebius, in his *Church History* from the early fourth century, described the three offices as follows: "so that all these have reference to the true Christ, the divinely inspired and heavenly Word, who is the only high priest of all, and the only King of every creature, and the Father's only supreme prophet of prophets" (1.3.8).

27. Barth earlier articulated this concern in his *Epistle to the Romans*, 8–9.

28. Revised translation from Garrett Green, *Karl Barth on Religion: The Revelation of God as the Sublimation of Religion* (London: T&T Clark, 2007), 44–45, translating I/2, 291, Barth's emphasis. The quotations from §17 that follow are taken from Garrett Green's translation. The page for Green's translation is listed last, preceded by the page numbers in the English translation of the *Dogmatics*, i.e., "(I/2, 280; 33)."

29. Jessica DeCou, "Relocating Barth's Theology of Culture: Beyond the 'True Words' Approach of *Church Dogmatics* IV/3," *International Journal of Systematic Theology* 15.2 (April 2013): 155.

30. Kathryn Tanner, *Theories of Culture: A New Agenda for Theology* (Minneapolis, MN: Fortress Press, 1997), 57.

31. Ibid.; original emphasis.

32. Barth defined theology "as the human logic of the divine Logos." See Karl Barth, *Evangelical Theology: An Introduction* (Grand Rapids, MI: Eerdmans, 1963), 49.

33. Tanner, *Theories of Culture*, 63.

34. For more on Barth's use of the *munus triplex* in English, see Bruce L. McCormack, "Karl Barth's Historicized Christology: Just How 'Chalcedonian' Is It?," in *Orthodox and Modern: Studies in the Theology of Karl Barth* (Grand Rapids, MI: Baker Academic, 2008), 202; Jones, *The Humanity of Christ*, 122–26; George Hunsinger, *Disruptive Grace: Studies in the Theology of Karl Barth* (Grand Rapids, MI: Eerdmans, 2000), 141–42 n. 18; Adam Neder, *Participation in Christ: An Entry into Karl Barth's Church Dogmatics* (Louisville, KY: Westminster John Knox, 2009), 74–75; Karin Bornkamm, "Die reformatorische Lehre vom Amt Christi und ihre Umformung durch Karl Barth," in *Zeitschrift für Theologie und Kirche*, ed. Eberhard Jüngel (Tübingen: Mohr Siebeck, 1986), 3–32; Karin Bornkamm, *Christus—König und Priester: Das Amt Christi bei Luther im Verhältnis zur Vor- und Nachgeschichte* (Tübingen: Mohr Siebeck, 1998), 382–85; Hans Urs von Balthasar, *The Theology of Karl Barth: Exposition and Interpretation*, trans. Edward T. Oakes (San Francisco: Ignatius, 1992), 391–92; Colin E. Gunton, *The Barth Lectures*, ed. Paul Brazier (New York: T&T Clark, 2007), 201; Anna Maria Schwemer, "Jesus Christus als Prophet, König und Priester: Das munus triplex und die frühe Christologie," in *Der messianische Anspruch Jesu und die Anfange der Christologie*, ed. Martin Hengel and Anna Maria Schwemer (Tübingen: Mohr Siebeck, 2001), 165–230; Jürgen Moltmann, "Trends in Eschatology," in *The Future of Creation: Collected Essays* (Minneapolis, MN: Fortress, 1979), 23–27. Also see Barth's alleged superficial misuse of the doctrine in Adam J. Johnson, "The Servant Lord: A Word of Caution Regarding the *munus triplex* in Karl Barth's Theology and the Church Today," *Scottish Journal of Theology* 65.2 (2012): 159–73.

35. In *Church Dogmatics* IV/3, §69, Barth presented "one of the most original (and least studied) tracts in the entire *Church Dogmatics*," in the words of John Webster (*Barth*, 2nd ed. [New York: Continuum, 2004], 131). The part-volume

proceeds in four subsections: §69.1: The Third Problem of the Doctrine of Reconciliation; §69.2: The Light of Life; §69.3: Jesus Is Victor; and §69.4: The Promise of the Spirit. The first three part-volumes present expositions of Christ as priest (IV/1), Christ as king (IV/2), and Christ as prophet (IV/3). The fourth part-volume containing Barth's ethics of reconciliation was never finished; portions of its first half were published as IV/4, §75, The Fragment on Baptism, and then §§74, 76, 77, and 78 as unedited drafts in Karl Barth, *The Christian Life: Church Dogmatics IV/4, Lecture Fragments*, ed. Hans-Anton Drewes and Eberhard Jüngel, trans. Geoffrey Bromiley (London: T&T Clark, 2004).

In IV/1, Barth employs the motif of humiliation, "The Lord as Servant: Jesus Christ, Son of God" (§59); and in IV/2, the motif of exaltation, "The Servant as Lord: Jesus Christ, Son of Man" (§64). In the pattern of IV/1 and IV/2, Barth again follows the Christological exposition with a discussion of sin: as falsehood opposed to the true witness of the prophet (§70). In turn, §71 considers the impact of Christ's prophetic activity on the human being. Whereas Christ's humiliation led to human justification in IV/1, §61, and Christ's exaltation led to human sanctification in IV/2, §66, the unity of the God-man and the proclamation of Jesus's life led to human calling or vocation in IV/3, §71. In the final sections on the Holy Spirit (§§72, 73), the sending of the Son by the Father in the incarnation is applied to the Christian community that exists *for* the world (§72) and that had previously experienced gathering (IV/1, §62) and upbuilding (IV/2, §67). To conclude his threefold exposition of the office of Jesus Christ in his doctrine of reconciliation, Barth meditated on the Holy Spirit and Christian hope (§73) following faith (§63) and love (§68).

36. From the question and answer period after John Godsey's paper, "The Architecture of Karl Barth's *Church Dogmatics*," in *Karl Barth's Table Talk*, ed. John Godsey (Richmond, VA: John Knox Press, 1963), 17.

37. Ibid.

38. For more on Barth's use of *Geschichte*, see Jones, *The Humanity of Christ*, 188–203. Jones identifies four closely related meanings of *Geschichte* in Barth's *Dogmatics*:

1. "God's pre-temporal elective intention [as it relates to Christ, is] … [b]asic to God's life, in a decision coordinate with God's self-assigned identity as three relating *Seinsweise* [modes of being]—God intends to create, sustain, and relate companionably to humankind" (189).

2. "a pair of closely related claims: (a) the life of Jesus Christ constitutes the identity of Jesus Christ, which, in turn, (b) God makes constitutive of the identity of God *qua* Son" (191).

3. "Christ's life as a reconciliatory event that mediates the relationship between God and humanity" (195).

4. "Christ's reconciling life-unto-death as the way of covenant fulfillment" (199).

39. For Barth, "He, Jesus Christ, lives. . . . His existence is act; that it is being in spontaneous actualization" (IV/3, 39, 40).

40. See G. C. Berkouwer, *The Triumph of Grace in the Theology of Karl Barth* (London: Paternoster Press, 1956), previously published in Dutch (1954) and in German (1957). Barth offered a preliminary response to Berkouwer's book in the preface to IV/2 and a more extended engagement in IV/3, 173–80.

41. In a somewhat perplexing passage in §11, Barth claims that "revelation is itself reconciliation," a position that, as noted above, he retracts in §69. See: "The fact that God can first tell us anything, this primary inconceivability in view of His wrath on sinful man, is in God's revelation the work of the Son or Word of God. The work of the Son or Word is the presence and declaration of God which, in view of the fact that it takes place miraculously in and in spite of human darkness, we can only describe as revelation. The term reconciliation is another word for the same thing. To the extent that God's revelation as such accomplishes what only God can accomplish, namely, restoration of the fellowship of man with God which we had disrupted and indeed destroyed; to the extent that God in the fact of His revelation treats His enemies as His friends; to the extent that in the fact of revelation God's enemies already are actually His friends, *revelation is itself reconciliation.* Conversely reconciliation, the restoration of that fellowship, the mercy of God in wrath triumphant over wrath, can only have the form of the mystery which we describe as revelation" (I/1, 409; emphasis added).

42. Significantly, the prophetic actualism and activity of Christ articulated in §69 follows Barth's insight in II/2 about Christ as the Elect One. While not necessarily required, the placing of election in the doctrine of God in II/2 surely adds clarity to *who* God as Son is, which is then explored in IV/3.

43. Here Barth also quoted "the introductory words to the Epistle to the Hebrews: πολυμερῶς καὶ πολυτρόπως πάλαι ὁ θεὸς λαλήσας τοῖς πατράσιν ἐν τοῖς προφήταις (Long ago God spoke to our ancestors in many and various ways by the prophets)" (I/2, 84).

44. See also: "Revelation remains revelation and does not become a revealed state. Revelation remains identical with Christ and Christ remains the object of Christian faith, even though He lives in Christians and they in Him" (I/2, 118).

45. Here we can recall Gregory of Nazianzus's fourth-century dictum (also in Athanasius): "the unassumed is the unhealed." Gregory Nazienzen, Letter 101, "To Cledonius the Priest against Apollinarius," in *The Nicene and Post-Nicene Fathers, Second Series*, vol. 7 (New York: C. Scribner's Sons, 1903), 839. Bediako twice cites this quotation; see Kwame Bediako, *Religion, Culture and Language: An Appreciation of the Intellectual Legacy of Dr. J. B. Danquah*, J. B. Danquah Memorial Lectures, Series 37, 2004, February 2–4, 2004 (Accra: Ghana Academy of Arts and Sciences, 2006), 36; and Kwame Bediako, "Thoughts on the Nature of the Project," *JACT* 11.2 (2008): 3.

46. In a distinct though not entirely unrelated vein, for more of Barth's use of simultaneities in the doctrines of justification and sanctification, see George Hunsinger, "A Tale of Two Simultaneities: Justification and Sanctification in Calvin, Luther and Barth," in *Conversing with Barth*, ed. Mike Higton and John C. McDowell (Burlington, VT: Ashgate, 2004), 68–89.

47. For scholarly discussions of Barth's understanding and use of "light" (*Licht*), see Hendrikus Berkhof and H. J. Kraus, *Karl Barths Lichtlehre* (Zurich: Theologischer Verlag, 1977); Henry Mottu, "La lumière et les lumières: Christ et le monde selon le dernier Barth, 1988," in *Un itinéraire théologique: Barth, Bonhoeffer et la théologie africaine-américane* (Geneva: Cahiers de la Revue de Théologie et de Philosophie 21, 2004), 36–48; Karl-Friedrich Wiggermann, "'Ein eigentümlich beschatter Bereich': Die Neuzeit in Karl Barths 'Lichterlehre,'" *Zeitschrift für Dialektische Theologie* 25.2 (2009): 119–38.

48. See also: "Yet the fact that the history of Israel can have no more continuations does not mean that it is outmoded, replaced or dissolved. It cannot be outmoded, because already the one covenant between God and man, instituted in the eternal election of Jesus Christ, was its basis, content and goal; because it was already actualized in it in this first form as national history; and because Jesus Christ already spoke and acted in it as His type, His pre-history and fore-word" (IV/3, 70).

49. Ivor Davidson, "Divine Light: Some Reflections after Barth," in *Trinitarian Theology after Barth*, ed. Myk Habets and Phillip Tolliday (Eugene, OR: Pickwick Publications, 2011), 65.

50. Ibid., 67, 68.

51. For an extended treatment of translatability by Bediako, see "Translatability and the Cultural Incarnations of the Faith," ch. 7 in *CiA*, 109–25.

52. As early as 1987 Bediako writes, "with what Professor Andrew Walls has taught us to call the Christian faith's 'infinite cultural translatability'" (Kwame Bediako, "Christ in Africa: Some Reflections on the Contribution of Christianity to the African Becoming," in *Proceedings of African Futures: 25th Anniversary Conference Held in the Centre of African Studies, University of Edinburgh, 9–11 December 1987*, ed. Christopher Fyfe and Chris Allen [Edinburgh: Centre of African Studies, 1987], 453). For Walls's usage, see Walls, *The Missionary Movement in Christian History: Studies in the Transmission of Faith* (Maryknoll, NY: Orbis Books, 1996), 22.

53. Kwame Bediako, "The Relevance of a Christian Approach to Culture in Africa," in *Christian Education in the African Context: Proceedings of the First Africa Regional Conference of the International Association for the Promotion of Christian Higher Education (IAPCHE), 4–9 March 1991, Harare, Zimbabwe* (Grand Rapids, MI: IAPCHE, 1991), 31.

54. See also Bediako, "The Relevance of a Christian Approach to Culture in Africa," 31; Kwame Bediako, "Biblical Exegesis in the African Context: The Factor and Impact of Translated Scriptures," *JACT* 6.1 (2003): 17.

55. Bediako's understanding of the translatability of the gospel shares distinct similarities with Lamin Sanneh, *Translating the Message: The Missionary Impact on Culture* (Maryknoll, NY: Orbis, 1989). Sanneh and Bediako overlapped in Aberdeen. When Bediako was a PhD student, Sanneh was a faculty member in the Department of Religious Studies; the department chair was Andrew Walls. It was Walls who asked Sanneh to teach courses in Christianity, outside of his graduate training in Islam.

56. Bediako, "Gospel and Culture: Some Insights for Our Time from the Experience of the Earliest Christians," *JACT* 2.2 (1999): 8.

57. Kwame Bediako, "Challenges of Ghana's Fourth Republic: A Christian Perspective," The William Ofori-Atta Memorial Lectures, lecture 2, October 7–9, 1992, 7.

58. Kwame Bediako, "The Church and the University: Some Reflections on the Rationale for a Christian Participation in Public Education in Africa," *ATF Bulletin* 16 (2003): 6; quoting Andrew Walls, "The Translation Principle in Christian History," in *The Missionary Movement in Christian History: Studies in the Transmission of Faith* (Maryknoll, NY: Orbis Books, 1996), 27.

59. See also Bediako, "The Relevance of a Christian Approach to Culture in Africa," 31.

60. For a tragic example of what can happen when Christian missionaries fail to allow the gospel to be translated into a host culture, see Hartman, "Lost in Translation."

61. Bediako, "Biblical Christologies in the Context of African Traditional Religion," 98.

62. Bediako, "The Willowbank Consultation," 29.

63. Kwame Bediako, "The Impact of the Bible in Africa," epilogue to Ype Schaaf, *On Their Way Rejoicing—The History and Role of the Bible in Africa* (Carlisle: Paternoster Press, 1995), 244.

64. Ibid.

65. The work of Cornelius Van Til first offered a number of these critiques and serves as a precedent for them.

66. See D. A. Carson's *Gagging of God: Christianity Confronts Pluralism* (Grand Rapids, MI: Zondervan, 1996) for just one prominent example. Byung Kato is the foremost African theologian articulating this critique.

67. See Mayra Rivera, *The Touch of Transcendence: A Postcolonial Theology of God* (Louisville, KY: Westminster John Knox Press, 2007), 4–5.

68. Recently, John Flett went so far as to argue that mission should be placed within the doctrine of God. See John Flett, *The Witness of God: The Trinity, Missio Dei, Karl Barth, and the Nature of Christian Community* (Grand Rapids, MI: Eerdmans, 2010).

69. Barth explicitly denies that he is a universalist in §70 when he writes, "No such postulate can be made even though we appeal to the cross and resurrection of Jesus Christ. Even though theological consistency might seem to lead our thoughts and utterances most clearly in this direction, we must not arrogate to ourselves that which can be given and received only as a free gift" (IV/3, 477).

70. See also in Barth that Christ "is Victor from the very outset" (IV/3, 229).

71. Bediako, "Understanding African Theology in the Twentieth Century," in *Jesus and the Gospel in Africa* (Oxford: Regnum, 2000), 56.

72. Ibid.

73. In *Theology and Identity*, Bediako treats four authors from the second century CE: Tatian, Tertullian, Justin Martyr, and Clement of Alexandria. All were first-generation converts to Christianity and reflected on how to interpret their pagan past in Greco-Roman religions in light of their faith in Jesus Christ (*TI*, 32). These second-century apologists saw "no more pressing problem to be faced by Gentile Christians in the Graeco-Roman world than the question of their heritage and historical roots" (*TI*, 35). The similar concerns of these apologists and the four modern African theologians (Bolaji Idowu, John S. Mbiti, Mulago gwa Cikala Musharhamina, and Byang Kato) form the basis for the book. In his analysis, Bediako's preference for the thought of Justin and Clement shines through.

74. Barth, *Epistle to the Romans*, 96.

75. Bediako draws this connection explicitly: as "St. Paul declared on Mars Hill, in Acts 17:27, in another time and place where a Christian account of the Transcendent was being forged in an encounter with a primal worldview, the Hellenistic worldview being essentially primal" (*CiA*, 101).

76. In his final public appearance, a tribute to Andrew Walls, Bediako compared himself to Clement of Alexandria and Walls to Clement's teacher, Pantaenus (Kwame Bediako, "Andrew F. Walls as Mentor," in *Understanding World Christianity: The Vision and Work of Andrew F. Walls*, ed. William R. Burrows, Mark R. Gornik, and Janice A. McLean [Maryknoll, NY: Orbis, 2011], 8).

77. Bediako, "'Missionaries did not bring Christ to Africa,'" 21.

FOUR. Contextual Reflection

1. The work of Afua Kuma has gone largely unexplored in the scholarly literature. For more on her and *Jesus of the Deep Forest*, see Richard Fox Young, "Clearing a Path through *Jesus of the Deep Forest*: Intercultural Perspectives on Christian Praise and Public Witness in Afua Kuma's Akan Oral Epic," *Theology Today* 70.1 (2013): 38–45; Philip Laryea, "Mother Tongue Theology: Reflections on Images of Jesus in the Poetry of Afua Kuma," *Journal of African Christian*

Thought 3.1 (2000): 50–60; Darren Middleton, "Jesus of Nazareth in Ghana's Deep Forest: The Africanization of Christianity in Madam Afua Kuma's Poetry," *Religion and the Arts* 9.1–2 (2005): 116–34. See also two engagements with Afua Kuma in broader essays: Kwame Bediako, "Cry Jesus! Christian Theology and Presence in Modern Africa," in *Jesus and the Gospel in Africa* (Oxford: Regnum, 2000), 8–15; Mercy Amba Oduyoye, "Jesus Christ," in *The Cambridge Companion to Feminist Theology*, ed. Susan Frank Parsons (Cambridge: Cambridge University Press, 2002), 153–55.

2. Afua Kuma, *Jesus of the Deep Forest: Prayers and Praises of Afua Kuma*, ed. Peter Kwasi Ameyaw, trans. Fr. Jon Kirby (Accra, Ghana: Asempa Publishers, 1980).

3. Ibid., 6.

4. Ibid., 30. For insightful analysis of this stanza, see Laryea, "Mother Tongue Theology," 51–52.

5. Bediako, *Jesus and the Gospel in Africa*, 11.

6. Ibid., 14–15.

7. Kuma, *Jesus of the Deep Forest*, 35, 37; cited in Bediako, *Jesus and the Gospel in Africa*, 15.

8. Bediako, *Jesus and the Gospel in Africa*, 8.

9. Ibid., 15.

10. Ibid., 9.

11. Kuma, *Jesus of the Deep Forest*, 38, 27, 32.

12. Young, "Clearing a Path through *Jesus of the Deep Forest*," 39.

13. Oduyoye, "Jesus Christ," 153–55.

14. Eugene H. Peterson, *The Message: The Bible in Contemporary Language* (Colorado Springs, CO: NavPress, 2005), 1441. See also Eugene H. Peterson, *Eat This Book: A Conversation in the Art of Spiritual Reading* (Grand Rapids, MI: Eerdmans, 2009), 172–73.

15. For an insightful treatment of the role of place in theological and personal self-understanding, see Mary McClintock Fulkerson, *Places of Redemption: Theology for a Worldly Church* (Oxford: Oxford University Press, 2007).

16. Recall the line repeated by the *New York Times* in Barth's obituary (cited in ch. 2) that no one can "responsibly ignore" Barth.

17. Gorringe, *Karl Barth*, 1.

18. Busch, *Karl Barth: His Life from Letters*, 421.

19. "Barth in Retirement," *Time* 81.22 (May 31, 1963): 60. Barth added, "A theologian should never be formed by the world around him—either East or West. He should make it his vocation to show both East and West that they can live without a clash. Where the peace of God is proclaimed, there peace on earth is implicit." This article was a follow-up to the cover article on Barth in *Time* 79.16 (April 20, 1962): 61–69.

20. Busch, *The Great Passion*, 31.

21. Ibid., 6.

22. Barth writes, "Think about John the Baptist in the crucifixion scene by Grünewald and the way his pointing hand is twisted in an almost impossible manner. It is this hand that is documented in the Bible" (Karl Barth, *The Word of God and Theology*, trans. Amy Marga [New York: T&T Clark, 2011], 82).

23. Busch, *The Great Passion*, 14.

24. Dietrich Bonhoeffer, *Barcelona, Berlin, New York: 1928–1931*, Dietrich Bonhoeffer Works, vol. 8 (Minneapolis, MN: Fortress Press, 2008), 64. Three days after this diary entry, Bonhoeffer wrote a letter in which he again mused about Barth's hypothetical response to Barcelona. See Bonhoeffer, *Barcelona, Berlin, New York*, 76.

25. Bonhoeffer attributed quite a significant shift in his own theological thinking to his time abroad. Near the end of his life, he wrote from prison to his friend Eberhard Bethge, "I don't think I have ever changed much, except at the time of my first impressions abroad, and under the first conscious influence of Papa's personality. It was then that a turning from the phraseological to the real ensued." Dietrich Bonhoeffer, *Letters and Papers from Prison*, Dietrich Bonhoeffer Works, vol. 10 (Minneapolis, MN: Fortress Press, 2010), 358.

26. Bediako, "The Willowbank Consultation," 28.

27. Ibid., 28.

28. Ibid.

29. Kwame Bediako, "Death and the Gospel in the Ghanaian Context," *Exchange* 20.2 (1991): 149.

30. See Anthony Ephrim-Donkor, *African Religion Defined: A Systematic Study of Ancestor Worship among the Akan* (New York: University Press of America, 2010); Anthony Ephirim-Donkor, *African Spirituality: On Becoming Ancestors* (Trenton, NJ: Africa World Press, 1997); Kofi Asare Opoku, *West African Traditional Religion* (Coraville, IA: FEP International, 1978).

31. This strain of thought can be traced back to Augustine (see *De civitate Dei* 4.34, 18.46) and is addressed by Barth in II/2, §34, "The Election of the Community."

32. Among others, Billy Graham encapsulated this viewpoint when he wrote, "[Consider] the novel thought that Christianity was not so much a 'religion' as a relationship with a Person." Billy Graham, *The Jesus Generation* (London: Hodder and Stoughton, 1972), 148.

33. See Barth's discussion of grace in Pure Land Buddhism in I/2, §17.3, 340 ff.; and the parables of the kingdom in §69.2.

34. Barth mentions Feuerbach forty-one times in the *Dogmatics*. The other significant treatment of Feuerbach is found in §45 (III/2, 240–41, 277–78).

35. John Glasse, "Barth on Feuerbach," *Harvard Theological Review* 57.2 (April 1964): 95. Glasse's article offers a significant and helpful engagement of all Barth's writings on Feuerbach.

36. This lecture was later attached as the "Introduction Essay" in the Torchbook edition of Ludwig Feuerbach, *Essence of Christianity*, trans. George Eliot, introd. Karl Barth, foreword H. Richard Niebuhr (New York: Harper & Row, 1957).

37. Glasse, "Barth on Feuerbach," 72.

38. Barth, "Introductory Essay," in *Essence of Christianity*, xxix, xix, xiv, xv.

39. Glasse, "Barth on Feuerbach," 72.

40. Here it is worth recalling Barth's early assertion in §69.2, "He, Jesus Christ, lives" (IV/3, 39).

41. Green, *Karl Barth on Religion*, 16.

42. Ibid., 20.

43. See Tom Greggs, *Theology against Religion: Constructive Dialogues with Bonhoeffer and Barth* (New York: Continuum, 2011), 91.

44. Questions surrounding Barth and the Jews are hotly debated. For two valuable views, see Katherine Sonderegger, *That Jesus Christ Was Born a Jew: Karl Barth's "Doctrine of Israel"* (University Park: Pennsylvania State University Press, 1992); Mark R. Lindsay, *Barth, Israel, and Jesus: Karl Barth's Theology of Israel*, Barth Studies Series (Aldershot: Ashgate, 2007); Mark R. Lindsay, *Reading Auschwitz with Barth: The Holocaust as Problem and Promise for Barthian Theology* (Eugene, OR: Pickwick Publications, 2014).

45. See Michael T. Dempsey, ed., *Trinity and Election in Contemporary Theology* (Grand Rapids, MI: Eerdmans, 2011), for a collection of essays debating this point in Barth studies.

46. Danquah, *The Akan Doctrine of God*, 169.

47. Ibid.

48. There is a long and sordid history of efforts by Christians to extract or minimize Jesus's identity as a Jew. As sympathetic as one might be to Bediako's motivations, there remain substantive theological reasons to object on this matter. See, e.g., J. Kameron Carter, *Race: A Theological Account* (New York: Oxford University Press, 2008).

49. Roar Fotland, "Ancestor Christology in Context: Theological Perspectives of Kwame Bediako" (PhD diss., University of Bergen, June 2005), 292–93.

50. Kwame Bediako, "Christian Faith and African Culture—An Exposition of the Epistle to the Hebrews," *Journal of African Christian Thought* 13.1 (June 2010): 45.

51. Bruce L. McCormack, "With Loud Cries and Tears: The Humanity of the Son in the Epistle to the Hebrews," in *The Epistle to the Hebrews and Christian Theology*, ed. Richard Bauckham et al. (Grand Rapids, MI: Eerdmans, 2009), 58; McCormack's emphasis.

52. Bediako, "One Song in Many Tongues," in *Jesus and the Gospel in Africa* (Oxford: Regnum, 2000), 78.

53. Bediako, "Thoughts on the Nature of the Project," 4.

54. Bediako, "Understanding African Theology in the Twentieth Century," 51.

55. Barth uses the word *primal* mostly in the sense of "original" and often connects it with "basic." There are eleven uses in §69, all but one using the wording, "the primal and basic form [*die Ur- und Grundgestalt*]." The other use is "the primal and basic form [*die Ur- und Grundgeform*]" (IV/3, 294). Other significant uses of the word in the *Dogmatics* are "first and primal [*das Uralte und Erste*]" when Barth is commenting on the Lord's Prayer, "This is the whole point with Jesus. His concern is not with something new but with that which is first and primal, with the God who wills to be God and to be known as God a second time in a different way, the God of Abraham, Isaac and Jacob, the God who wills to be revealed in His name and hallowed in His name" (I/1, 319); "primal knowledge [*prima sciencia*]" (I/2, §17, 289); "primal revelation [*Uroffenbarung*]" (I/2, §17, 307); "primal history [*Urgeschichte*]" of the covenant in the Exodus (II/1, §31, 600); "primal decision [*Urentscheidung*]" (II/2, §32, 50). In II/2, §32, *primal* appears twenty-one times, most often in relation to *Urentscheidung*. In II/2, §33, there are an additional sixteen uses as "primal decision [*Urentscheidung*]" and "primal and basic plan [*Ur- und Grundplan*]." Overall, there is significant overlap between Barth's use of "primal" and Bediako's use of "primal religions" and "primal imagination." The "primal" is that which is original—going back to the earliest human ancestors, Adam and Eve—and encompasses issues of religion and culture, in addition to revelation—as Barth uses it above in IV/3, 281.

56. Bediako, "Death and the Gospel in the Ghanaian Context," 148; original emphasis.

57. Kwame Gyeke, *Essay on African Philosophical Thought: The Akan Conceptual Scheme* (Cambridge: Cambridge University Press, 1987), 69; quoted in Bediako, *Religion, Culture and Language*, 8.

58. Bediako, "Understanding African Theology in the Twentieth Century," 51.

59. See II/2, §33.1, "Jesus Christ, Electing and Elected."

60. Jones, *The Humanity of Christ*, 252.

61. For an excellent exposition and application of Barth's postmetaphysical doctrine of God, see Kevin Hector, *Theology without Metaphysics: God, Language, and the Spirit of Recognition* (Cambridge: Cambridge University Press, 2011).

62. For more on Barth and universalism, see Tom Greggs, "'Jesus Is Victor': Passing the Impasse of Barth on Universalism," *Scottish Journal of Theology* 60.2 (May 2007): 196–212.

63. In Gillian Mary Bediako's collection of his sermons, there is a whole grouping labeled "revivals/evangelistic."

64. J. Kwabena Asamoah-Gyadu, "Kwame Bediako and the Eternal Christological Question," in *Seeing New Facets of the Diamond: Christianity as a Universal Faith: Essays in Honour of Kwame Bediako*, ed. Gillian M. Bediako, Benhardt Y. Quarshie, and J. Kwabena Asamoah-Gyadu (Eugene, OR: Wipf and Stock, 2014), 51.

65. Cyril Okorocha, "The Meaning of Salvation: An African Perspective," in *Emerging Voices in Global Christian Theology*, ed. William Dyrness (Grand Rapids, MI: Zondervan, 1994), 76.

66. John Mbiti, *Bible and Theology in African Christianity* (Nairobi: Oxford University Press, 1986), 158–59.

67. John Mbiti, "Some Reflections on African Experience of Salvation Today," in *Living Faith and Ultimate Goals*, ed. S. J. Samartha (Geneva: World Council of Churches, 1974), 112–13. See also Kofi Asare Opoku, "Toward a Holistic View of Salvation," in *Healing for God's World: Remedies from Three Continents* (New York: Friendship Press, 1991), 41–60.

68. Kofi Asare Opoku, "Post-Colonial Church Cultures in Multicultural Societies," Plenary Panel address, Transatlantic Roundtable on Religion and Race, Accra, Ghana, July 31, 2013.

69. Hunsinger's description of Barth's position as either "exclusivism without triumphalism" or "inclusivism without compromise" is also apt. See George Hunsinger, *How to Read Karl Barth* (New York: Oxford University Press, 1991), 278.

70. Kwame Bediako, "Response to Taber: Is There More than One Way to Do Theology?," *Gospel in Context* 1.1 (1978): 13–14.

71. Ibid., 14.

72. Bediako, "[Response to] David Hesselgrave," 13.

73. Bediako, "The Willowbank Consultation," 28.

74. Bediako defended his dissertation in July 1983. The dissertation was 536 pages, not including the bibliography, and was later published in 1992 as *Theology and Identity*.

75. Bediako, "The Willowbank Consultation," 31.

76. See also *CiA*, 265; Bediako, "'In the Bible, Africa walks on familiar ground,'" 34; Kwame Bediako, "Types of African Theology," in *Christianity in Africa in the 1990s*, ed. C. Fyfe and A. Walls (Edinburgh: University of Edinburgh, Centre for African Studies), 56.

77. Actual quote in Jack Newfield, *A Prophetic Minority* (New York: Signet Book, 1966), 111.

FIVE. Cultural Reflection

1. See Kelton Cobb, *Blackwell Guide to Theology and Popular Culture* (Malden, MA: Blackwell, 2005), for more on his helpful distinctions between types of culture: high culture, folk culture, and popular culture.

2. Busch, *Karl Barth: His Life from Letters*, 395.

3. Philip Stoltzfus, *Theology as Performance: Music, Aesthetics, and God in Western Thought* (New York: T&T Clark, 2006), 117.

4. Karl Barth to H. Scholz, May 24, 1953. Cited in Busch, *Karl Barth: His Life from Letters*, 395.

5. Karl Barth, *Wolfgang Amadeus Mozart*, trans. Clarence K. Pott (Grand Rapids, MI: Eerdmans, 1986), 16; Busch, *Karl Barth: His Life from Letters*, 498–99.

6. Barth, *Wolfgang Amadeus Mozart*, 16.

7. Karl Barth, *How I Changed My Mind* (Richmond, VA: John Knox Press, 1966), 72. Barth even wrote a public letter of thanks to Mozart; see Barth, "A Letter of Thanks to Mozart, Basel, December 23, 1955," in *Wolfgang Amadeus Mozart*, 37.

8. Karl Barth, *Wolfgang Amadeus Mozart*, 43–60.

9. Karl Barth, "Mozart's Freedom," in *Wolfgang Amadeus Mozart*, 56–57. For the German, see Karl Barth, "Mozarts Freiheit," in *Wolfgang Amadeus Mozart* (Zurich: Theologischer Verlag, 1982), 43.

10. Barth, "Mozart's Freedom," 57; Barth's emphasis. Barth quipped, "There are probably very few theologians' studies in which the pictures of Calvin and Mozart are to be seen hanging next to each other and at the same height." Barth, *How I Changed My Mind*, 72.

11. Barth is said to have owned records of every piece of Mozart's work that had been recorded. He would fall asleep and was awakened to Mozart's music as well. Barth "died peacefully some time in the middle of the night [December 9–10, 1968]. He lay there as asleep, with his hands gently folded from his evening prayers. So his wife found him in the morning, while in the background a record was playing the Mozart with which she had wanted to waken him" (Busch, *Karl Barth: His Life from Letters*, 498–99).

12. Busch referred to the beginning of Barth's work on IV/3, §69, in 1956 as "a happy coincidence that while Barth was preoccupied with Mozart in this way, his dogmatics lectures (from the beginning of the winter semester he had begun on the material for a new volume, IV/3) were an extended and thoroughgoing discussion of the theological problem of the 'parables of the kingdom of heaven' in the human and earthly realm" (Busch, *Karl Barth: His Life from Letters*, 410).

13. Karl Barth, *Theology and Church: Shorter Writings 1920–1928* (London: SCM Press, 1962), 337.

14. Ibid., 338.

15. DeCou, "Relocating Barth's Theology of Culture," 155; original emphasis. See also Paul Metzger, *The Word of Christ and the World of Culture: Sacred and Secular through the Theology of Karl Barth* (Grand Rapids, MI: Eerdmans, 2003); Robert J. Palma, *Karl Barth's Theology of Culture: The Freedom of Culture for the Praise of God* (Allison Park, PA: Pickwick Publications, 1983).

16. Kwame Bediako, "Culture," in *New Dictionary of Theology*, eds. Sinclair Ferguson and David Wright (Downers Grove, IL: InterVarsity Press, 1988), 183–85.

17. Ibid., 183.

18. Ibid.; see also Kwame Bediako, "Gospel and Culture: Some Insights for Our Time from the Experience of the Earliest Christians," *JACT* 2.2 (1999): 8.

19. Bediako, "Gospel and Culture," 8.

20. Ibid.

21. Ibid.

22. Bediako, "Scripture as the Hermeneutics of Culture and Tradition," 2.

23. Bediako, "Gospel and Culture," 9.

24. Ibid.

25. Ibid., 8–9.

26. Kwame Bediako, "Gospel and Culture: Guest Editorial," *JACT* 2.2 (1999): 1.

27. See Bediako, "African Identity: The Afrikania Challenge," in *CiA*, 17–38.

28. Bediako, "Gospel and Culture," 12.

29. Bediako, "The Willowbank Consultation," 26.

30. Bediako, "Understanding African Theology in the Twentieth Century," 53.

31. Ibid., 51.

32. See also Bediako, "Understanding African Theology in the Twentieth Century," 53.

33. For more on Bediako's theology of négritude, see Tim Hartman, "An Act of Theological Négritude: Kwame Bediako on African Christian Identity," in *Religion, Culture and Spirituality in Africa and the African Diaspora*, ed. William Ackah, Jualynne E. Dodson, and R. Drew Smith (New York: Routledge, 2018), 81–95.

34. Gyeke, *Essay on African Philosophical Thought*, 69. Bediako sought to connect the death of Jesus with its impact in the spiritual world. Bediako wrote, "The victory of the Cross was achieved in the realm of spiritual power, that is, in the very realm where ancestors, spirit-powers and magical forces are believed to operate." Since Jesus's death has spiritual ramifications, his death can affect the ancestors and the spiritual realm in which they are understood to preside. See Bediako, *Religion, Culture and Language*, 8.

35. Bediako borrowed the term "primal imagination" from C. G. Baëta's *Christianity in Tropical Africa*.

36. Bediako, *Religion, Culture and Language*, 36.

37. Bediako, "Thoughts on the Nature of the Project," 4.

38. Ibid.

39. Ibid.

40. Ibid.

41. Bediako, "Understanding African Theology," 51. See *TI*, 4.

42. More of Bediako's understanding of Odwira is explored in ch.6, including how he understands the crucifixion as the fulfillment of the traditional Odwira

festival: "The *Odwira* to end all *odwiras* has taken place through the death of Jesus Christ" (JAC, 33).

43. Bediako, *Jesus and the Gospel in Africa*, 9.

44. Bediako, "'Their past is also our present,'" 8.

45. Kwame Bediako, "Recognizing the Primal Religions" (Stone Lecture No. 2, Princeton Theological Seminary, Princeton, NJ), October 21, 2003.

46. Kwame Bediako, "The Holy Spirit, the Christian Gospel and Religious Change: The African Evidence for a Christian Theology of Religious Pluralism," in *Essays in Religious Studies for Andrew Walls*, ed. James Thrower (Aberdeen: Department of Religious Studies, University of Aberdeen, 1986), 47.

47. Ibid.

48. On this point, see also Patrick J. Ryan, "'Arise O God!': The Problem of 'Gods' in West Africa," *Journal of Religion in Africa* 11.3 (1980): 161–71.

49. Kwame Bediako, "The Significance of Modern African Christianity—A Manifesto," *Studies in World Christianity* (*Edinburgh Review of Theology and Religion*) 1.1 (1995): 54. Also in Bediako, "Cry Jesus!," 16–17.

50. See also Bediako, "Understanding African Theology in the Twentieth Century," 59; Bediako, "The Impact of the Bible in Africa," 248.

51. Bediako, "Understanding African Theology in the Twentieth Century," 59; Bediako, "The Impact of the Bible in Africa," 248.

52. Bediako, "Understanding African Theology in the Twentieth Century," 59.

53. Ibid.

54. Ibid.

55. Ibid.

56. Ibid.

57. In his 1894 Christmas Eve sermon, "The Light of the World," Christoph Blumhardt described "the shadow which is cast over all Christendom" as a result of Christianity's selfish exploitation of "these sublime words—'come into the flesh, come into the world.'" Christoph Blumhardt, *Christoph Blumhardt and His Message*, ed. R. Lejeune (Rifton, NY: Plough Publishing House, 1963), 137.

58. Barth pairs "reconciliation" and "revelation" twenty-nine times in IV/3, §69.

59. The initial use of *der sprechende, der leuchtende Gott*, literally, "the talking, shining God," is in IV/3, 79. In *Church Dogmatics*, the phrase "eloquent and radiant" appears eight times, all within three pages in §69, IV/3, 79–81.

60. See again Blumhardt's 1894 Christmas Eve sermon, "The Light of the World," 141–42.

61. For more on the use and meaning of "eloquent and radiant" in §69, see John Webster, "'Eloquent and Radiant': The Prophetic Office of Christ and the Mission of the Church," in his *Barth's Moral Theology: Human Action in Barth's Thought* (Grand Rapids, MI: Eerdmans, 1998), 125–50.

62. Hunsinger, *How to Read Karl Barth*, 234–80. See also Glenn A. Chestnutt, *Challenging the Stereotype: The Theology of Karl Barth as a Resource for Inter-Religious Encounter in a European Context* (Oxford: Peter Lang, 2010), esp. chs. 3 and 4; Geoff Thompson, "'As open to the world as any theologian could be . . .'? Karl Barth's Account of Extra-Ecclesial Truth and Its Value to Christianity's Encounter with Other Religious Traditions" (PhD diss., University of Cambridge, 1995); Geoff Thompson, "Religious Diversity, Christian Doctrine and Karl Barth," *International Journal of Systematic Theology* 8.1 (January 2006): 3–24; Greggs, *Theology against Religion*, esp. ch. 4, 74–98.

63. Hunsinger, *How to Read Karl Barth*, 235.

64. Ibid., 255.

65. See also Barth's discussion of John 10 a bit earlier in §69.2: *Church Dogmatics* IV/3, 95.

66. Clifford J. Green, *Karl Barth: Theologian of Freedom* (San Francisco: Collins, 1989), 43.

67. See *Church Dogmatics* IV/3, 114 x2; 117 x2; 120; 122; 125; 128; 130; 143.

68. There are two additional uses outside the dogmatics of minor significance. Barth speaks of some New Testament parables (the Lost Son and the Good Samaritan) as parables of the kingdom in his 1956 lecture on the humanity of God (Barth, *Humanity of God*, 51). Barth had spoken about theological beliefs translated into political terms as "examples of parables, analogies and corollaries of the Kingdom of God" in his 1946 lecture, "The Christian Community and the Civil Community, §27," in Green, *Karl Barth: Theologian of Freedom*, 289.

69. Translated from *Die christliche Lehre nach dem Heidelberger Katechismus* (Zollikon-Zurich: Evangelisher Verlag, 1948) by Shirley Guthrie, in Karl Barth, *Learning Jesus Christ through the Heidelberg Catechism* (Grand Rapids, MI: Eerdmans, 1964), 62–63; emphasis added.

70. Barth cited this book as C. H. Dodd, *The Parables of the Kingdom* (New York: Scribner, [1935] 1961): Karl Barth, "12 Gespräch mit Vertretern der Herrnhuter Brüdergemeinde (12.10.1960)," in *Karl Barth Gesamtausgabe: Gespräche 1959–1962 (GA IV/25)*, ed. Eberhard Busch (Zurich: Theologischer Verlag Zürich, 1995), 146.

71. Karl Barth, "An Prof. Dr. Jean Daniélou S.J., Paris, 1948," in *Offene Briefe 1945–1968 (GA V.15)*, ed. Diether Koch (Zurich: Theologischer Verlag Zürich, 1984), 169. Barth and Willem Visser't Hooft also corresponded about Dodd's work both in 1948 and in 1957.

72. Webster, "'Eloquent and Radiant,'" 141.

73. Barth expresses the relationship this way: "In sum, the New Testament parables are as it were the prototype of the order in which there can be other true words alongside the one Word of God, created and determined by it, exactly corresponding to it, fully serving it and therefore enjoying its power and authority" (IV/3, 113).

74. See Barth's discussion of these texts in IV/3, 112.

75. Hunsinger, *How to Read Karl Barth*, 262. For Hunsinger's understanding of "uncreated light" in Barth, see "Uncreated Light: From Irenaeus and Torrance to Aquinas and Barth," in *Light from Light: Scientists and Theologians in Dialogue*, ed. Gerald O'Collins and Mary Ann Meyers (Grand Rapids, MI: Eerdmans, 2012), 208–35. In his chapter, Hunsinger rightfully claims that "Barth's controlling metaphor was not creation but resurrection" (222).

76. Hunsinger, *How to Read Karl Barth*, 264.

77. Ibid., 265.

SIX. Constructive Reflection

1. Kwame Bediako, "Christ, Our Odwira," sermon preached on September 30, 1990 (and again on October 22, 1995), on Odwira Sunday, Mpeiase, Akropong, 1. In the personal collection of sermons on the Epistle to the Hebrews of Gillian Mary Bediako in Akropong-Akuapem, Ghana.

2. "Speech by Oseadeeyo Addo Dankwa III, Okuapehene on the occasion of the 1990 *Odwira* Durbar," at Akropong-Akuapem, Friday, September 28, 1990, 1. In the personal collection of sermons on the Epistle to the Hebrews of Gillian Mary Bediako in Akropong-Akuapem, Ghana.

3. For more on the connection between the Odwira festival and the Christian faith, see Frank Kwesi Adams, *Odwira and the Gospel: A Study of the Asante Odwira Festival and Its Significance for Christianity in Ghana* (Oxford: Regnum, 2010).

4. For examples, see Lesslie Newbigin, *The Other Side of 1984: Questions for the Churches* (Geneva: World Council of Churches, 1983), 23; and more pejoratively, D. A. Carson, *Becoming Conversant with the Emerging Church: Understanding a Movement and Its Implications* (Grand Rapids, MI: Eerdmans, 2009), esp. 200–202.

5. John Calvin, *Institutes of the Christian Religion*, trans. Ford Lewis Battles (Philadelphia: Westminster John Knox, 1960), I.11.13.

6. There is one use of "syncretism" in the *Church Dogmatics* in I/2, §17, 334 (Green, *Karl Barth on Religion*, 94) and four uses of "syncretistic," one each in I/1, III/1, III/3, and IV/2.

7. I am indebted to Ross Kane for this idea of syncretism as expanding the gospel. See Ross Kane, "Social Healing through Hybrid and Syncretic Sacrifice in South Sudan," paper presented at the Annual Meeting of the American Academy of Religion, Atlanta, 2015. See also Ross Kane, "Ritual Formation of Peaceful Publics: Sacrifice and Syncretism in South Sudan (1991–2005)," *Journal of Religion in Africa* 44.3–4 (2014): 386–410.

8. For more on selecting ancestors: "Not all the dead are ancestors. . . . For ancestors become so not solely by association in blood lineage, but also by quality

of life, by the social significance and impact of their work; in other words, the dead become ancestors by achievement in life and not solely for having lived in the community" (*CiA*, 80).

9. Ephirim-Donkor, *African Religion Defined*, v.

10. Bediako, "Death and the Gospel in the Ghanaian Context," 147.

11. C. G. Baëta, "The Challenge of African Culture to the Church and the Message of the Church to African Culture," in *Christianity and African Culture* (Accra: Christian Council of the Gold Coast, 1955), 59; original emphasis. Also cited in *CiA*, 60.

12. See Harry Sawyerr, "Ancestor Worship I: The Mechanics," *Sierra Leone Bulletin of Religion* 6.2 (December 1964); John S. Pobee, *Toward an African Theology* (Nashville, TN: Abingdon, 1979); Charles Nyamiti, *Christ as Our Ancestor: Christology from an African Perspective* (Gweru, Zimbabwe: Mambo Press, 1984).

13. Bediako, "Death and the Gospel in the Ghanaian Context," 148.

14. Bediako, "Challenges of Ghana's Fourth Republic," Lecture 2, 13.

15. Bediako, "Death and the Gospel in the Ghanaian Context," 147.

16. Danquah, *The Akan Doctrine of God*, 168; quoted in Kwame Bediako, "Religion and National Identity: Assessing the Discussion from Cicero to Danquah," Bediako Law and Religion Inaugural Lecture, June 25, 1997, Ghana Academy of Arts and Sciences, Accra, 14.

17. Bediako, "'Their past is also our present,'" 2.

18. Baëta, "The Challenge of African Culture to the Church," 59; original emphasis. Also *CiA*, 60.

19. Bediako, "Challenges of Ghana's Fourth Republic," Lecture 3, 4–5.

20. Bediako, "Religion and National Identity," 6.

21. Robert Owusu Agyarko, "God's Unique Priest (*Nyamesofopreko*): Christology in the Akan Context" (PhD diss., University of the Western Cape, 2009).

22. Ephirim-Donkor, *African Religion Defined*, v.

23. For Roman Catholic perspectives, see Edward Fasholé-Luke, "Ancestor Veneration and the Communion of Saints," in *New Testament Christianity for Africa and the World*, ed. Mark Glasswell and Edward Fasholé-Luke (London: SPCK, 1974); Nyamiti, *Christ as Our Ancestor.*

24. Bediako, "Challenges of Ghana's Fourth Republic," Lecture 3, 8.

25. Ibid., 5.

26. Tinyiko Sam Maluleke, "African Traditional Religions in Christian Mission and Christian Scholarship: Re-Opening a Debate That Never Started," *Religion and Theology* 5.2 (1998): 131.

27. Ibid. For the original use of "intellectual smugglers," see Okot p'Bitek, *African Religions in Western Scholarship* (Kampala: East African Literature Bureau, 1970), 88.

28. Tinyiko Sam Maluleke, "Black and African Theologies in the New World Order: A Time to Drink from Our Own Wells," *Journal of Theology for Southern Africa* 96 (November 1996): 16.

29. Bediako, "'Missionaries did not bring Christ to Africa,'" 25.

30. Ibid., 25–26. For more on Akan thrones, or stools, see Peter Sarpong, *The Sacred Stools of the Akan* (Accra-Tema: Ghana Pub. Corp., 1971).

31. Bediako, "'Missionaries did not bring Christ to Africa,'" 26.

32. Ibid.

33. Bediako, "'Their past is also our present.'"

34. According to Bediako, "For the African theologian, however, the traditional religions, even if they constitute his past, are of the nature of an 'ontological' past, which means that together with the profession of the Christian faith, it gives account of the same entity—namely the history of the religious consciousness of the African Christian" (*CiA*, 258).

35. See also Bediako: "African indigenous knowledge systems lie at the heart of the academic study of the emergence of African Christianity, for they help to explain the way Africans live out their Christian faith. [. . .] African indigenous knowledge systems—the traditional wisdom, knowledge, skills and understandings of the universe that have continued with African societies [. . .] operate within a world-view in which to live is to be connected to the Transcendent and to people—the living, the living dead and those yet to come. Might this be part of the explanation why so much of our African Christianity seems to live beyond the Enlightenment frame and seems not to wait for verification by Enlightenment procedures?" Bediako, "A New Era in Christian History," 3, 4, and 7.

36. Homi Bhabha, *Location of Culture* (London: Routledge, 1994).

37. Bediako, "'Whose Religion Is Christianity?,'" 48.

38. Ibid., 47.

39. Bediako, "'In the Bible . . . Africa walks on familiar ground,'" 38.

40. See Gustavo Gutiérrez, *We Drink from Our Own Wells* (Maryknoll, NY: Orbis, 1984).

41. See Bediako, "The Willowbank Consultation," 25–26.

42. Kofi Asare Opoku, personal interview, Ghana Institute of Management and Public Administration, Accra, Ghana, July 31, 2013.

43. Bediako, "Gospel and Culture: Guest Editorial," 1; Bediako's emphasis.

44. Karl Barth, *Göttingen Dogmatics*, vol. 1, trans. Geoffrey W. Bromiley (Grand Rapids, MI: Eerdmans, [1924] 1991), 258, 259. See also Barth's description of the work of interpretation: "Free thinking with the help of authorities" (260).

45. Bruce L. McCormack, "The Identity of the Son: Karl Barth's Exegesis of Hebrews 1.1–4 (and Similar Passages)," in *Christology, Hermeneutics, and Hebrews:*

Profiles from the History of Interpretation, ed. Jon Laansma and Daniel Treier (London: T&T Clark, 2012), 157.

46. See IV/3, 48; 232; 266; 235 x2; 236; 293; 301.

47. More generally, Barth identifies Jesus Christ with the prophetic office by citing the biblical witness: John 6:14; 1 Timothy 2:16; 2 Corinthians 1:20 (IV/3, 12).

48. Bediako, "Biblical Christologies in the Context of African Traditional Religions," 101; JAC, 25.

49. Bediako, "Religion and National Identity," 6.

50. Jean-Marc Éla, *My Faith as an African*, trans. John Pairman Brown and Susan Perry (Maryknoll, NY: Orbis, 1988), 20.

51. Barth had planned to lecture on Hebrews during the summer semester of 1922 at the University of Göttingen but found that his main lecture course on Calvin was too demanding and canceled his plan. See McCormack, "The Identity of the Son," 155.

52. Bruce L. McCormack, "The Significance of Karl Barth's Theological Exegesis of Philippians," in Karl Barth, *The Epistle to the Philippians: 40th Anniversary Edition* (Louisville, KY: Westminster John Knox Press, 2002), v–xxv.

53. See 1:1, six uses (I/2, 84; III/1, 115; III/2, 462; IV/3, 93; and IV/3, 584); 1:2, twelve uses (I/2, 401 x2; 442; I/2, 148; II/1, 416; II/2, 99; III/1, 19, 51, 53; III/2, 483; IV/2, 34; IV/3, 93); 1:3, twenty-one uses (I/1, 360, 386, 429; I/2, 379; II/1, 416, 606, 661; II/2, 99 x2; III/1, 54; III/2, 466; III/3, 10, 35, 59, 439 x2, 441; IV/1, 44; IV/3, 195, 767); and 1:4, three uses (I/2, 379; III/2, 14; III/3, 453).

54. McCormack, "The Identity of the Son," 156; original emphasis.

55. Bediako's views on the Epistle to the Hebrews are most clearly expressed in three published works: "Jesus in African Culture: A Ghanaian Perspective," first published in 1990 and republished in *Jesus and the Gospel in Africa*, from which the citations here are taken; *Christianity in Africa*, ch. 12, "Christian Religion and the African World-View: Will Ancestors Survive?," 210–34; and the posthumously published article, "Christian Faith and African Culture—An Exposition of the Epistle to the Hebrews," *JACT* 13.1 (June 2010), 45–57. There are also a number of helpful unpublished sermons on Hebrews held in the personal archive of Bediako's widow, Dr. Gillian Mary Bediako.

56. Bediako, "Christian Faith and African Culture," 47.

57. Ibid.

58. Ibid.

59. The questions surrounding the authorship of the Epistle to the Hebrews are unresolved. Though many had long assumed that Paul had written the letter, the current scholarly consensus opposes that view but does stress that the author was a Hellenistic Jew.

60. McCormack, "The Identity of the Son," 156.

61. Bediako, "Biblical Christologies in the Context of African Traditional Religion," 100–101; see the same text, slightly edited, in JAC, 24.

SEVEN. Collaborative Reflection

1. Ivan Illich, "To Hell with Good Intentions," in *Combining Service and Learning: A Resource Book for Community and Public Service*, ed. Jane C. Kendall (Raleigh, NC: National Society for Internships and Experiential Education, 1990), 320.

2. For more on Barth's understanding of the Holy Spirit, see Tim Hartman, "The Promise of an Actualistic Pneumatology: Beginning with the Holy Spirit in African Pentecostalism and Karl Barth," *Modern Theology* 33.3 (July 2017): 333–47.

3. For examples, see Brian McLaren, "The Method, the Message, and the Ongoing Story," in *The Church in Emerging Culture: Five Perspectives* (Grand Rapids, MI: Zondervan, 2003), 191–234.

4. Bediako, "Africa and Christianity on the Threshold of the Third Millennium," 316.

5. Ibid.

6. Bediako, "Biblical Exegesis in the African Context," 20.

7. Ibid.

8. Ibid.

9. For more on Bediako's understanding of the Hellenistic parallels, see Bediako, "Religion and National Identity," 3.

10. Bediako, "The Significance of Modern African Christianity—A Manifesto," 62.

11. Kwame Bediako, "The Unique Christ in the Plurality of Religions," in *The Unique Christ in Our Pluralist World*, ed. Bruce Nichols (Grand Rapids, MI: Baker, 1994), 55.

12. Ibid. See also Bediako, "Islam and the Kingdom of God," 6.

13. Also in Bediako, "Understanding African Theology in the Twentieth Century," 52.

14. See also *CiA*, 265; Bediako, "'In the Bible . . . Africa walks on familiar ground,'" 34; Bediako, "Types of African Theology," 56.

15. Bediako, "Islam and the Kingdom of God," 3.

16. John Mbiti, "Theological Impotence and the Universality of the Church," in *Mission Trends No.3: Third World Theologies*, ed. Gerald Anderson and Thomas Stransky (Grand Rapids, MI: Eerdmans, 1976), 16.

17. Bonhoeffer, *Letters and Papers from Prison*, 382–83.

18. This is the insight of Peter Berger's *The Heretical Imperative*.

BIBLIOGRAPHY

Aboagye-Mensah, Robert. "Socio-Political Thinking of Karl Barth: Trinitarian and Incarnational Christology as the Ground for His Social Action and Its Implications for Us Today." PhD dissertation, University of Aberdeen, 1984.

Adams, Frank Kwesi. *Odwira and the Gospel: A Study of the Asante Odwira Festival and Its Significance for Christianity in Ghana*. Oxford: Regnum, 2010.

Adogame, Afe. "Sub-Saharan Africa." In *Religion, Globalization, and Culture*, edited by Peter Beyer and Lori Beaman, 527–48. Leiden: Brill, 2007.

African Christianity Rising. Directed by James Ault. James Ault Productions, Northampton, MA, 2013.

Agyarko, Robert Owusu. "God's Unique Priest (*Nyamesofopreko*): Christology in the Akan Context." PhD dissertation, University of the Western Cape, 2009.

Aimé Césaire, une voix pour l'histoire. Directed by Euzhan Palcy. JMJ Productions, Martinique, [1994] 2006.

"America's Changing Religious Landscape." Pew Research Center. May 12, 2015. www.pewforum.org/2015/05/12/americas-changing-religious-landscape/.

Asad, Talal. *Formations of the Secular*. Stanford, CA: Stanford University Press, 2003.

Asamoah-Gyadu, J. Kwabena. *African Charismatics: Current Developments within Independent Pentecostalism in Ghana*. Leiden: Brill, 2005.

———. "Bediako of Africa: A Late 20th Century Outstanding Theologian and Teacher." *Mission Studies* 26 (2009): 5–16.

———. *Contemporary Pentecostal Christianity: Interpretations from an African Context*. Oxford: Regnum, 2013.

———. "Kwame Bediako and the Eternal Christological Question." In *Seeing New Facets of the Diamond: Christianity as a Universal Faith: Essays in Honour of Kwame Bediako*, edited by Gillian M. Bediako, Benhardt Y. Quarshie, and J. Kwabena Asamoah-Gyadu, 38–55. Eugene, OR: Wipf and Stock, 2014.

Ashcroft, Bill, Gareth Griffiths, and Helen Tiffin. *The Empire Writes Back: Theory and Practice in Post-Colonial Literature*. London: Routledge, 1989.

Baëta, C. G. "The Challenge of African Culture to the Church and the Message of the Church to African Culture." In *Christianity and African Culture*, 51–61. Accra: Christian Council of the Gold Coast, 1955.

———. *Christianity in Tropical Africa*. Oxford: Oxford University Press, 1968.

Balthasar, Hans Urs von. *The Theology of Karl Barth: Exposition and Interpretation*. Translated by Edward T. Oakes. San Francisco: Ignatius, 1992.

Barrett, David. "AD 2000: 350 Million Christians in Africa." *International Review of Mission* 59.233 (January 1970): 39–54.

Barth, Karl. Afterword to *Action in Waiting*, by Christoph Blumhardt, 217–22. Rifton, New York: Plough Publishing House, 2012.

———. "An Prof. Dr. Jean Daniélou S.J., Paris, 1948." In *Offene Briefe 1945–1968 (GA V.15)*, edited by Diether Koch, 167–75. Zurich: Theologischer Verlag Zürich, 1984.

———. *The Christian Life: Church Dogmatics IV.4, Lecture Fragments*. Edited by Hans-Anton Drewes and Eberhard Jüngel, translated by Geoffrey Bromiley. London: T&T Clark, 2004.

———. "Christianity or Religion?" In *Fragments Grave and Gay*, 27–31. London: Fontana, 1971.

———. *Church Dogmatics*. 4 vols. Edinburgh: T&T Clark, 1956–75.

———. *Epistle to the Romans*. 2nd ed. Translated by Edwyn C. Hoskyns. London: Oxford University Press, [1933] 1968.

———. *Evangelical Theology: An Introduction*. Grand Rapids, MI: Eerdmans, 1963.

———. "Evangelical Theology in the 19th Century." In *Humanity of God*, 11–36. Louisville, KY: Westminster John Knox Press, 1960. Translated from Karl Barth, "Evangelische Theologie im 19. Jahrhundert." *Theologische Studien*, Heft 49. Zollikon-Zurich: Evangelischer Verlag, 1957.

———. *Das Evangelium in der Gegenwart*. Munich: Chr. Kaiser Verlag, 1935.

———. "Extra Nos—Pro Nobis—In Nobis." Translated by George Hunsinger. *The Thomist* 50.4 (October 1986): 497–511.

———. "Extra Nos—Pro Nobis—In Nobis." In *Hören und Handeln: Festschrift für Ernst Wolf zum 60. Geburtstag*, edited by Helmut Gollwitzer and Hellmut Traub, 15–27. Munich: Chr. Kaiser Verlag, 1962.

———. *Fakultätsalbum der Evangelisch-theologischen Fakultät*. Muenster, 1927.

———. *Fragments Grave and Gay*. London: Fontana, 1971.

———. *Göttingen Dogmatics*, vol. 1. Translated by Geoffrey W. Bromiley. Grand Rapids, MI: Eerdmans, [1924] 1991.

———. *How I Changed My Mind*. Richmond, VA: John Knox Press, 1966.

———. *Humanity of God*. Louisville, KY: Westminster John Knox Press, 1960.

————. "Introductory Essay." In Ludwig Feuerbach, *Essence of Christianity*, x–xxxii. New York: Harper & Row, 1957.

————. *Karl Barth's Table Talk*. Edited by John Godsey. Richmond, VA: John Knox Press, 1963.

————. *Learning Jesus Christ through the Heidelberg Catechism*. Translated by Shirley Guthrie. Grand Rapids, MI: Eerdmans, 1964. Originally published as *Die christliche Lehre nach dem Heidelberger Katechismus*. Zollikon-Zurich: Evangelisher Verlag, 1948.

————. "Mozart's Freedom." In *Wolfgang Amadeus Mozart*, 43–60. Grand Rapids, MI: Eerdmans, 1986.

————. "No Boring Theology! A Letter from Karl Barth." *South East Asian Journal of Theology* 11 (Autumn 1969): 3–5.

————. *Der Römerbrief*. 1st ed. Bern: G. A. Bäschlin, 1919.

————. "A Theological Dialogue." *Theology Today* 19.2 (July 1962): 171–77.

————. *Theological Existence Today*. Translated by R. Birch Hoyle. Lexington, KY: ATLA, [1933] 1962.

————. "Theological Existence Today!" In *A Church Undone: Documents from the German Christian Faith Movement, 1932–1940*, edited and translated by Mary Holberg, 81–100. Minneapolis, MN: Fortress Press, 2015.

————. *Theology and Church: Shorter Writings 1920–1928*. London: SCM Press, 1962.

————. *Theology of Schleiermacher*. Grand Rapids, MI: Eerdmans, 1982.

————. "Unscientific Concluding Post-Script." In *Theology of Schleiermacher*, 261–79. Grand Rapids, MI: Eerdmans, 1982.

————. *Wolfgang Amadeus Mozart*. Translated by Clarence K. Pott. Grand Rapids, MI: Eerdmans, 1986.

————. *The Word of God and Theology*. Translated by Amy Marga. New York: T&T Clark, 2011.

————. "12 Gespräch mit Vertretern der Herrnhuter Brüdergemeinde (12.10.1960)." In *Karl Barth Gesamtausgabe: Gespräche 1959–1962 (GA IV/25)*, edited by Eberhard Busch. Zurich: Theologischer Verlag Zürich, 1995.

Bediako, Gillian Mary. *Primal Religion and the Bible: William Robertson Smith and His Heritage*. London: Bloomsbury Academic, 1997.

Bediako, Gillian M., Benhardt Y. Quarshie, and J. Kwabena Asamoah-Gyadu, eds. *Seeing New Facets of the Diamond: Christianity as a Universal Faith. Essays in Honour of Kwame Bediako*. Eugene, OR: Wipf and Stock, 2014.

Bediako, Kwame. "Africa and Christianity on the Threshold of the Third Millennium: The Religious Dimension." *African Affairs* 99 (2000): 303–23.

————. "Andrew F. Walls as Mentor." In *Understanding World Christianity: The Vision and Work of Andrew F. Walls*, edited by William R. Burrows, Mark R. Gornik, and Janice A. McLean, 7–10. Maryknoll, NY: Orbis, 2011.

————. "Biblical Christologies in the Context of African Traditional Religion." In *Sharing Jesus in the Two-Thirds World*, edited by Vinay Samuel and Chris Sugden, 81–121. Grand Rapids, MI: Eerdmans, 1984.

————. "Biblical Exegesis in the African Context: The Factor and Impact of Translated Scriptures." *JACT* 6.1 (2003): 15–23.

————. "Challenges of Ghana's Fourth Republic: A Christian Perspective." The William Ofori-Atta Memorial Lectures, October 7–9, 1992.

————. "Christian Faith and African Culture—An Exposition of the Epistle to the Hebrews." *JACT* 13.1 (June 2010): 45–57.

————. "Christian Tradition and the African God Revisited: A Process in the Exploration of a Theological Idiom." In *Witnessing to the Living God in Contemporary Africa*, edited by David Gitari and Patrick Benson, 77–97. Nairobi: Uzima Press, 1986.

————. *Christianity in Africa: The Renewal of a Non-Western Religion*. Edinburgh: Edinburgh University Press, 1995.

————. "Christ in Africa: Some Reflections on the Contribution of Christianity to the African Becoming." In *Proceedings of African Futures: 25th Anniversary Conference Held in the Centre of African Studies, University of Edinburgh, 9–11 December 1987*, edited by Christopher Fyfe and Chris Allen, 447–58. Edinburgh: Centre of African Studies, 1987.

————. "The Church and the University: Some Reflections on the Rationale for a Christian Participation in Public Education in Africa." *ATF Bulletin* 16 (2003): 5–7.

————. "Conclusion: The Emergence of World Christianity and the Remaking of Theology." In *Understanding World Christianity: The Vision and Work of Andrew F. Walls*, edited by William R. Burrows, Mark R. Gornik, and Janice A. McLean, 243–56. Maryknoll, NY: Orbis, 2011.

————. "Cry Jesus! Christian Theology and Presence in Modern Africa." In *Jesus and the Gospel in Africa*, 8–15. Oxford: Regnum, 2000.

————. "Culture." In *New Dictionary of Theology*, edited by Sinclair Ferguson and David Wright, 183–84. Downers Grove, IL: InterVarsity Press, 1988.

————. "Death and the Gospel in the Ghanaian Context." *Exchange* 20.2 (1991): 147–49.

————. "The Doctrine of Christ and the Significance of Vernacular Terminology." *International Bulletin of Missionary Research* 22.3 (July 1998): 110–11.

————. "Education and Human Values in Ghana—A Christian Reflection on Our Common Future." *JACT* 18.2 (December 2015): 50–62.

————. "The Emergence of World Christianity and the Remaking of Theology." *JACT* 12.2 (2009): 50–55.

————. "An Evaluation of the Achievement of the Christian Ideal in Education in Ghana from the 19th Century to the Early 20th Century." In *Educating a*

Nation: A Christian Perspective for Our Time, 1–26. The Andrew McCutcheon Atkinson Memorial Lectures, delivered at the Presbyterian Church of the Resurrection, Accra, Ghana, December 1, 1993.

———. "Gospel and Culture: Guest Editorial." *JACT* 2.2 (1999): 1.

———. "Gospel and Culture: Some Insights for Our Time from the Experience of the Earliest Christians." *JACT* 2.2 (1999): 8–17.

———. "The Holy Spirit, the Christian Gospel and Religious Change: The African Evidence for a Christian Theology of Religious Pluralism." In *Essays in Religious Studies for Andrew Walls*, edited by James Thrower, 44–56. Aberdeen: Department of Religious Studies, University of Aberdeen, 1986.

———. "The Impact of the Bible in Africa." Epilogue to Ype Schaaf, *On Their Way Rejoicing—The History and Role of the Bible in Africa*, 243–54. Carlisle: Paternoster Press, 1995.

———. "'In the Bible . . . Africa walks on familiar ground': Why the World Needs Africa." *AICMAR Bulletin* 6 (2007): 32–50.

———. "Islam and the Kingdom of God." *JACT* 7.2 (2004): 3–7.

———. *Jesus and the Gospel in Africa*. Oxford: Regnum, 2000.

———. "Memorandum to Christian Service College Council on the Work of the College." May 29, 1978. Unpublished archival document.

———. "'Missionaries did not bring Christ to Africa—Christ brought them': Why Africa Needs Jesus Christ." *AICMAR Bulletin* 6 (2007): 17–31.

———. "Négritude et Surréalisme: Essai sur l'oeuvre poétique de Tchicaya U Tam'si." MA thesis, T.E.R., Bordeaux III, 1970.

———. "A New Era in Christian History—African Christianity as Representative Christianity: Some Implications for Theological Education and Scholarship." *JACT* 9.1 (2006): 3–12.

———. "New Paradigms on Ecumenical Co-Operation: An African Perspective." *International Review of Mission* (July 1992): 375–79.

———. "Reading Signs of the Kingdom." Stone Lecture No. 1, Princeton Theological Seminary, Princeton, NJ, October 20, 2003.

———. "Recognizing the Primal Religions." Stone Lecture No. 2, Princeton Theological Seminary, Princeton, NJ, October 21, 2003.

———. "The Relevance of a Christian Approach to Culture in Africa." In *Christian Education in the African Context: Proceedings of the First Africa Regional Conference of the International Association for the Promotion of Christian Higher Education (IAPCHE), 4–9 March 1991, Harare, Zimbabwe*, 24–35. Grand Rapids, MI: IAPCHE, 1991.

———. "Religion and National Identity: Assessing the Discussion from Cicero to Danquah." Bediako Law and Religion Inaugural Lecture, June 25, 1997. Ghana Academy of Arts and Sciences, Accra.

————. *Religion, Culture and Language: An Appreciation of the Intellectual Legacy of Dr. J. B. Danquah.* J. B. Danquah Memorial Lectures, Series 37, 2004, February 2–4, 2004. Ghana Academy of Arts and Sciences, Accra, 2006.

————. "[Response to] David Hesselgrave: Dialogue on Contextualization Continuum." *Gospel in Context* 2.3 (1979): 12–13.

————. "Response to Taber: Is There More than One Way to Do Theology?" *Gospel in Context* 1.1 (1978): 13–14.

————. "Review of *African Theology en Route.*" *Journal of Religion in Africa* 11.2 (1980): 158–59.

————. "Scripture as the Hermeneutics of Culture and Tradition." *JACT* 4.1 (2001): 2–11.

————. "The Significance of Modern African Christianity—A Manifesto." *Studies in World Christianity* (*Edinburgh Review of Theology and Religion*) 1.1 (1995): 51–67.

————. "'Their past is also our present': Why All Christians Have Need of Ancestors: Making a Case for Africa." *AICMAR Bulletin* 6 (2007): 1–16.

————. *Theology and Identity: The Impact of Culture on Christian Thought in the Second Century and Modern Africa.* Oxford: Regnum, 1992.

————. "Thoughts on the Nature of the Project." *JACT* 11.2 (2008): 3–4.

————. "Types of African Theology." In *Christianity in Africa in the 1990s,* edited by C. Fyfe and A. Walls, 56–69. Edinburgh: University of Edinburgh, Centre for African Studies.

————. "Understanding African Theology in the Twentieth Century." In *Jesus and the Gospel in Africa,* 49-62. Oxford: Regnum, 2000.

————. "The Unique Christ in the Plurality of Religions." In *The Unique Christ in Our Pluralist World,* edited by Bruce Nichols, 47–56. Grand Rapids, MI: Baker, 1994.

————. "L'Univers interior de Tchicaya U Tam'si." PhD dissertation, T.E.R., Bordeaux III, 1973.

————. "'Whose Religion Is Christianity?': Reflections on Opportunities and Challenges for Christian Theological Scholarship as Public Discourse—The African Dimension." *JACT* 9.2 (2006): 43–48.

————. "The Willowbank Consultation, January 1978—A Personal Reflection." *Themelios* 5.2 (January 1980): 25–32.

————. "Worship as Vital Participation: Some Personal Reflections on Ministry in the African Church." *JACT* 8.2 (2005): 3–7.

————. "'Why has the summer ended and we are not saved?': Encountering the Real Challenge of Christian Engagement in Primal Contexts." *JACT* 11.2 (2008): 5–8.

Bediako, Kwame, and Gillian Mary Bediako. "'Ebenezer, this is how far the Lord has helped us': Reflections on the Institutional Itinerary of the Akrofi-Christaller

Memorial Centre for Mission Research & Applied Theology (1974–2005)."Unpublished handbook. ACI, Akropong-Akuapem, 2005.

Bellah, Robert, Richard Madsen, William Sullivan, Ann Swidler, and Steven Tipton. *Habits of the Heart: Individualism and Commitment in American Life.* Berkeley: University of California Press, [1985] 2007.

Bennett, Louise. *Selected Poems.* Kingston, Jamaica: Sangster's Book Stores, 1982.

Berger, Peter L. *The Heretical Imperative: Contemporary Possibilities of Religious Affirmation.* Garden City, NY: Anchor Press, 1979.

———. *The Sacred Canopy: Elements of a Sociological Theory of Religion.* New York: Anchor Books, 1990.

Berkhof, Hendrikus, and H. J. Kraus. *Karl Barths Lichtlehre.* Zurich: Theologischer Verlag, 1977.

Berkouwer, G. C. *The Triumph of Grace in the Theology of Karl Barth.* London: Paternoster Press, 1956.

Beyer, Peter, and Lori Beaman, eds. *Religion, Globalization, and Culture.* Leiden: Brill, 2007.

Bhabha, Homi. *Location of Culture.* London: Routledge, 1994.

Blumhardt, Christoph. *Christoph Blumhardt and His Message.* Edited by R. Lejeune. Rifton, NY: Plough Publishing House, 1963.

Blumhardt, Christian. "Die 'Instruction.'" *Evangelisches Missionsmagazin (EMM)* (1830).

Bonhoeffer, Dietrich. *Barcelona, Berlin, New York: 1928–1931.* Dietrich Bonhoeffer Works, vol. 8. Minneapolis, MN: Fortress Press, 2008.

———. *Letters and Papers from Prison.* Dietrich Bonhoeffer Works, vol. 10. Minneapolis, MN: Fortress Press, 2010.

Bornkamm, Karin. *Christus — König und Priester: Das Amt Christi bei Luther im Verhältnis zur Vor- und Nachgeschichte.* Tübingen: Mohr Siebeck, 1998.

———. "Die reformatorische Lehre vom Amt Christi und ihre Umformung durch Karl Barth." In *Zeitschrift für Theologie und Kirche,* edited by Eberhard Jüngel, 3–32. Tübingen: Mohr Siebeck, 1986.

Bouchard, Larry. "On Contingency and Culpability: Is the Postmodern Post-Tragic?" In *Evil after Postmodernism: Histories, Narratives, and Ethics,* edited by Jennifer L. Geddes, 24–44. London: Rutledge, 2001.

———. *Tragic Method, Tragic Theology: Evil in Contemporary Drama and Religious Thought.* University Park: Pennsylvania State University Press, 2010.

Brathwaite, Kamau. "History of the Voice." In *Roots: Essays in Caribbean Literature,* 2729–33. Ann Arbor: University of Michigan Press, 1993.

Brown, Robert McAfee. Introduction to *Portrait of Karl Barth,* by Georges Casalis, 1–37. Garden City, NY: Doubleday and Co., 1963.

Bujo, Bénézet. *African Theology in Its Social Context.* Translated by John O'Donohue. Maryknoll, NY: Orbis Books, 1992.

Busch, Eberhard. *The Great Passion: An Introduction to Karl Barth's Theology.* Grand Rapids, MI: Eerdmans, 2004.

———. *Karl Barth: His Life from Letters and Autobiographical Texts.* Philadelphia: Fortress, 1976.

———. *Karl Barths Lebenslauf: Nach Seinen Briefen und Autobiograph Texten.* Munich: Kaiser, 1975.

"Call to Glory." Funeral program for Kwame Bediako. July 2008.

Calvin, John. *Institutes of the Christian Religion.* Translated by Ford Lewis Battles. Philadelphia: Westminster John Knox, 1960.

Campbell, George Van Pelt. "Religion and Phases of Globalization." In *Religion, Globalization, and Culture,* edited by Peter Beyer and Lori Beaman, 281–302. Leiden: Brill, 2007.

Carson, D. A. *Becoming Conversant with the Emerging Church: Understanding a Movement and Its Implications.* Grand Rapids, MI: Eerdmans, 2009.

———. *Gagging of God: Christianity Confronts Pluralism.* Grand Rapids, MI: Zondervan, 1996.

Carter, J. Kameron. *Race: A Theological Account.* New York: Oxford University Press, 2008.

Casanova, José. *Public Religions in the Modern World.* Chicago: University of Chicago Press, 1994.

———. "Public Religions Revisited." In *Religion: Beyond a Concept,* edited by Hent de Vries, 101–19. New York: Fordham University Press, 2008.

———. "Rethinking Secularization: A Global Comparative Perspective." *Hedgehog Review* 8.1–2 (Spring–Summer 2006): 7–22.

———. "The Secular, Secularizations, Secularisms." In *Rethinking Secularism,* edited by Craig Calhoun, Mark Juergensmeyer, and Jonathan van Antwerpen, 54–74. New York: Oxford University Press, 2011.

Césaire, Aimé. *Discourse on Colonialism.* New York: Monthly Review Press, [1950] 1972.

———. *Notebook of a Return to My Native Land = Cahier d'un retour au pays natal.* Translated by Mireille Rosello and Annie Pritchard. Newcastle upon Tyne: Bloodaxe Books, 1995.

———. *Notebook of a Return to the Native Land.* Translated and edited by Clayton Eshleman and Annette Smith. Middletown, CT: Wesleyan University Press, 2001.

Chestnutt, Glenn A. *Challenging the Stereotype: The Theology of Karl Barth as a Resource for Inter-Religious Encounter in a European Context.* Oxford: Peter Lang, 2010.

Chidester, David. *Savage Systems: Colonialism and Comparative Religion in Southern Africa.* Charlottesville: University Press of Virginia, 1996.

Christaller, J. G. *A Dictionary of the Asante and Fante Language Called Tshi (chwee, Twi): With a Grammatical Introduction and Appendices on the Geography of the*

Gold Coast and Other Subjects. Basel: Printed for the Evangelical Missionary Society, 1881.

————. *A Grammar of the Asante and Fante Language Called Twi Based on the Akuapem Dialect with Reference to the Other (Akan and Fante) Dialects*. Basel: Printed for the Evangelical Missionary Society, 1875.

Christensen, Torben, and William R. Hutchinson, eds. *Missionary Ideologies in the Imperialist Era: 1880–1920*. Copenhagen: Aros, 1982.

Clarke, Peter B. *West Africa and Christianity*. London: Edward Arnold, 1986.

Clerk, N. T. "A Short Centenary Sketch: The Settlement of West Indian Immigrants on the Goldcoast under the Auspices of the Basel Mission 1843–1943." Basel Mission Archives, ref. no. D.076 (1943).

Cobb, Kelton. *Blackwell Guide to Theology and Popular Culture*. Malden, MA: Blackwell, 2005.

Cochrane, Arthur. *The Church's Confession under Hitler*. Philadelphia: Westminster Press, 1962.

Colby, Sandra L., and Jennifer M. Ortman. "Projections of the Size and Composition of the U.S. Population: 2014 to 2060," Current Population Reports, P25-1143, U.S. Census Bureau, Washington, DC, 2014.

Collins Winn, Christian T. *Jesus Is Victor! The Significance of the Blumhardts for the Theology of Karl Barth*. Eugene, OR: Pickwick Publications, 2009.

Cone, James. *God of the Oppressed*. Minneapolis, MN: Seabury Press, 1975.

Danker, William J. *Profit for the Lord: Economic Activities in Moravian Missions and the Basel Mission Trading Company*. Grand Rapids, MI: Eerdmans, 1971.

Danquah, J. B. *The Akan Doctrine of God: A Fragment of Gold Coast Ethics and Religion* (1944). Reprint of 1968 2nd ed. New York: Routledge, 2006.

Danso, Yaw. *The Basel Mission in Anum 1863–1918*. Osu, Ghana: Heritage Publications, 2013.

Davidson, Ivor. "Divine Light: Some Reflections after Barth." In *Trinitarian Theology after Barth*, edited by Myk Habets and Phillip Tolliday, 48–69. Eugene, OR: Pickwick Publications, 2011.

Debrunner, Hans W. *A History of Christianity in Ghana*. Accra, Ghana: Waterville Publishing House, 1967.

DeCou, Jessica. "Relocating Barth's Theology of Culture: Beyond the 'True Words' Approach of *Church Dogmatics* IV/3." *International Journal of Systematic Theology* 15.2 (April 2013): 154–71.

Dempsey, Michael T., ed. *Trinity and Election in Contemporary Theology*. Grand Rapids, MI: Eerdmans, 2011.

Dinkelaker, Bernhard. *How Is Jesus Christ Lord? Reading Kwame Bediako from a Postcolonial and Intercontextual Perspective*. Bern: Peter Lang, 2017.

Dodd, C. H. *The Parables of the Kingdom*. New York: Scribner, [1935] 1961.

Dorrien, Gary J. *Kantian Reason and Hegelian Spirit: The Idealistic Logic of Modern Theology.* Oxford: Wiley-Blackwell, 2012.

Durkheim, Émile. *The Elementary Forms of Religious Life.* Translated by Karen E. Fields. New York: Free Press, 1995.

Éla, Jean-Marc. *My Faith as an African.* Translated by John Pairman Brown and Susan Perry. Maryknoll, NY: Orbis, 1988.

Ephirim-Donkor, Anthony. *African Religion Defined: A Systematic Study of Ancestor Worship among the Akan.* New York: University Press of America, 2010.

———. *African Spirituality: On Becoming Ancestors.* Trenton, NJ: Africa World Press, 1997.

Eusebius. "Life of Constantine." In *Eusebius: Church History, Life of Constantine the Great, and Oration in Praise of Constantine*, vol. 1, *The Nicene and Post-Nicene Fathers*, 2nd ser., 405–610. New York: Christian Literature Company, 1890; Peabody, MA: Hendrickson Publishers, 1999.

Fanon, Frantz. *Black Skin, White Masks.* New York: Grove Press, [1952] 2008.

———. *The Wretched of the Earth.* New York: Grove Press, [1961] 2004.

Fasholé-Luke, Edward. "Ancestor Veneration and the Communion of Saints." In *New Testament Christianity for Africa and the World*, edited by Mark Glasswell and Edward Fasholé-Luke, 209–21. London: SPCK, 1974.

Ferguson, James. *Global Shadows: Africa in the Neoliberal World Order.* Durham, NC: Duke University Press, 2006.

Feuerbach, Ludwig. *Essence of Christianity.* Translated by George Eliot. Introduction by Karl Barth. Foreword by H. Richard Niebuhr. New York: Harper & Row, 1957.

Finke, Roger. "Innovative Returns to Tradition: Using Core Teachings as the Foundation for Innovative Accommodation." *Journal for the Scientific Study of Religion* 43.1 (March 2004): 19–34.

Fiske, Edward B. "Karl Barth Dies in Basel; Protestant Theologian, 82." *New York Times*, December 11, 1968, 1, 42.

Flett, John. *The Witness of God: The Trinity, Missio Dei, Karl Barth, and the Nature of Christian Community.* Grand Rapids, MI: Eerdmans, 2010.

Fotland, Roar. "Ancestor Christology in Context: Theological Perspectives of Kwame Bediako." PhD dissertation, University of Bergen, 2005.

Frei, Hans. "The Doctrine of Revelation in the Thought of Karl Barth, 1909 to 1922: The Nature of Barth's Break with Liberalism." PhD dissertation, Yale University, 1956.

Fretheim, Sara. *Kwame Bediako and African Christian Scholarship: Emerging Religious Discourse in Twentieth-Century Ghana.* Eugene, OR: Pickwick Publications, 2018.

Friedman, Thomas. *The World Is Flat: A Brief History of the Twenty-First Century.* Updated and expanded ed. New York: Farrar, Straus and Giroux, 2007.

Fulkerson, Mary McClintock. *Places of Redemption: Theology for a Worldly Church.* Oxford: Oxford University Press, 2007.

Gauchet, Marcel. *The Disenchantment of the World: A Political History of Religion.* Translated by Oscar Burge. Princeton, NJ: Princeton University Press, 1997.

Gitari, David, and Patrick Benson, eds. *Witnessing to the Living God in Contemporary Africa.* Nairobi: Uzima Press, 1986.

Glasse, John. "Barth on Feuerbach." *Harvard Theological Review* 57.2 (April 1964): 69–96.

"Global Christianity—A Report on the Size and Distribution of the World's Christian Population." Pew Research Center, December 19, 2011. www.pewforum.org/2011/12/19/global-christianity-exec/.

Godsey, John. "The Architecture of Karl Barth's *Church Dogmatics.*" In *Karl Barth's Table Talk,* edited by John Godsey. Richmond, VA: John Knox Press, 1963.

Gornik, Mark. *Word Made Global: Stories of African Christianity in New York City.* Grand Rapids, MI: Eerdmans, 2011.

Gorringe, Timothy. *Karl Barth: Against Hegemony.* New York: Oxford University Press, 1999.

Graham, Billy. *The Jesus Generation.* London: Hodder and Stoughton, 1972.

Green, Clifford J. *Karl Barth: Theologian of Freedom.* San Francisco: Collins, 1989.

Green, Garrett. *Karl Barth on Religion: The Revelation of God as the Sublimation of Religion.* London: T&T Clark, 2007.

Greggs, Tom. "'Jesus Is Victor': Passing the Impasse of Barth on Universalism." *Scottish Journal of Theology* 60.2 (May 2007): 196–212.

———. *Theology against Religion: Constructive Dialogues with Bonhoeffer and Barth.* New York: Continuum, 2011.

Gunn, G. G. *A Hundred Years 1848–1948: The Story of the Presbyterian Training College Akropong.* Akropong, Akwapim, Gold Coast: Presbyterian Training College, 1948.

Gunton, Colin E. *The Barth Lectures.* Edited by Paul Brazier. New York: T&T Clark, 2007.

Gussman, Wilhelm. *Quellen und Forschungen zur Geschichte des Augsburgischen Glaubensbekenntnisses.* Leipzig: B. G. Teubner, 1911.

Gutiérrez, Gustavo. *We Drink from Our Own Wells.* Maryknoll, NY: Orbis, 1984.

Gyeke, Kwame. *Essay on African Philosophical Thought: The Akan Conceptual Scheme.* Cambridge: Cambridge University Press, 1987.

Habermas, Jürgen. "A Conversation about God and the World." In *Religion and Rationality: Essays on Reason, God, and Modernity,* edited by Eduardo Mendieta. Cambridge, MA: MIT Press, 2002.

Habets, Myk, and Phillip Tolliday, eds. *Trinitarian Theology after Barth*. Princeton Theological Monograph Series. Eugene, OR: Pickwick Publications, 2011.

Harnack, Adolf von. *What Is Christianity?* Translated by Thomas Bailey Saunders. New York: Harper & Brothers, [1900] 1957.

Hartman, Tim. "An Act of Theological Négritude: Kwame Bediako on African Christian Identity." In *Religion, Culture and Spirituality in Africa and the African Diaspora*, edited by William Ackah, Jualynne E. Dodson, and R. Drew Smith, 81–95. New York: Routledge, 2018.

———. "Humanity and Destiny: A Theological Comparison of Karl Barth and African Traditional Religions." In *Karl Barth and Comparative Theologies*, edited by Martha Moore-Keish and Christian Collins Winn, 228–47. New York: Fordham University Press, 2019.

———. "Lost in Translation: Postcolonial Reflections on 'The Panare Killed Jesus Christ.'" *Cross Currents* 63.3 (September 2013): 328–49.

———. "The Promise of an Actualistic Pneumatology: Beginning with the Holy Spirit in African Pentecostalism and Karl Barth." *Modern Theology* 33.3 (July 2017): 333–47.

Hastings, Adrian. *The Church in Africa: 1450–1950*. Oxford: Clarendon Press, 1994.

———. *A History of African Christianity, 1950–1975*. Cambridge: Cambridge University Press, 1979.

———. "A New Voice out of Ghana: A Review of Kwame Bediako's *Christianity in Africa*." *Church Times* (January 1996): 15.

Hector, Kevin. *Theology without Metaphysics: God, Language, and the Spirit of Recognition*. Cambridge: Cambridge University Press, 2011.

Hengel, Martin, and Anna Maria Schwemer, eds. *Der messianische Anspruch Jesu und die Anfange der Christologie*. Tübingen: Mohr Siebeck, 2001.

Hepprich, Brigit. *Pitfalls of Trained Incapacity: The Unintended Effects of Integral Missionary Training in the Basel Mission on Its Early Work in Ghana (1828–1840)*. Eugene, OR: Pickwick Publications, 2016.

Higton, Mike, and John C. McDowell, eds. *Conversing with Barth*. Burlington, VT: Ashgate, 2004.

Holberg, Mary, trans. and ed. *A Church Undone: Documents from the German Christian Faith Movement, 1932–1940*. Minneapolis, MN: Fortress Press, 2015.

Hübinger, Gangolf. *Kulturprotestantismus und Politik: Zum Verhältnis von Liberalismus und Protestantismus im Wilhelminischen Deutschland*. Tübingen: J. C. B. Mohr, 1994.

Hunsinger, George. *Disruptive Grace: Studies in the Theology of Karl Barth*. Grand Rapids, MI: Eerdmans, 2000.

———. *How to Read Karl Barth*. New York: Oxford University Press, 1991.

———. "A Tale of Two Simultaneities: Justification and Sanctification in Calvin, Luther and Barth." In *Conversing with Barth*, edited by Mike Higton and John C. McDowell, 68–89. Burlington, VT: Ashgate, 2004.

———. "Uncreated Light: From Irenaeus and Torrance to Aquinas and Barth." In *Light from Light: Scientists and Theologians in Dialogue*, edited by Gerald O'Collins and Mary Ann Meyers, 208–35. Grand Rapids, MI: Eerdmans, 2012.

Hunter, James Davison. *American Evangelicalism: Conservative Religion and the Quandary of Modernity*. New Brunswick, NJ: Rutgers University Press, 1983.

———. "The Culture War and the Sacred/Secular Divide: The Problem of Pluralism and Weak Hegemony." *Social Research* 76.4 (Winter 2009): 1307–22.

———. *Evangelicalism: The Coming Generation*. Chicago: University of Chicago Press, 1987.

———. *To Change the World: The Irony, Tragedy, and Possibility of Christianity in the Late Modern World*. New York: Oxford University Press, 2010.

Idowu, Bolaji. *African Traditional Religion: A Definition*. Maryknoll, NY: Orbis Books, 1973.

———. *Towards an Indigenous Church*. London: Oxford University Press, 1965.

Illich, Ivan. "To Hell with Good Intentions." In *Combining Service and Learning: A Resource Book for Community and Public Service*, edited by Jane C. Kendall, 314–20. Raleigh, NC: National Society for Internships and Experiential Education, 1990.

Jay, Paul. *Global Matters*. Ithaca, NY: Cornell University Press, 2010.

Jansen, John Frederick. *Calvin's Doctrine of the Work of Christ*. London: J. Clark, 1956.

Jenkins, Philip. *The New Faces of Christianity: Believing the Bible in the Global South*. New York: Oxford University Press, 2006.

———. *The Next Christendom: The Rise of Global Christianity*. New York: Oxford University Press, 2002.

Jenson, Robert. "Karl Barth." In *Modern Theologians: An Introduction to Christian Theology in the Twentieth Century*, 2nd ed., edited by David F. Ford, 21–36. Oxford: Blackwell, 1997.

Johnson, Adam J. "The Servant Lord: A Word of Caution Regarding the *munus triplex* in Karl Barth's Theology and the Church Today." *Scottish Journal of Theology* 65.2 (2012): 159–73.

Johnson, William Stacy. *The Mystery of God: Karl Barth and the Postmodern Foundations of Theology*. Louisville, KY: Westminster John Knox, 1997.

Jones, Iwan Russell. "Following the Footprints of God: Kwame Bediako, 1945–2008." www.ship-of-fools.com/features/2008/kwame_bediako.html. Accessed September 1, 2018.

Jones, Paul Dafydd. *The Humanity of Christ: Christology in Karl Barth's Church Dogmatics*. New York: T&T Clark, 2008.

Jones, Robert P. *The End of White Christian America*. New York: Simon & Schuster, 2016.

Jüngel, Eberhard. *Karl Barth: A Theological Legacy*. Translated by Garrett E. Paul. Philadelphia: Westminster Press, 1986.

———, ed. *Zeitschrift für Theologie und Kirche*. Tübingen: Mohr Siebeck, 1986.

Kalu, Ogbu. *The History of Christianity in West Africa*. London: Longman Group, 1980.

Kane, Ross. "Ritual Formation of Peaceful Publics: Sacrifice and Syncretism in South Sudan (1991–2005)." *Journal of Religion in Africa* 44.3–4 (2014): 386–410.

———. "Social Healing through Hybrid and Syncretic Sacrifice in South Sudan." Paper presented at the Annual Meeting of the American Academy of Religion, Atlanta, 2015.

Kuma, Afua. *Jesus of the Deep Forest: Prayers and Praises of Afua Kuma*. Edited by Peter Kwasi Ameyaw, translated by Fr. Jon Kirby. Accra, Ghana: Asempa Publishers, 1980.

Kutter, Hermann. *They Must: Or, God and the Social Democracy. A Frank Word to Christian Men and Women*. American ed. Chicago: Co-operative Printing Co., 1908.

Lactantius. "On the Deaths of the Persecutors." In *Fathers of the Third and Fourth Centuries*, vol. 7, *The Ante-Nicene Fathers*, 301–22. Buffalo, NY: Christian Literature Company, 1886; Peabody, MA: Hendrickson, 1999.

Laryea, Philip. "Mother Tongue Theology: Reflections on Images of Jesus in the Poetry of Afua Kuma." *Journal of African Christian Thought* 3.1 (2000): 50–60.

Lindsay, Mark R. *Barth, Israel, and Jesus: Karl Barth's Theology of Israel*. Barth Studies Series. Aldershot: Ashgate, 2007.

———. *Reading Auschwitz with Barth: The Holocaust as Problem and Promise for Barthian Theology*. Eugene, OR: Pickwick Publications, 2014.

Mahmood, Sara. "Can Secularism Be Other-Wise?" In *Varieties of Secularism in a Secular Age*, edited by Michael Warner, Jonathan Van Antwerpen, and Craig Calhoun, 282–99. Cambridge, MA: Harvard University Press, 2010.

———. *Religious Difference in a Secular Age: A Minority Report*. Princeton, NJ: Princeton University Press, 2016.

Maluleke, Tinyiko Sam. "African Traditional Religions in Christian Mission and Christian Scholarship: Re-Opening a Debate That Never Started." *Religion & Theology* 5.2 (1998): 121–37.

———. "Black and African Theologies in the New World Order: A Time to Drink from Our Own Wells." *Journal of Theology for Southern Africa* 96 (November 1996): 3–19.

Marquardt, Friedrich-Wilhelm. *Theologie und Sozialismus: Das Beispiel Karl Barths*. 3rd ed. Munich: Chr. Kaiser, 1972.

Marsh, Charles. *Reclaiming Dietrich Bonhoeffer: The Promise of His Theology*. New York: Oxford University Press, 1994.

Mbiti, John. *African Religions and Philosophy*. 2nd rev. and enl. ed. Oxford: Heinemann, 1990.

———. *Bible and Theology in African Christianity*. Nairobi: Oxford University Press, 1986.

———. *New Testament Eschatology in an African Background: A Study of the Encounter between New Testament Theology and African Traditional Concepts*. Oxford: Oxford University Press, 1971.

———. "Some Reflections on African Experience of Salvation Today." In *Living Faith and Ultimate Goals*, edited by S. J. Samartha, 108–19. Geneva: World Council of Churches, 1974.

———. "Theological Impotence and the Universality of the Church." In *Mission Trends No. 3: Third World Theologies*, edited by Gerald Anderson and Thomas Stransky, 6–18. Grand Rapids, MI: Eerdmans, 1976.

McCormack, Bruce L. "The Identity of the Son: Karl Barth's Exegesis of Hebrews 1.1–4 (and Similar Passages)." In *Christology, Hermeneutics, and Hebrews: Profiles from the History of Interpretation*, edited by Jon Laansma and Daniel Treier, 155–72. London: T&T Clark, 2012.

———. *Karl Barth's Critically Realistic Dialectical Theology: Its Genesis and Development 1909–1936*. Oxford: Clarendon Press, 1995.

———. "Karl Barth's Historicized Christology: Just How 'Chalcedonian' Is It?" In *Orthodox and Modern: Studies in the Theology of Karl Barth*, 201–34. Grand Rapids, MI: Baker Academic, 2008.

———. *Orthodox and Modern: Studies in the Theology of Karl Barth*. Grand Rapids, MI: Baker Academic, 2008.

———. "Revelation and History in Transfoundationalist Perspective: Karl Barth's Theological Epistemology in Conversation with a Schleiermachian Tradition." In *Orthodox and Modern: Studies in the Theology of Karl Barth*, 21–40. Grand Rapids, MI: Baker Academic, 2008.

———. "The Significance of Karl Barth's Theological Exegesis of Philippians." In Karl Barth, *The Epistle to the Philippians: 40th Anniversary Edition*, 89–105. Louisville, KY: Westminster John Knox Press, 2002.

———. "With Loud Cries and Tears: The Humanity of the Son in the Epistle to the Hebrews." In *The Epistle to the Hebrews and Christian Theology*, edited by Richard Bauckham, Daniel Driver, Trevor Hart, and Nathan MacDonald, 37–68. Grand Rapids, MI: Eerdmans, 2009.

McCulloh, Gerald W. *Christ's Person and Life-Work in the Theology of Albrecht Ritschl with Special Attention to* Munus Triplex. Lanham, MD: University Press of America, 1990.

McLaren, Brian. "The Method, the Message, and the Ongoing Story." In *The Church in Emerging Culture: Five Perspectives*, edited by Leonard Sweet and Andy Crouch, 191–234. Grand Rapids, MI: Zondervan, 2003.

Metzger, Paul. *The Word of Christ and the World of Culture: Sacred and Secular through the Theology of Karl Barth*. Grand Rapids, MI: Eerdmans, 2003.

Middleton, Darren. "Jesus of Nazareth in Ghana's Deep Forest: The Africanization of Christianity in Madam Afua Kuma's Poetry." *Religion and the Arts* 9.1–2 (2005): 116–34.

Miller, Jon. *Missionary Zeal and Institutional Control: Organizational Contradictions in the Basel Mission on the Gold Coast, 1828–1917*. Grand Rapids, MI: Eerdmans, 2003.

Modern, John Lardas. *Secularism in Antebellum America*. Chicago: University of Chicago Press, 2011.

Moltmann, Jürgen. *The Future of Creation: Collected Essays*. Minneapolis, MN: Fortress, 1979.

Mottu, Henry. "La lumière et les lumières: Christ et le monde selon le dernier Barth, 1988." In *Un itinéraire théologique: Barth, Bonhoeffer et la théologie africaine-américane*, 39–54. Geneva: Cahiers de la Revue de Théologie et de Philosophie 21, 2004.

Naumann, Friedrich. *Das Soziale Programm der evangelischen Kirche*. Erlangen: Deichert, 1891.

Nazienzen, Gregory. Letter 101, "To Cledonius the Priest against Apollinarius." In *The Nicene and Post-Nicene Fathers, Second Series*, vol. 7. New York: C. Scribner's Sons, 1903.

Neder, Adam. *Participation in Christ: An Entry into Karl Barth's Church Dogmatics*. Louisville, KY: Westminster John Knox, 2009.

Neff, David. "Theologian Kwame Bediako Dies." *Christianity Today Online*. June 13, 2008. www.christianitytoday.com/gleanings/2008/june/theologian-kwame -bediako-dies.html. Accessed September 1, 2018.

Newbigin, Lesslie. *The Other Side of 1984: Questions for the Churches*. Geneva: World Council of Churches, 1983.

Newfield, Jack. *A Prophetic Minority*. New York: Signet Books, 1966.

Nichols, Bruce, ed. *The Unique Christ in Our Pluralist World*. Grand Rapids, MI: Baker, 1994.

Nyamiti, Charles. *Christ as Our Ancestor: Christology from an African Perspective*. Gweru, Zimbabwe: Mambo Press, 1984.

O'Collins, Gerald, and Mary Ann Meyers, eds. *Light from Light: Scientists and Theologians in Dialogue*. Grand Rapids, MI: Eerdmans, 2012.

Oduyoye, Mercy Amba. "Jesus Christ." In *The Cambridge Companion to Feminist Theology*, edited by Susan Frank Parsons, 151–70. Cambridge: Cambridge University Press, 2002.

Okorocha, Cyril. "The Meaning of Salvation: An African Perspective." In *Emerging Voices in Global Christian Theology*, edited by William Dyrness, 59–92. Grand Rapids, MI: Zondervan, 1994.

Olabimtan, Kehinde. "'Is Africa Incurably Religious?' II: A Response to Jan Platvoet and Henk van Rinsum." *Exchange* 32.4 (2003): 322–39.

Olupona, Jacob K., and Regina Gemignani. *African Immigrant Religions in America.* New York: New York University Press, 2007.

Opoku, Kofi Asare. "Post-Colonial Church Cultures in Multicultural Societies." Transatlantic Roundtable on Religion and Race, Accra, Ghana, July 31, 2013.

———. "Toward a Holistic View of Salvation." In *Healing for God's World: Remedies from Three Continents,* edited by Kofi Asare Opoku and Yong-Bok Kim, 41–60. New York: Friendship Press, 1991.

———. *West African Traditional Religion.* Coraville, IA: FEP International, 1978.

Ortiz, Fernando. *Cuban Counterpoint: Tobacco and Sugar.* Translated by Harriet de Onís. New York: Knopf, 1947.

Palma, Robert J. *Karl Barth's Theology of Culture: The Freedom of Culture for the Praise of God.* Allison Park, PA: Pickwick Publications, 1983.

p'Bitek, Okot. *African Religions in Western Scholarship.* Kampala: East African Literature Bureau, 1970.

Pannenberg, Wolfhart. *Jesus: God and Man.* Translated by Lewis L. Wilkins and Duane A. Priebe. London: SCM, 1968.

———. *Systematic Theology,* vol. 2. Translated by Geoffrey Bromiley. Grand Rapids, MI: Eerdmans, 1991.

Parrinder, Geoffrey. *Religion in Africa.* Harmondsworth: Penguin Books, 1969.

Peterson, Eugene H. *Eat This Book: A Conversation in the Art of Spiritual Reading.* Grand Rapids, MI: Eendmans, 2009.

———. *The Message: The Bible in Contemporary Language.* Colorado Springs, CO: NavPress, 2005.

Pfleiderer, Georg. "Das 'prophetische Amt' der Theologie: Zur systematischen Rekonstruktion der Theologie Karl Barths und ihres Entwicklungsgangs." *Zeitschrift für Dialektische Theologie* 17.2 (January 2001): 112–38.

Platvoet, Jan, and Henk van Rinsum. "Is Africa Incurably Religious? Confessing and Contesting an Invention." *Exchange* 32.2 (2003): 123–53.

Pobee, John S. *Religion in a Pluralistic Society.* Leiden: Brill, 1976.

———. *Toward an African Theology.* Nashville, TN: Abingdon, 1979.

Porter, Andrew. *Religion versus Empire? British Protestant Missionaries and Overseas Expansion, 1700–1914.* Manchester: Manchester University Press, 2004.

Quartey, Seth. *Missionary Practices on the Gold Coast, 1832–1895: Discourse, Gaze and Gender in the Basel Mission in Pre-Colonial West Africa.* Youngstown, NY: Cambria Press, 2007.

Rah, Soong-Chan. *The Next Evangelicalism: Freeing the Church from Western Cultural Captivity.* Grand Rapids, MI: InterVarsity Press, 2009.

Reardon, Bernard M. G. *Liberal Protestantism.* Stanford, CA: Stanford University Press, 1968.

Reid, Jennifer, ed. *Religion, Postcolonialism, and Globalization: A Sourcebook*. New York: Bloomsbury Academic, 2015.

Rennstich, Karl. "The Understanding of Mission, Civilisation and Colonialism in the Basel Mission." In *Missionary Ideologies in the Imperialist Era: 1880–1920*, edited by Torben Christensen and William R. Hutchinson, 94–103. Copenhagen: Aros, 1982.

Rieff, Philip. "The American Transference: From Calvin to Freud." In Philip Rieff, *The Feeling Intellect: Selected Writings*, edited by Jonathan Imber, 10–14. Chicago: University of Chicago Press, 1990.

———. "The Evangelist Strategy." In Philip Rieff, *The Feeling Intellect: Selected Writings*, edited by Jonathan Imber, 123–29. Chicago: University of Chicago Press, 1990.

———. *The Feeling Intellect: Selected Writings*. Edited by Jonathan Imber. Chicago: University of Chicago Press, 1990.

———. "Reflections on Psychological Man in America." In Philip Rieff, *The Feeling Intellect: Selected Writings*, edited by Jonathan Imber, 3–9. Chicago: University of Chicago Press, 1990.

———. *Triumph of the Therapeutic: Uses of Faith after Freud*. Chicago: University of Chicago Press, 1987.

Rieger, Joerg. *Globalization and Theology*. Nashville, TN: Abingdon, 2010.

Rivera, Mayra. *The Touch of Transcendence: A Postcolonial Theology of God*. Louisville, KY: Westminster John Knox Press, 2007.

Robertson, Roland. *Globalization: Social Theory and Global Culture*. London: Sage, 1992.

———. "Global Millennialism: A Postmortem on Secularization." In *Religion, Globalization, and Culture*, edited by Peter Beyer and Lori Beaman, 9–34. Leiden: Brill, 2007.

Rumscheidt, Martin. Foreword to *Fragments Grave and Gay*, by Karl Barth. London: Fontana, 1971.

Ryan, Patrick J. "'Arise, O God!': The Problem of 'Gods' in West Africa." *Journal of Religion in Africa* 11.3 (1980): 161–71.

Samuel, Vinay, and Chris Sugden, eds. *Sharing Jesus in the Two-Thirds World*. Grand Rapids, MI: Eerdmans, 1984.

Sanneh, Lamin. *Translating the Message: The Missionary Impact on Culture*. Maryknoll, NY: Orbis, [1989] 2009.

Santos, Boaventura de Sousa. *Epistemologies of the South: Justice against Epistemicide*. Boulder, CO: Paradigm Publishers, 2014.

Sarpong, Peter. *The Sacred Stools of the Akan*. Accra-Tema: Ghana Pub. Corp., 1971.

Sawyerr, Harry. "Ancestor Worship I: The Mechanics." *Sierra Leone Bulletin of Religion* 6.2 (December 1964): 25–33.

Schaaf, Ype. *On Their Way Rejoicing: The History and Role of the Bible in Africa*. Carlisle, PA: Paternoster Press, 1995.

Schalter, Wilhelm. *Geschichte der Basler Mission: Mit besonderer Berücksichtigung der ungedruckten Quellen.* Basel: Verlag der Basler Missionsbuchhandlung, 1916.

Schweitzer, Peter. *Survivors on the Gold Coast: The Basel Missionaries in Colonial Ghana.* Accra, Ghana: Smartline, 2000.

Schwemer, Anna Maria. "Jesus Christus als Prophet, König und Priester. Das munus triplex und die frühe Christologie." In *Der messianische Anspruch Jesu und die Anfange der Christologie,* edited by Martin Hengel and Anna Maria Schwemer, 165–230. Tübingen: Mohr Siebeck, 2001.

Sen, Amartya. "How to Judge Globalism." *American Prospect* 13.1 (Winter 2002).

Shirky, Clay. *Cognitive Surplus: Creativity and Generosity in a Connected Age.* New York: Penguin Press, 2010.

———. "Monkeys with Internet Access: Sharing, Human Nature, and Digital Data." Paper presented at SXSW (South by Southwest), Austin, TX, March 14, 2010. www.shirky.com/weblog/2010/04/the-collase-of-complex-business -models/.

Smith, Noel. *The Presbyterian Church of Ghana, 1835–1960: A Younger Church in a Changing Society.* Accra: Ghana Universities Press, 1966.

Sonderegger, Katherine. *That Jesus Christ Was Born a Jew: Karl Barth's "Doctrine of Israel."* University Park: Pennsylvania State University Press, 1992.

Stam, Robert, and Ella Shohat. "Whence and Whither Postcolonial Theory?" *New Literary History* 43 (2012): 371–90.

Stanley, Brian. *The World Missionary Conference, Edinburgh 1910.* Grand Rapids, MI: Eerdmans, 2009.

Stoltzfus, Philip. *Theology as Performance: Music, Aesthetics, and God in Western Thought.* New York: T&T Clark, 2006.

Sturch, Richard. *The Word and the Christ: An Essay in Analytic Christology.* Oxford: Clarendon Press, 1991.

Tanner, Kathryn. *Theories of Culture: A New Agenda for Theology.* Minneapolis, MN: Fortress Press, 1997.

Taylor, Charles. *A Secular Age.* Cambridge, MA: Belknap Press of Harvard University Press, 2007.

Taylor, John V. *The Primal Vision: Christian Presence amid African Religion.* Philadelphia: Fortress Press, 1963.

Thompson, Geoff. "'As open to the world as any theologian could be . . .'? Karl Barth's Account of Extra-Ecclesial Truth and Its Value to Christianity's Encounter with Other Religious Traditions." PhD dissertation, University of Cambridge, 1995.

———. "Religious Diversity, Christian Doctrine and Karl Barth." *International Journal of Systematic Theology* 8.1 (January 2006): 3–24.

Thrower, James, ed. *Essays in Religious Studies for Andrew Walls.* Aberdeen: Department of Religious Studies, University of Aberdeen, 1986.

Visser, Hans, and Gillian M. Bediako. Introduction to *Jesus and the Gospel in Africa*, xi–xvii. Oxford: Regnum, 2000.

Wainright, Geoffrey. *For Our Salvation: Two Approaches to the Work of Christ.* Grand Rapids, MI: Eerdmans, 1997.

Walls, Andrew F. "The Gospel as Prisoner and Liberator of Culture." In *The Missionary Movement in Christian History: Studies in the Transmission of Faith,* 3–15. Maryknoll, NY: Orbis Books, 1996.

———. "Kwame Bediako and Christian Scholarship in Africa." *International Bulletin of Missionary Research* 32.4 (2008): 188–93.

———. *The Missionary Movement in Christian History: Studies in the Transmission of Faith.* Maryknoll, NY: Orbis Books, 1996.

———. "Structural Problems in Mission Studies." *International Bulletin of Missionary Research* 15.4 (October 1991): 146–55.

———. "Towards Understanding Africa's Place in Christian History." In *Religion in a Pluralistic Society*, edited by J. S. Pobee, 180–89. Leiden: Brill, 1976.

———. "The Translation Principle in Christian History." In *The Missionary Movement in Christian History: Studies in the Transmission of Faith*, 26–42. Maryknoll, NY: Orbis Books, 1996.

Ward, Graham. *Barth, Derrida and the Language of Theology.* Cambridge: Cambridge University Press, 1995.

Webster, John. *Barth.* 2nd ed. New York: Continuum, 2004.

———. "'Eloquent and Radiant': The Prophetic Office of Christ and the Mission of the Church." In *Barth's Moral Theology: Human Action in Barth's Thought*, 125–50. Grand Rapids, MI: Eerdmans, 1998.

Welch, Claude. *Protestant Thought in the Nineteenth Century.* 2 vols. New Haven, CT: Yale University Press, 1972.

Wiggermann, Karl-Friedrich. "'Ein eigentümlich beschatter Bereich': Die Neuzeit in Karl Barths 'Lichterlehre.'" *Zeitschrift für Dialektische Theologie* 25.2 (2009).

Williams, David T. *The Office of Christ and Its Expression in the Church: Prophet, Priest, King.* Lewiston, NY: Edwin Mellen Press, 1997.

"Witness to an Ancient Truth." *Time* 79.16 (April 20, 1962): 61–69.

Woodard-Lehman, Derek. "Democratic Faith: Barth, Barmen, and the Politics of Reformed Confession" in *Thy Kingdom Come: The Contemporary Relevance of the Barmen Declaration*, edited by Frank Dallmayr, 74–116. Lanham, MD: Rowman and Littlefield, 2019.

World Council of Churches. www.oikoumene.org/en/member-churches/presbyterian-church-of-ghana. Accessed September 1, 2018.

Young, Richard Fox. "Clearing a Path through *Jesus of the Deep Forest*: Intercultural Perspectives on Christian Praise and Public Witness in Afua Kuma's Akan Oral Epic." *Theology Today* 70.1 (2013): 38–45.

INDEX

Aboagye-Mensah, Robert, 212n63
"adult form of Christianity," Barth on, 74, 75, 216n22
African Christianity
  ATRs as ontological past for, 143, 235n34 (*see also* African traditional religions)
  continuity with Christian past, 96–99, 223n73
  ethnocentrism of European missionary efforts, as response to, 134–35
  primal imagination as substructure of, 141–46 (*see also* primal imagination)
  as syncretism/synthesis, 48, 103
  twin heritage of, 69, 71, 96–99, 144, 145, 165, 171
  See also Bediako, Kwame
African cosmologies, spiritual world in, 41, 123, 128, 129, 165, 168, 230n34
African Independent/Initiated Churches (AICs), 21, 109
African traditional religions (ATRs)
  Akan religion, 121

ancestor cults and Bediako's ancestor theology, 108–9, 121, 123, 124, 127–29, 163–71, 179, 180, 233n8
  Christological reflection on, 69, 72–73, 98
  contextual theological reflection on, 12, 107–9, 119, 123–25
  cultural reflection on, 141, 143–44, 145–48
  juxtaposition of Barth/Bediako and understanding of, 189–90
  as ontological past for African Christians, 143, 235n34
  as *praeparatio evangelica*, 119, 165, 169, 171, 174, 215n18
  primal imagination and, 141, 143–44
  salvation, relationship to Bediako's understanding of, 130–32
  terminological considerations, 215n10
  transcultural theology and, 38, 47, 60, 205n82
Afrikania, 69
Agyarko, Robert Owusu, 167

TIM HARTMAN
is assistant professor of theology at Columbia Theological Seminary.

CPSIA information can be obtained
at www.ICGtesting.com
Printed in the USA
LVHW052122201119
638029LV00009B/148/P